THE GOLDEN CENTURY

THE
GOLDEN
CENTURY

—

CLASSIC
MOTOR
YACHTS

1830 – 1930

ROSS
MacTAGGART

W. W. NORTON & COMPANY

NEW YORK · LONDON

To Thomas and Audrey MacTaggart, who introduced me to things-that-float

The text of this book is composed in Miller (designed by Matthew Carter)
and Interstate Condensed (designed by Tobias Frere-Jones) with the
display type set in Univers Thin Ultra Condensed (designed by Adrian Frutiger)
and Engraver's Gothic (designed by Morris Fuller Benton).

Manufacturing by Mondadori Printing, Verona

Book design by Robert L. Wiser
Archetype Press, Washington, D.C.

Library of Congress Cataloging-in-Publication Data
MacTaggart, Ross.
The golden century: classic motor yachts, 1830–1930 / Ross MacTaggart.
　　p.　cm.
Includes bibliographical references and index.
ISBN 0-393-04949-3
1. Yachts—History. I. Title.
VM331.M17　2000
623.8′2314—dc21　　　　　　　　　　　　00-055100

W. W. Norton & Company, Inc., 500 Fifth Avenue, New York, N.Y. 10110
www.wwnorton.com
W. W. Norton & Company Ltd., 10 Coptic Street, London WC1A 1PU

1　2　3　4　5　6　7　8　9　0

CONTENTS

ACKNOWLEDGMENTS

This book progressed beyond fantasy due to my editor, Jim Mairs. I discovered Jim when reading the preface to *The World's Most Extraordinary Yachts*, by Jill Bobrow and Dana Jinkins, distributed by W. W. Norton. The authors gave Jim the credit for urging them "to produce a book on classic motor yachts." Yet they decided not to limit themselves "to the classic or old."

I wanted to produce just such a book.

People had been telling me that getting a publisher was near impossible, that one needed a phalanx of college degrees, as well as connections and a good agent. I had none of this. But it was apparent that a kindred spirit existed high in the clouds at 500 Fifth Avenue, just a subway ride from my apartment. When I called Norton, Jim did four extraordinary things. First, he took my call immediately. Second, he asked if I could come in the next day. Third, he offered, from that very first meeting, words dear to a would-be writer: "Ross, I guarantee we will publish your book." Fourth, when my life later took a dramatic, unexpected turn and this volume was put into a rusty filing cabinet as a result, causing me to miss my deadline by many years, Jim never scolded, badgered, or harassed. He simply said, repeatedly, that he had confidence that I would finish. For all this I remain grateful.

I also wish to thank other individuals who helped bring this book into being: Susan Carlson and Nina Gielen of W. W. Norton, copyeditor Janet Byrne, Eric Fuentecilla for a beautiful cover, and Robert L. Wiser for such an elegant layout.

As a surprising dividend of that unexpected turn in my life, I found myself living in rural Kansas after decades on the East Coast, finally finding the peace of mind—and the stunningly low overhead that rural America can offer—to continue writing. Yet, unlike authors blessed with financial support from universities, foundations, spouses, inherited wealth, or savings, I still needed help and found it from my community. To my surprise and delight, the local grocery store, owned by Kay Lauer—on the classic block-long Main Street—let me run a tab for the year it took to finally finish the book, as did the adjacent hardware store (right out of a 1930s movie), owned by Jim and Glenda Fink. When I needed to make endless photocopies, the locally owned Kansas Graphics also allowed a tab, and I thank its owners, Vicki and Marvin Adcock and Jane and Ron Scott.

This support would have been impossible from businesses owned by distant multinational corporations—a testament to a vanishing and precious way of life.

Richard Janopaul, another member of my community and a friend, gave me a loan to buy my first computer.

Beverly Pinkston was my heretofore secret Muse for resuming the book after its long hiatus.

Emily Hunter, brave girl, deserves a special thanks for inviting me to Kansas; Stan Amick offered refuge.

While it's hoped that the collective words I've slaved over will be both enjoyable and informative, it's understandable that people will buy this book for the pretty pictures. Accessing such images is, I've learned, an art form in itself. The majority of images in this volume have never been published, and some took over a decade to find. Because this book is the first of a planned eight-volume set, I suspect that I've driven more than a few archivists to the brink of madness with my endless requests, large orders, obscure queries, and persistence ("Are you *sure* the pictures don't exist?"). These archivists, researchers, volunteers, librarians, and department heads *are* the pretty pictures.

Because this project was twelve years in gestation, some of the people listed on the opposite page may no longer be affiliated with the same organization. And, this list is specific to this volume; many others of invaluable help will be thanked in the later volumes enriched by their assistance.

Barge House Museum
Pat Bausell
Peter Tasi

Bath Iron Works
John Poulin
Rusty Robertson

Boston Public Library
Aaron Schmidt

Glasgow Museums
Winnie Tyrell

Hagley Museum
and Library
Barbara Hall

Historical Collections
of the Great Lakes
Bowling Green State
    University
Robert Graham

Lyndhurst, A National
Trust Historic Site
Irene Epstein

Maine Maritime
Museum
Nathan R. Lipfert
Susan Russell

Mariners' Museum
Lisa Flick
Heather Friedle
Claudia Jew
Charlotte Valentine

Maritime Museum
Association
of San Diego
Craig Arnold
Chuck Bencik

Millicent Library
Carolyn Longworth

Morgan Library
Debbie Coutavas
Christine Nelson

Museum of the
City of New York
Elizabeth Ellis
Eileen K. Morales

Mystic Seaport
Philip L. Budlong
Mary Anne Stets

A special thanks
to Peggy Tate Smith,
who brought clarity
to muddled matters.

National Maritime
Museum
Meredith Sampson

The Rosenfeld
Collection:
Deborah M. DiGregorio
Jack (The Intrepid)
    MacFadyen
Elizabeth Rafferty
Victoria R. Sharps

Ships' Plans:
Ellen C. Stone
Pat Wilbur

New York Yacht Club
Joseph Jackson
Bill Watson

San Francisco
Maritime National
Historic Park
Heather Hawkins
William Kooiman

Suffolk County
Vanderbilt Museum
Florence Ogg

University of Glasgow
Simon Bennett
George Gardner

I'd also like to thank yacht designer Jay Benford (a kindred spirit), who supplied images; Jim Mairs for taking images of *Cigarette* and allowing their publication; Ineke Bruynooghe, whose family has undertaken the restoration of *Delphine* and who graciously supplied images; Urbain Ureel and Cynthia D'Vincent, who graciously supplied images of *Delphine* and *Acania*, respectively; William Kooiman, who contributed a first-hand account of being aboard the *Hussar;* Lucia del Sol Knight, editor of the *Encyclopedia of Yacht Designers* (see Sources), who supplied biographical information on John H. Wells; and an old friend, Colleen Babington, who gave me the best writing advice I ever received. When I was struggling to start this book many years ago, she said, "Ross, stop *thinking* about the perfect way to say things before you put anything on paper and *write* whatever comes to mind, whenever. Don't worry if it's right, and don't worry if it's the beginning, middle, or end of the book. Just put it down!" I began, oddly, by writing the caption for *Vidor* on page 90.

Authors Jay Ottinger, C. Philip Moore, and Bill Robinson graciously allowed me to quote them on several occasions, their words making a point better than mine.

There were two books of enormous assistance. Erik Hofman's groundbreaking *The Steam Yachts,* published in 1970, was an inspiration and a wealth of information. Fred M. Walker's *Song of the Clyde: A History of Clyde Shipbuilding* provided biographical information on the many Scottish shipbuilders who launched hundreds of splendid motor yachts.

And, to a friend whose presence enhances my spirit, a special thanks to Christina.

Note: The addresses for the organizations shown above are listed in Sources.

FOREWORD

They were remarkable. The men and women who commissioned the palatial yachts depicted in these pages, and the people who designed and built them, were, in a word, extraordinary. When I began this volume thirteen years ago it was the yachts themselves that captivated me. I knew little about their owners, less about their designers, and nothing about their builders, inanimate apparently being more interesting than animate. Yet curiosity overcame me. For example, in looking at the unique profile, interiors, and size of *Lysistrata,* I thought: Who would commission such a vessel? It developed that a remarkable man, a "controlled alcoholic sociopath," ordered her—James Gordon Bennett. The more I read about him (the accuracy of the literature is suspect), the more fascinated I became. To my surprise, his yacht, by extension, became more interesting. I could no longer look at the alluring images of *Lysistrata* out of context. The yacht was not an isolated creation to be admired only for her size and appearance but a manifestation of a particular personality, and a rather larger-than-life one at that.

Indeed, the people detailed in these pages all seemed larger than life—a psychological prerequisite for yacht ownership?

There are the unanswered questions that draw one's attention. Why did Cornelius K. G. Billings *(Vanadis)* go to the trouble of ordering a huge new 240-foot yacht, only to then sell her shortly after her launching? And why has he—one of the richest men of his day—almost disappeared from the historical record? Did John Jacob Astor IV or his son Vincent add a second funnel to *Noma,* and why? Who was Anson W. Hard *(Avalanche),* and why did he order one of the most advanced yachts ever designed? What made Anna Dodge continue with the building of the 258-foot *Delphine* after the death of her husband, Horace (a founder of the Dodge Motor Company)? And, even after a disastrous sinking and, later, war service drastically altered the elegant yacht, what made this elegant Grosse Pointe matron spend hundreds of thousands of dollars to refurbish her beloved *Delphine*? Another interesting character—and enigma—is Annie Henrietta Yule, better known as Lady Yule, who, just a year after the

death of her husband, ordered one of the largest and most palatial steam yachts ever launched, the 300-foot *Nahlin.* Who was this woman, and why did she undertake such a dramatic and expensive . . . statement? Sadly, the answers to these intriguing questions remain locked in that most difficult-to-access of archives: the passage of time.

In trying to unearth answers, I got wrapped up in people's lives. Ransom E. Olds *(Mettamar)* was fascinating; I knew his company's name—Oldsmobile—but didn't know he predated Henry Ford in building cars in Detroit and introducing mass production techniques. I'd heard of that monstrous nineteenth-century robber baron Jay Gould *(Atalanta)* and knew he was responsible for myriad dastardly schemes to enrich himself at the expense of "the people." Yet in researching Gould I learned that almost all of what I'd been told, read, or taught wasn't true. His yacht, *Atalanta,* ceased to be a beautiful but distasteful symbol of the spoils of ill-gotten gain and assumed her true nature. She had represented a way for a man dying of tuberculosis to escape a press intent on destroying him and a public—lied to by the press—that hounded him. John Pierpont Morgan *(Corsair)* is another character we all "know" who emerged, through research, quite different than depicted. I always liked the beautiful black-hulled *Corsair*s (there were four)—and liked 'em better when I grew to like their owner. And then there is a yacht like *Edamena IV,* chosen simply to illustrate a point. She wasn't big, palatial, or famous and, like thousands of such vessels, is forgotten. I also knew nothing about her owner and wasn't concerned. Yet when I typed Earle P. Charlton into a new-fangled invention called the Internet, it took just seconds to re-create this man who died in 1930, a man who started with fifty dollars' worth of goods, opened what became known as a five & dime, and later became a founder of Woolworth's. The fact that he was generous with his resulting fortune intrigued me, and even more delightful was the fact that his grandson and namesake had recently donated three million dollars to an obscure college in honor of his grandfather to help "people from all walks of life who are just trying to make a better life for themselves." Somehow, in a way I can't explain but believe to be a truth, *Edamena IV*, forever frozen in a pretty picture, became more beautiful.

Today (Earle P. Charlton II's gift aside) children are taught that they can't succeed in life without a college degree. It was always a pleasure to learn of so many yacht owners who, without higher education, a high school diploma, or well-connected relatives, amassed great fortunes through hard work and creative thinking. Six brothers (*Margaret F III*) grew up the sons of a small-town blacksmith and went on to create a company, Body by Fisher, that was sold just two decades later to General Motors for $208 million. Tommy Lipton (better known as Sir Thomas) was born to poor Irish parents and, starting with a single small grocery store, went on to create an international business—Drink Lipton's! Walter Chrysler (*Frolic II* and *III*) skipped college and in a span of just two decades increased his annual income from $4,100 to $1 million; all this *before* he created the automotive giant that still bears his name. Thomas Lawson (*Dreamer*) was the son of a carpenter who had little schooling, yet he created a fortune of $50 million by the time he was forty through stock trading. Jesse L. Livermore (*Athero II*) followed a similar path (his first trade was for ten dollars—he made a profit of three dollars) and he went on to amass, and lose, four separate fortunes.

While self-made personalities make for interesting research (and, I hope, reading), many people of inherited wealth, obviously, played an important role in this century of grand motor yachts. Morton Freeman Plant (*Iolanda*) sold off inherited business interests and shifted his attentions to yachting. In his twenty-second year John Hay Whitney (*Aphrodite II*) found himself $179 million richer and used this remarkable dividend to pursue his love of yachting, even building a lavish, mansion-like, three-story boathouse. And, of course, no story about millionaires would be complete without a Vanderbilt or two. The patriarch of the family commissioned the first motor yacht in the United States—*North Star*. His descendants, including the brothers William Kissam II (*Alva II*) and Harold Stirling (*Vara*), owned a dizzying array of impressive vessels.

The naval architects who designed these floating mansions and cottages were, more often than not, also without benefit of college degrees or the kind of education considered essential today. William Gibbs, after quitting his career as a lawyer, went on—completely self-taught—to design not only some of the most elegant motor and auxiliary yachts ever launched (such as *Hussar*, known as *Sea Cloud*) but the largest ocean liner built in America and the fastest in the world: the SS *United States*. George L. Watson started as an apprentice in an established shipyard when he was sixteen, becoming one of the most famous and brilliant designers of racing and steam yachts. John Alden is another well-known example of a great talent nurtured through the apprentice system, while others seemed to benefit from college, such as the prolific motor yacht designer John H. Wells and Harvard graduate Clinton Crane. (Is the ancient but now abandoned apprentice system, where one learns by doing, a better way to teach than the system that has replaced it—college?)

The people who built these yachts of wood and steel also make for stories larger than life. Consider the Horatio Alger quality of men like Harry J. Defoe, who whittled hulls as a child and went on—again totally self-taught—to built 300-foot steel naval vessels as well as beautiful motor yachts. Is such a thing possible today? Imagine the builders who began in an age of wooden ships and, the industrial revolution hard upon them, learned how to build out of iron, a material infinitely more difficult to work with, to say nothing of the quantum shift in technique from largely man-made to machine-made. Robert Napier was one such builder, the son of a blacksmith who began as an apprentice at sixteen. He went on to a brilliant career designing steam engines and building ships, becoming known as the father of Clyde River shipbuilding. And then there are characters such as the Marquis of Ailsa, who, deciding to create a shipyard, conveniently did so directly under the looming presence of his home, Culzean Castle, in Ayrshire.

The most important contributors to this book, however, are the photographers. Of the over two hundred images in these pages, the majority were taken by two men—both self-taught—Edwin Levick and Morris Rosenfeld.

Although born in London in 1868, Levick spent an exotic childhood near the Red Sea in Egypt; his father was the British consul in Suez, and he grew up surrounded by water and boats—an early experience that would leave an indelible imprint. Educated in France, Levick immigrated to America at the turn of the century and earned a livelihood by writing news stories. On occasion, he would illustrate an article with a photograph, and eventually he discovered that his editors were more interested in his photography talents than his writing abilities. He opened his own studio and employed, among others, a young Morris Rosenfeld. For many years Levick was the official photographer for the New York and New Rochelle Yacht Club cruises, and in 1928 he won the Photographer's Association blue ribbon for one of his images. After Levick's death in 1929, his son John carried on the business of Edwin Levick, Inc., for another decade. Later, the Mariners' Museum, in Newport News, Virginia (see Sources), was able to acquire over forty thousand Levick images.

The work of Morris Rosenfeld, born in 1885 on New York's Lower East Side, dominates this volume. When he was thirteen he won a five-dollar prize for an image he'd taken of a bark in dry dock. As a freelance photographer, Rosenfeld took a wide variety of images and worked for Edwin Levick as well as the German-American newspaper *Staats Zeitung*. By 1910 Rosenfeld had his own company, with prestige clients such as AT&T, major shipping lines, the New York Parks Department, and various real-estate developers. Yet his passion was yachting photography, and he soon focused his attentions there. His son Stanley remembers going out on Long Island Sound "like hunters" in search of yachts to capture on film. After the death of Edwin Levick in 1929, Rosenfeld became the acknowledged leader in the field of marine photography and, with sons Stanley, Bill, and Dave, prowled the waters in *Photo III*, a 33-footer designed by Fred Lord and built by the Kanno Yard, in City Island, New York. The firm of Morris Rosenfeld & Sons went on through the 1970s; its archive of almost a million images was later purchased by Mystic Seaport and now comprises the Rosenfeld Collection (see Sources).

All my research never answered the question that most intrigued me about these diverse people: Were they happy? Their obituaries recited their many club memberships, how many companies they founded or sat on the board of, their marriage (or marriages), and children. But these dry dissertations of facts don't reveal who they were, leaving us to wonder. Were they nice? Did they love their spouses and children? Were they loved in return? Even biographies don't usually answer such questions, and if they do, one must remain cautious: a writer (including this one) can make a person out to be a devil or a saint, depending on motivation and personal neurosis.

Another question obscured by time is: Why did these men and women order a yacht? A few answers have trickled down through the decades—for Gould, Morgan, and various Vanderbilts—but for others the question will likely remain as such.

What began as a dispassionate observation regarding the design of grand motor yachts evolved into a broader work encompassing the people involved in their creation; this book is better for their stories. Rather than detailing the dry biographies of people long dead, I have tried to focus on their legacies. If magnificent homes, such as the dramatic Art Deco mansion of Sir Stephen Courtauld *(Virginia)*, are extant and open to the public, I offer this information in Sources at the end of this volume. If entire museums were donated to the American people, such as by Charles Lang Freer, this, too, is listed. If they had interesting or entertaining descendants, they are detailed. If they underwrote hospitals, libraries, and parks that can still help us, teach us, and soothe us, then these lasting creations are chronicled.

This volume is dedicated to all these extraordinary individuals.

INTRODUCTION

In a musty basement, my hands are covered with thin cotton gloves as I carefully remove the delicate paper envelope from the treasure it protects and obscures. Slowly, the content of the white envelope—a small piece of glass—is revealed. But this is no ordinary glass. When the fragile item is held in front of the overhead lightbulb, its value is revealed. Like magic, the dim light transforms the glass and exposes an image. An image that likely hasn't been seen by anyone since it was first photographed decades, or perhaps even a century, before.

I look in wonder at the glass negative, stored, like many millions more, in dark, cold, and rarely accessed archival vaults in a handful of museums across the globe. These negatives document a forgotten century, one where palatial ships ranging from fifty feet to over four hundred feet plied the waters of vast oceans, great lakes, and rivers; set speed records on calmer bays and sounds, and carried the monied few on leisurely tours around a world that was far less familiar than it is today.

To me, these images and the ships they represent all have one common point of desirability. They are motor yachts, their engines either steam, gas, or diesel fired. As such, they are now forgotten, unlike their companions upon the waters of the world: classic ships blessed with acres of canvas to propel them with the grace of wind. Sailing vessels and racing yachts (particularly the latter) are the subject of much lore, romance, and documentation. So are the behemoths of the world's waters: ocean liners, their sheer size captivating our attention, or, better yet, remembered for dramatically smashing into an iceberg on a maiden voyage (and creating a cottage industry). Even tugboats are the object of fascination and enjoy a cult following.

But ... the story of motor yachts has been neglected. While hundreds of books detail the history of famous and beautiful sailing vessels, no comparable record exists for motor yachts. This selective historical memory belies the fact that a century ago motor yachts were enormously popular, much more so than ships of sail. Lord and Lady Brassey's *Sunbeam** traveled the world exploring then exotic lands, and when Lady Brassey chronicled these exploits—which vast sums of money could buy—in a series of books, they became best-sellers. During this now forgotten century of motor yachting, rich men vied with one another to have the fastest, longest, and most up-to-date yachts—only to be one-upped by a woman who commissioned the largest private yacht ever built. Yacht envy. (This record was finally broken in 1999 with the launching of the 462-foot *Mipos*—a project name meaning "Mission Impossible.")

It was an Englishman, Thomas Assheton-Smith, who commissioned the first known motor yacht, in 1830: the 120-foot steam-powered *Menai*, designed by Robert Napier. This new-fangled mode of travel was received with less than enthusiasm by members of the British aristocracy. The *Herald* of 1825 wrote of commercial steam vessels: "Such clouds of smoke as completely obscures all distant objects. Murky vomitings of the furnaces covered the surface of Southampton water from side to side." Moreover, the august Royal Yacht Squadron had enacted strict rules against the ownership of steam-powered yachts. Assheton-Smith, a member, resigned before commissioning *Menai*. And, apparently unconcerned by such a social setback, he went on to commission eight more steam yachts by 1850, including *Fire King*, the fastest in his fleet.

*As couples went, Anna and Thomas Brassey were unusual. Anna was the most famous female yachting enthusiast of her day. When she died (from malaria) aboard *Sunbeam* in 1887, her burial was at sea. Thomas, later Lord Brassey, was the captain of their yacht in an age when a hired master was a rule. After his wife's death, Brassey continued making extensive cruises aboard *Sunbeam* until delivering the aging vessel to India in 1916, where she was used as a hospital ship. After the war, *Sunbeam* was purchased by Lord Runciman, who enjoyed the famous vessel until she was scrapped in 1929, after fifty-five years of service.

MENAI

The first private steam yacht was ordered in 1830 by Thomas Assheton-Smith, who later commissioned eight more steam yachts. *Sporting Magazine* once commented that Assheton-Smith "has determined to take his future aquatic excursions in a steam vessel of extraordinary power …"

120 feet and built in 1830 for Thomas Assheton-Smith. Designed by Robert Napier. Engine by Robert Napier.

Robert Napier (1791–1876), who designed *Menai* and built her engines, was known as the father of Clyde River shipbuilding. He created his first steam engine (extant) for the PS *Levan* in 1823, and his involvement with *Menai* represented a significant breakthrough. Mr. Assheton-Smith, *Menai*'s owner, introduced Napier to important contacts, and the designer soon had work from overseas governments, the East India Company, and, later, the British Admiralty. The first four ships built by Samuel Cunard involved Napier, and this experience convinced him to construct entire vessels (he had previously contracted out most of the building). In 1841 Napier started building in the Burgh of Govan (which later became part of Glasgow) at the Govan Old Yard and, after relocating to Govan East ship-

yard in 1850, became a profound influence, building the PS *Persia* in 1855, the ironclad *Black Prince* in 1861, and then the HMS *Warrior,* also in 1861, the first such British vessel. Although Napier died in 1876, the company continued, producing almost 500 vessels during its history until being taken over by William Beardmore in 1900. Yet, as Fred M. Walker writes in *Song of the Clyde: A history of Clyde shipbuilding,* "Without [Napier's] drive and initiative the Clyde would have been a quieter place, and fewer of the shipbuilders who were to become great would have had the all-around training that made their businesses flourish. Truly, Napier was the father of the industry on the river." (The Govan East shipyard was later taken over by Harland & Wolff, the company that built the *Titanic*.)

*Rudder Magazine (1898–1970) was popular, influential, and edited for many years by Thomas Fleming Day (1861–1927), a "hard-bitten deepwater sailor." Day was a champion of ocean sailing in small craft and sailed from Providence, Rhode Island, to Rome, Italy, aboard Sea Bird, a 25-foot gaff-rigged yawl. He chronicled his voyage in "a chatty, nothing-to-it" account, Across the Atlantic in Sea Bird, published in 1911. Day also used the magazine to needle his readers, scolding them for rarely making voyages without land in sight. In 1912 Day skippered (along with a crew of three) Detroit, a 35-foot vessel with a 240-square-foot sail and 16-hp engine, on a 6,000-mile voyage from Detroit, Michigan, to Saint Petersburg, Russia.

Assheton-Smith would be inadvertently assisted in his passion for motor yachting by none other than Queen Victoria. In the summer of 1842, on a sailing trip to Scotland, the queen wasn't amused by the sight of passenger steamers repeatedly plowing past the *Royal George* as she drifted, becalmed by the wind. "How annoying and provoking this is!" Victoria exclaimed in her diary. For her return home, the queen chartered a steam yacht and lost no time in ordering the 225-foot paddlewheel steamer *Victoria and Albert*. Only after Victoria commissioned a second *V&A* in 1853 did English society accept the ownership of steam yachts. Such acceptance was, no doubt, assisted by Cornelius Vanderbilt, the richest man in the world (leaving a fortune estimated, in today's dollars, at $95.9 billion). Vanderbilt's 270-foot *North Star*, the first American motor yacht, completed an unprecedented 15,024-mile world cruise, also in 1853. The voyage attracted international publicity and was made in a record four months; it would have taken a year in a sailing vessel. In one dramatic stroke, it became impossible to dismiss the practicality that motor yachts afforded.

Assheton-Smith's *Menai* was a paddlewheel vessel, her huge wheels grafted on to a traditional clipper hull. The early *Victoria and Albert* and *North Star*, among others, were also such hybrids. The advent of the screw propeller enabled motor yachts to develop along more graceful lines. The prototype for the screw motor yacht was, it appears, *Archimedes*, built in 1838. This early vessel didn't revolutionize yacht design overnight; it took an unusual tug-of-war to accomplish such a feat. In 1844 Their Lords Commissioners of the British Admiralty wanted to know: What was more efficient, the paddle wheel or the screw propeller? To ascertain this, two vessels were built, the paddlewheel steamer *Alecto* and the screw steamer *Rattler*. After launching, the two were tied to each other at their sterns. The *Alecto* started her paddle wheel and was soon pulling the other vessel at 2 knots. The *Rattler* then started her engines and, with the *Alecto* at full speed, managed to bring her to a complete stop before then pulling her at a steady speed.

Thus the screw motor yacht was legitimized, although two more decades passed before the first American screw motor yacht, the *Clarita*, was built, in 1864, for Leonard W. Jerome. In that same year steam yachts were first registered in the New York Yacht Club yearbook, although there were only two. Almost two decades later (1882) the New York Yacht Club listed 23 steam yachts; by 1900 the number had jumped to 189. So, while this book covers a century of grand motor yachts, it was a phenomenon that blossomed in the 1880s and died in the 1930s—a mere fifty years.

Motor yacht owners in England were, initially, "old money" landowners with enormous acreage. As such, they had plenty of time to spare for different seasons: racing, fishing, hunting and shooting, and, of course, the London season. The advent of motor yachts created a heretofore unknown cruising season, and vastly wealthy landowners took to leisurely voyages lasting months and even years. It would not prove important that their yachts were fast, for two other features were more desirable: reliability and comfort. The English yacht owners (as opposed to their American counterparts) were "blessed with a more restful disposition," or so said the 1902 *Rudder*.* English-built motor yachts were primarily designed as good seaboats, able to withstand rough seas and still offer comfortable, even palatial, accommodations.

*William Picard (W. P.) Stephens (1854–1946) was a well-known naval architect, boat builder, author, and editor. His collection of over 2,000 plans is located at Mystic Seaport Museum.

Across the Atlantic, however, a different sensibility existed. Few Americans could afford a relaxing lifestyle—a dividend of inherited wealth—and financiers, industrialists, and rail tycoons were busy *earning* their fortunes. "The yacht owner in America appears to understand only one thing—the speed attained by his vessel," as W. P. Stephens* commented. Because American yachts (protected by inland waterways such as Long Island Sound) seldom encountered rough water or heavy weather, hulls could be made distinctly lighter than British versions, and thus faster. Yet speed also required vast amounts of hull space for boilers, engines, and coal bunkers. For Americans, accommodations and comfort were secondary.

As the twentieth century dawned the difference between American and European yachts became less distinct. The industrial age spawned a new breed of Englishman, such as Sir Thomas Lipton, who, by his self-made nature, was a match for his American counterparts. Americans ordered yachts from English yards, which offered the advantage of better-trained engineers, while the yards themselves had experience steeped in centuries, and (at the turn of the century) competitive prices: they could build a $700,000 vessel for $100,000 less than in America. As the price of coal escalated in England, this savings was erased, and distinctions between English and American vessels were further blurred in the 1920s, when a number of grand yachts were built by Krupp-Germaniawerft in Kiel, Germany.

During this century of motor yachting, rich Americans vied with one another for two objectives: size and speed. J. P. Morgan owned three successive black-hulled yachts, all recognized for their beauty, and all named *Corsair;* his son commissioned a fourth—a 343-foot beauty. Morton Plant took advantage of his inheritance, sold off his business interests, and devoted himself to, among other interests, yachting; he owned a number of grand vessels, including the 318-foot *Iolanda.* William K. Vanderbilt II (a grandson of "Commodore" Vanderbilt) enjoyed the 285-foot *Alva,* while William Astor apparently made do with the 232-foot German-built *Nourmahal.* Emily Roebling Cadwalader routed this male-dominated race when she commissioned within just five years three successive yachts named *Savarona,* the last being the largest private yacht then launched, at an imposing 407 feet. Lady Annie Henrietta Yule also made an impressive showing with the 300-foot *Nahlin.*

While the yachts of such tycoons (and old money such as Cadwalader, of the Brooklyn Bridge Roeblings) are the stuff of legend and romance, the people who worked for them—the company vice presidents, lawyers, and managers—also had yachts, albeit a tad smaller. The names of these vessels are no longer remembered, yet they live on in the photographs that document this age, particularly its latter half. Those moderately wealthy could afford the 68-foot *Alondra,* the 93-foot *Trail,* the 124-foot *Zapala,* or even the 171-foot *Athero II* (all detailed in these pages). After World War I, few palatial motor yachts hundreds of feet long were built, while the market for smaller vessels boomed.

This book ends in 1930 for several reasons. During the 1920s steam was largely replaced by diesel, which required far less space for engines, coal bunkers, and boilers. As such, accommodations increased, while overall length decreased (which helped fuel the market in yachts for those of moderate wealth). All this, in turn, brought about a radical change in how yachts were designed, a change that, to me, made them less attractive. Sweeping countersterns, such as the *Titanic*'s, disappeared, as did clipper bows, varnished deckhouses, multiple smokestacks, and masts set at rakish angles. The interiors of yachts also changed. By the late 1920s main saloons and staterooms no longer looked like English manor houses inexplicably afloat. History was ignored as a new era in design became the rule, one that looked toward the future and disdained the past. Today this influence still prevails. Yachts look like they could fly into space, the waters they ply an anachronism and a hindrance.

Other events had a negative effect on yachts by the 1930s: the advent of the automobile and good roads. In the nineteenth century and early twentieth, roads were dirt, and, as such, often impassable quagmires during rainy seasons. As Erik Hofman observes in his book *The Steam Yachts,* while the rich could afford private trains as a mode of comfortable travel, even this choice had its limitations; trains had to go where the *rails* went, not where *you* wanted. Moreover, rail sidings were dirty, noisy places, often in unappealing parts of town. So, while you might've arrived in style, your destination could be decidedly less stylish.

Having a motor yacht made all this moot. Suddenly, one could travel the world in any degree of comfort and have as many servants, stewards, crew, and officers as one wanted and could afford. For old money in England, long cruises became a way of life. In America, newly rich industrialists and financiers would board high-speed commuters ranging from 50 feet to well over 300 (such as the fourth Morgan *Corsair*) and be whisked to their palatial homes on Long Island, the Hudson River, Lake Saint Clair, or in the suburbs of Boston. Who had time for leisure? There were fortunes to be made!

And then Henry Ford came along. By the 1920s cars were transforming travel, and with their popularity, roads were steadily improved. Private yachts were no longer the fastest way to travel. They also cost an enormous amount to build, operate, and maintain, and were somewhat less attractive when income taxes were first levied in 1914.

Finally, this book ends in 1930 for an overwhelming reason: the Great Depression. In an instant, grand yachts became a thing of the past. Just three months prior to the stock market crash of October 1929, the respected yacht design and brokerage firm of Henry J. Gielow (pronounced Jill-ow) had taken the unprece-

CURMUDGEON COMMENTS:

The vast majority of the yachts depicted in this volume no longer exist. This seems extraordinarily wasteful to me, yet I should not be surprised. Western culture is gleeful in its destruction of the natural beauty that surrounds us and in the casual discarding of human-made creations built with love, pride, and craftsmanship. Books such as *Lost New York* detail this latter madness. *Cityscapes of Boston*, by Robert Campbell and Peter Vanderwarker, shows before-and-after images of Boston, the "after" always worse than the "before."

dented step of ordering, on speculation, five 190-foot yachts to be built by the Bath Iron Works. The heady 1920s had "proven" the market for such a move, but this kind of optimism would die before year's end. It took a decade to find a buyer for the last Gielow yacht, *Aletes*. Her buyer? The United States Navy. No one else could afford her.

By the early 1930s yachts that had once sold for hundreds of thousands of dollars could almost not be given away. Few people had the $50,000 to $100,000 a year it took to maintain the average yacht, to say nothing of the maintenance cost of such a white elephant as the 407-foot *Savarona*. (To save on import duties, *Savarona* was never brought into American waters, even though Emily Cadwalader, her owner, lived in Pennsylvania.)

During the ensuing decades less than a handful of large yachts were commissioned, while hundreds of vessels were sacrificed in World War II, scrapped due to old age or neglect, or lost in any one of the innumerable mishaps that can befall a vessel (the last Morgan *Corsair* foundered on rocks near Acapulco, slowly fell onto her side, and was declared a total loss). The photographs documenting this century of yachting were relegated to storerooms and occasionally purchased by or donated to museums that could properly house the millions of motor yacht images that few people wanted to see. As the decades ensued, a remarkable era and a way of life were largely forgotten, a century lost.

ELUCIDATION

I am, among other distractions, an architectural designer and, as such, see the world through a lens of scale, proportion, and standards of beauty that are, obviously, highly subjective. As a designer, how things *look* is a fundamental preoccupation; a mechanical engineer, for example, would have written a very different book on yachts.

Also, the reader may note the absence of some famous yacht, or the seemingly short shrift given another. Indulgence is requested, as this is the first volume of an intended multi-volume set. The vessel you yearn for will likely appear later in the series.

Please note that the length listed for each yacht, unless otherwise noted, is length overall—LOA.

THE DESIGN OF MOTOR YACHTS, 1830—1930

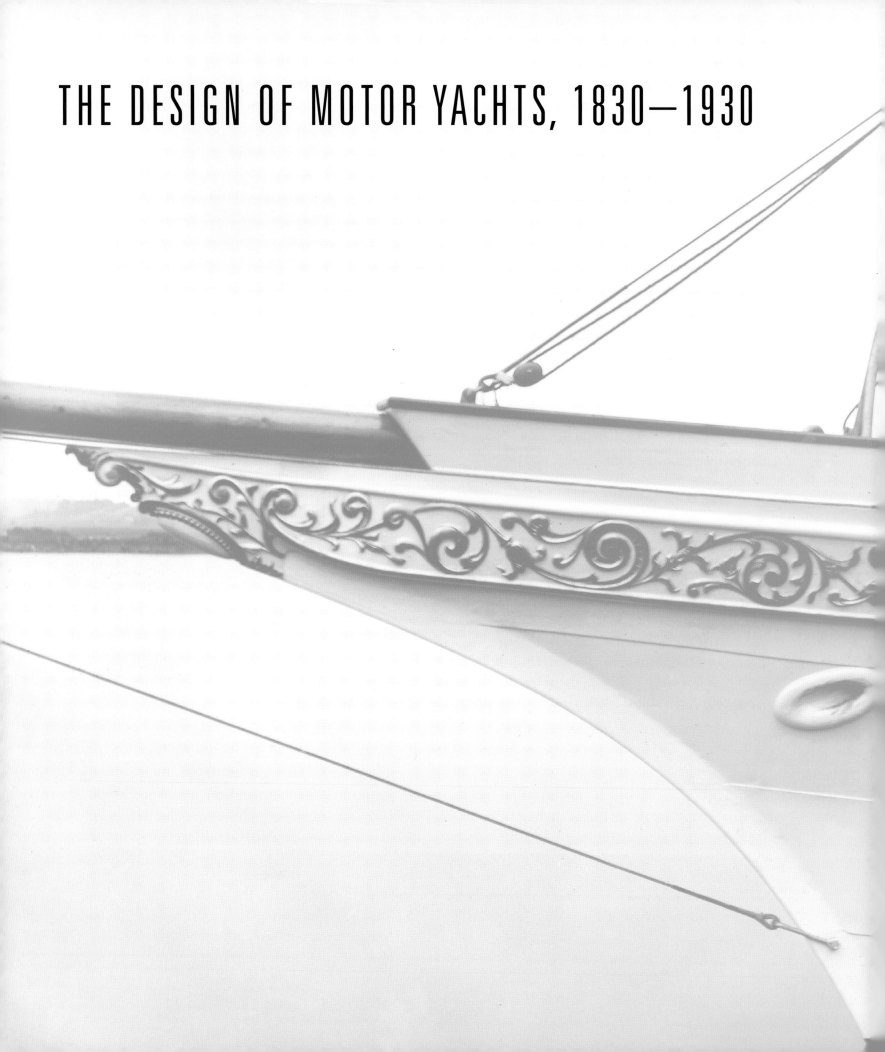

Few realize the difficulties of steam yacht design. The naval architect who would be successful as a designer of modern steam yachts must have universal qualifications. He must possess sufficient artistic taste to combine a beautiful hull with an efficient one, and in carrying out his work he must exercise and draw upon sound, practical experience of a dozen trades. From the preliminary weight estimates to the finishing coat of topside enamel he must, theoretically and practically, have the work at his fingers' ends. His client will have comfort, economy, and with every modern luxury, and all within a floating house which has no two points equal in dimension or shape.

The Yachting Monthly, October 1906

From 1830 to 1930 the design of motor yachts metamorphosed from vessels utilizing clipper-ship–type hulls (with paddle wheels awkwardly grafted on), to peculiar hybrids (which appeared both sailing yacht and steamer), and finally to streamlined creations never seen before. By the 1920s motor yacht design reached a level of grace and beauty that remains unsurpassed even seven decades later.

ONEIDA

138 feet and built in 1883. Designed and built by John Roach & Son, of Chester, Pennsylvania.

1883 · LAUNCHED AS UTOWANA

Early steam yachts in the mid-range size were like strange hermaphrodites, not quite clipper ship, not quite steamship. Accommodations were in the hull with only a very small cabin or two on deck, if that. Still, *Oneida* had a delightfully jaunty appearance, although her tiny stack looked as if it was embarrassed at being visible.

Not everyone agreed that *Oneida*'s small deck cabin was an aesthetic asset. *Century Magazine* (August 1882) commented that "the tendency of Americans to crowd their decks with houses is excusable when it results from a question of dollars and cents, as in a freight or passenger vessel. But we cannot understand why, when a gentleman builds for pleasure a craft in which beauty of lines and decoration are especially considered, he should so often disfigure it with clumsy excrescences called cabins, so formed and placed as to ruin the general grace of outline."

Oneida was owned by a Wall Street financier, Elias Cornelius Benedict, who took up yachting in his early fifties on the advice of his doctor. "I had reached such a state that my physician said that I would have to do something . . . to save my life," he said. That something developed into a passion; one *Oneida* log

recorded 240,000 miles. Benedict later owned a successive vessel; and at 583 gross tons, this *Oneida* was considerably larger than her predecessor (141 tons). Benedict was elected commodore of the Seawanhaka Corinthian Yacht Club in 1895, and for the first time a commodore's pennant could be seen flying on a member's steam yacht. (The SCYC was founded in 1871 as a small-boat sailing club. Steam so proved its popularity that, by 1895, steam yachts predominated as a type.)

The first *Oneida* was the setting for a famous, if clandestine, event in American history when she was offered to President Grover Cleveland (a friend of Benedict's) as the perfect setting for the removal of a cancerous growth in his jaw. The president feared that if the public knew about his condition, a financial panic would result. *Oneida*'s elegant main saloon was readied for this secret surgery (it proved successful), and the American public simply assumed their president had enjoyed a cruise aboard a friend's yacht.

Benedict enjoyed *Oneida* for three decades, selling her in 1917. He had the second *Oneida* for just three years before his death, in November 1920, at his Indian Harbor estate in Greenwich, Connecticut.

John Roach & Sons, which built *Oneida*, had its beginnings when John Roach (1815–87) began making castings for marine engines at one dollar a day. He later purchased a small New York foundry and within four years had amassed $30,000 in savings. An 1856 boiler explosion destroyed the foundry, and, unable to recover the insurance, Roach found himself penniless after paying debts. Nonetheless, he rebuilt the company and installed equipment capable of building the largest marine engines then known. Some notable vessels with Roach-built engines included the enormous steamboats *Bristol* and *Providence*. In 1868 the business significantly expanded with the purchase of several foundries in New York and in 1871 Roach also purchased a Chester, Pennsylvania, shipyard (where *Oneida* was built); it was later headed by his son, John Baker Roach. The company built a wide variety of vessels, including the steam yachts *Viking* and *Utowana*.

In 1883 Roach & Sons began construction of the despatch-boat *Dolphin* for the U.S. Navy, as well as three cruisers. When the *Dolphin* was completed, the new secretary of the navy, William C. Whitney, refused to accept the vessel, for reasons unexplained, even though she had been accepted by the naval board. The turn of events was disastrous to the company; John Roach, in the years to come, was never able to discuss what had happened without "uncontrollable emotion."

ATALANTA

Jay Gould commissioned one of the earliest, grandest private steam yachts built, and the most advanced in existence at the time, the black-hulled *Atalanta* (which included two Herreshoff-designed and -built steam launches, 27-foot and 35-foot LOA). For her launching, a special train brought the Gould family, dignitaries, and even the commodore of the New York Yacht Club (remarkable considering that the club had blackballed Gould as a member, forcing him to found a competing club, the American Yacht Club). *Atalanta*'s crew of 52 were accommodated with quarters as plush as passenger quarters on other yachts.

Blessed with a long life, *Atalanta* was eventually sold to the Venezuelan Navy until being dropped from *Jane's* in 1950, ancient at sixty-seven.

Commissioning a yacht seemed a strange choice for Gould, a workaholic. The nineteenth-century press was baffled, refusing to believe that Gould, their favored punching bag, would ever take a break. Unknown to the press, or even close friends, Gould had been diagnosed with tuberculosis in the early 1880s and was advised to curtail his business activities in order to recover.

Today, even a century after his death in 1892, Gould is remembered as the worst of the nineteenth-century robber barons. Yet this reputation, as detailed by Maury Klein in his 1986 book *The Life and Legend of Jay Gould*, was almost wholly fabricated by the media and bears little relation to the life of Gould. In sharp contrast to his reputation as a destroyer of companies through stock manipulation, Klein details a man obsessed with building a powerful transportation and communications empire. He eventually controlled half the rail mileage in the Southwest, New York's elevated rail system, and the Western Union Company.

Exceedingly private and shy, Gould was devoted to his wife and six children, and upon his death left his ample estate (estimated at $42.1 billion, in today's dollars) in roughly equal terms to his children. (In contrast, "Commodore" Vanderbilt left the vast bulk of his $95.9 billion estate [in today's dollars] to just one of his eleven surviving children.)

Gould also loved his Hudson River estate, Lyndhurst, and spent many hours carefully nurturing the camellias, ferns, and orchids in its massive greenhouse, the largest in private hands.

Five of the Gould children went on to own dozens of sailing and steam yachts, including the spectacular steam yachts *Niagara* and *Valhalla*, and sons George and Howard became noted yachtsmen and America's Cup supporters. Indeed, the Gould family is eclipsed only by the Vanderbilt family in terms of number of vessels owned.

Today, Lyndhurst is owned by the National Trust for Historic Preservation and is open to the public (see Sources).

William Cramp & Sons, the company that built *Atalanta*, as well as the first *Corsair* (see page 146), was the premier shipbuilder of Philadelphia. The company began in 1830 during an age of wood ships and ended over a century later in an era of steel. The founder of the firm, William Cramp (1807–79), was passionate about wooden ship construction and its associated skills; it was his son, Charles H. Cramp (1828–1913), who brought the company into the industrial age. Cramp & Sons was awarded eight government contracts during the Civil War, and their most famous contribution was the *New Ironsides*, a 232-foot wood hull (the largest yet constructed in the United States) sheathed with four inches of iron plating and powered by a steam engine and single screw. Beginning with *Corsair* (hull #211) in 1880, Cramp went on to built eight steam yachts, although this type of vessel was in the minority of the over 500 ships launched by the yard. After Charles died in 1913 the company passed out of family control, and in 1927 the ship manufacturing branch was closed, only to be reactivated during World War II with an impressive workforce of 18,000. After the war, the yard was again closed, this time permanently.

235 feet (15 feet was soon added) and built in 1883 for Jay Gould. Designed and built by William Cramp & Sons, Philadelphia. Powered by a steam engine that drove her at 17 knots.

In this extraordinary, unidentified image (opposite), *Atalanta* was possibly at the yard of her builder, William Cramp & Sons, in Philadelphia (where three well-dressed teenagers were unsuccessful in trying to look casual). Note the narrow beam, which was typical of yachts until the 1930s, the spiderweb-like wing bridge, and the name *Atalanta* embossed on the capstan.

On occasion, a researcher is rewarded with images such as the one above, highlighting the stern of *Atalanta*. The launch is powered by a steam or naptha engine and has two curious awnings (variously referred to as pram-type or melon-type hoods), presumably to keep occupants dry and shaded. Note the pitted nature of the black-painted hull, a condition quite inexplicable. No self-respecting owner or crew would tolerate such a condition, as hull finishes were usually maintained to a mirror-like brilliance. Was this image taken after one of Gould's trips abroad, or at the end of a season?

Of course, *Atalanta*'s crew would have had a difficult time maintaining a fine hull finish due to the fact that they, on a regular basis, plowed the yacht into other objects. One such memorable occasion occurred in September 1883, when *Atalanta* sliced the tugboat *General Hawley* in two; the unfortunate vessel sank at once, spilling its five crew members into the water. Unable to stop quickly, the yacht then struck a schooner anchored at a mooring before coming to a halt. *Atalanta* then lowered two boats, which rescued the crew from the *General Hawley*.

In 1889 a miscommunication between *Atalanta*'s captain and engineer resulted in the yacht's crashing into Pier 51 in New York City, causing considerable damage to the pier.

1

Concurrent with the building of his new yacht, Gould had purchased a Renaissance Revival mansion on New York's Fifth Avenue at Forty-seventh Street. For his new home (the Goulds had lived across the street since 1869), Gould ordered furniture from the fashionable decorating firm Herter Brothers, which did interiors for J. Pierpont Morgan (see page 146) and the William H. Vanderbilt mansion (Vanderbilt's grandsons were noted yachtsmen; see pages 83 and 95). Herter also supplied two bedroom suites for Gould's estate, Lyndhurst.

A man named W. W. Smith, of whom nothing is known, is credited with the interiors of *Atalanta*, as well as the first *Corsair*. Was Herter also involved in the interiors for *Atalanta*, such as this opulent dining saloon below her main deck (1)? As the Herter records from this period are largely lost, this intriguing question will likely remain as such.

The large trophy on the dining table is, to date, unidentified.

Atalanta's pantry (2) featured fine joinerwork, designed to hold every item of china or crystal in specially

fitted compartments—a necessary diligence considering the extreme rolling and pitching that early yachts such as *Atalanta* experienced.

Atalanta's galley (3) featured an impressive "French range," while a sizable skylight offered ample light and ventilation.

The steam engine (4) powering *Atalanta* protruded above the main deck and into the deckhouse, topped by a skylight. Note painting on bulkhead; *Atalanta?*

The interior images of *Atalanta* have never been published.

The aft section of *Atalanta*'s deckhouse was the location for Captain John W. Shackford's (formerly of the White Star Line) private stateroom, which was surprisingly plush (1). His berth sank out of sight when not in use and was then covered with a velvet settee.

Besides the captain, *Atalanta* had a crew consisting of "three engineers, two mates, four quartermasters, two boatswains, three oilers, twelve firemen, a steward, three cooks, six servants, and 18 sailors." These men were located in quarters distinctly less inviting than the captain's.

Opposite (2) is one of the very few images that document such quarters. The protruding mast and hull shape indicate that the crew was located aft.

The photograph of this unidentified cabin opposite (3) is marked "deck stateroom," although its location and intended occupant are unknown. Was this Gould's study?

Opposite (4), another unidentified, but extremely opulent, stateroom aboard *Atalanta*. Was this Jay Gould's? A contemporary account describes such a cabin as being "furnished with polished mahogany and other hard woods, Persian carpets, a satin couch, rosewood cabinets, and damask hangings."

The built-in berth surrounded by tufted satin panels and enclosed by thick drapes must have been supremely cocoon-like—a warm haven on cool nights, a furnace on hot, humid nights.

2

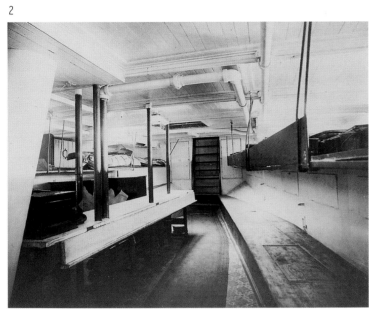

3

4

CLERMONT

1892

Clermont was built well after screw propellers became the standard for steam yacht propulsion. The fact that her owner and designer, Alfred Van Santvoord, was the principal owner of the Hudson River Day Line—nearly all paddlewheelers—may have predisposed him to go against the tide.

This delightful image highlights the extraordinary stack of *Clermont*, as well as her formidable masts.

Van Santvoord (1819–1901) began his career at sixteen as a clerk in his father's shipping office. He was later employed by the People's Line as a secretary and treasurer and was an agent for an Albany, New York, passenger barge line. In 1850 he designed a new type of towboat that became a universal model for towboat construction. In 1859 Van Santvoord became the managing director of the Hudson River Steamboat Company (succeeding his father), which was known for its elegant fleet of vessels, including the *City of Albany* and the *River Queen* (which became famous during the Civil War when President Lincoln and the vice president of the Confederacy, Alexander H. Stephens, met on board to discuss peace terms in 1865). The Hudson River Day Line was incorporated in 1879, with Van Santvoord serving as president until his death; the company itself lasted almost a century. Two of the line's most well-known steamboats included the *Chauncey Vibbard* and the *Mary Powell* (known as the "Queen of the Hudson"), the latter the fastest boat of her class, with a speed of 26 miles an hour. Other Van Santvoord interests included the directorship of several railroads, and he was a founder and vice president of the Lincoln National Bank in New York City.

Married in 1852 to the former Anna Margaret Townsend, the couple had five children: Elizabeth, Charles Townsend, Katherine Lawrence, Sarah, and Anna Townsend.

Van Santvoord died aboard *Clermont* in 1901. The yacht was converted into a excursion steamer on the Hudson after 1912 and remained as such until being scrapped in the early 1920s.

160 feet (another 15 feet later added) and built in 1892 for Alfred Van Santvoord, who also designed her. Built by H. Lawrence, Greenpoint. Powered by a paddle beam that drove her at 16 knots.

HOHENZOLLERN

1893

Royal yachts were invariably in a class by themselves, a result of their nature, size, and design. The Imperial yacht *Hohenzollern* was an impressive symbol of German supremacy, and surely intended as such. Her battleship-type bow, triple masts, and distinctive funnels set her apart. But it was her bulk, more than anything, that inspired awe. At 382 feet she was one of the largest yachts afloat, outstripping other royal yachts, such as Britain's 250-foot *Victoria and Albert (II)*, and private yachts like Jay Gould's 250-foot *Atalanta*. Only the Egyptian royal yacht *Mahroussa* (extant) was larger—she was launched with a length of 423 feet.

Hohenzollern was designed as a dispatch vessel; the German admiralty—as well as the Socialists in the Reichstag, no doubt—were taken aback when Kaiser Wilhelm II announced at the launching ceremony that the new vessel would be his personal yacht. She replaced a previous *Hohenzollern* (268 feet, built in 1875, and later renamed *Kaiseradler*) and was adorned with a mighty Imperial Eagle on her bow, while another eagle at her stern—with outstretched wings—held aloft a balcony. Deep in her hull, eight Scotch boilers supplied steam to a pair of massive Vulcan-Stettin triple-expansion engines.

The Kaiser (born Frederick Wilhelm Viktor Albert of Hohenzollern in 1859) had unexpectedly risen to power. After the March 1888 death of Emperor Wilhelm I, Frederick III was crowned emperor. However, Frederick III had throat cancer and later fell into a coma. His son, Wilhelm II, succeeded him in mid-1888. It seemed that the new Kaiser was intimidated by his sudden prominence and illustrious relations. Queen Victoria was his grandmother, King Edward VII was an uncle, and King George V and Czar Nicholas II were cousins. Nor could his withered left arm (a birth defect) have helped matters. Wilhelm II became

382 feet and built in 1893 for the German Admiralty. Designed by the German Admiralty. Built by Vulcan-Stettin. Powered by two Vulcan-Stettin triple-expansion steam engines, which drove her at 21 knots.

Hohenzollern (opposite), unique in many ways, featured an extraordinary element: a balcony encircling her stern, shaded by a canvas awning, and secured, in part, by an Imperial Eagle.

Rising high above the main deck, even higher than the bridge, was the Kaiser's personal bridge (below), a setting ideal for intensifying Teutonic pride.

famed for his disparaging and belligerent remarks about his relations, having "the least inhibited tongue in Europe," as historian Barbara Tuchman writes.

The Kaiser took to his new yacht with enthusiasm, traveling extensively. Being *the* impressive presence at Britain's Cowes Week and Germany's Kiel Week must have delighted the Kaiser no end (in photographs of such occasions, *Hohenzollern* startles the viewer with her obvious bulk, easily dwarfing all other yachts).

Hohenzollern made at least one trip to the United States, in 1902. The Kaiser, and his brother, Prince Henry, had come abroad for the launching of *Meteor (III)*, the Kaiser's latest racing schooner (designed by Cary Smith). In advance of the voyage, the Kaiser had cabled noted photographer Joseph Byron to immortalize his beloved *Hohenzollern*. The opening image on page 32, taken at the West Thirty-fourth Street pier, as well as the remaining shots of *Hohenzollern* are the result. To the author's knowledge, these remarkable photographs have never been published.

Above, the lower landing. Note the sisal runners, the lone sensible detail among wonderful extravagance.

Opposite, the main companionway, lighted by a skylight, featured numerous paintings, etchings, and drawings of German events, places, and buildings.

Byron n.y. 12892

1

2

Hohenzollern's conference room (1), while opulent, was, like the remaining interiors of the Imperial yacht, quite subdued for the era. Compare these images with those of *Atalanta* (pages 22–29) to appreciate the difference. However, the decor of the British *Victoria and Albert (II)* was more subdued than that of *Hohenzollern*.

In the "Working Room" (2), or the Kaiser's study, aboard *Hohenzollern*, the tumblehome (the inward cant of the hull) gave this elegant setting an obvious nautical flavor. Note, again, the plethora of paintings, drawings, and etchings.

Another view of the Kaiser's study (3).

The "Music Room" (4) featured velvet-covered columns, but no musical instruments are discernible in this image (although a grand piano may have been lurking under the draped fabric at the extreme right upper corner).

3

4

Above, a cozy corner in the "Music Room."

The distinction afforded *Hohenzollern* due to her size was erased after the launching of the 420-foot Russian royal yacht *Standart* in 1895 and the 430-foot British *Victoria and Albert (III)* in 1899. In 1913, the Kaiser had hoped to rectify this untenable situation—being one-upped by relations—when he ordered a yacht that would easily eclipse all other royal vessels: a 520-foot *Hohenzollern (III)* (her length is estimated). Unfortunately, while his new yacht was under construction, and while aboard *Hohenzollern* during the Kiel Regatta in June 1914, the Kaiser received a telegram. Informed that Archduke Franz Ferdinand of Austria had been assassinated, the Kaiser could not have foreseen that this message would bring an end to his world. When World War I erupted, the Kaiser's grandiose new yacht was never completed; her empty hulk was broken up in the early 1920s.

The Kaiser was forced to abdicate in 1918 as part of the Armistice. He moved to Holland, where he died in 1941. One wonders about his reaction to events in Germany between the years 1918 and 1941.

The fate of the Kaiser's beloved *Hohenzollern* is unknown.

287 feet and built in 1896 for Ignatio Florio of Palermo. Designed and built by Scott Shipbuilding & Engine, Ltd., Greenock. Powered by a 4-cylinder triple-expansion steam engine that drove her at 15 knots.

ERIN

1896 · LAUNCHED AS AEGUSA

Lipton (1) being photographed aboard the SS *Victoria* in 1920.

The first of Lipton's five *Shamrock*'s (2) on the wind while *Erin,* like a mother hen, watches respectfully at a distance.

1

As steam propulsion continued to prove itself, designers were emboldened to highlight the features that made a steam yacht, well, a steamer. The stack on *Erin* was a notable design feature, as opposed to the timid version on *Oneida*.

The outboard profile of *Erin* was typical of large steam yachts before the turn of the century: a long, lean, clipper-style hull; small, separate deckhouses; the prominent stack; open pilot station; and a pair of masts with vestigial sails. While these features were typical, *Erin*'s owner was hardly so.

Sir Thomas Lipton was born to poor Irish parents in 1850 and at fifteen emigrated to America. He worked at a number of jobs and moved frequently in search of a career, but returned to Glasgow a few years later with only a barrel of flour and a rocking chair for his mother. (This reverse migration was unusual. When people left for America, they rarely returned.) Through hard work, clever marketing, and good prices, Lipton built a small grocery store into a national chain. He had also learned that by cutting out the middleman and producing his own products for the store, he could increase profit and at the same time lower prices. This idea later manifested itself, rather dramatically, when he applied these principles to a very humble product: tea. Moreover, Lipton originated the idea of individual tea bags instead of selling only in bulk. From this simple idea an international business was created, one that earned Lipton an enormous fortune.

Lipton was a workaholic to the extreme and for many years lived a simple life, often sleeping in one of his stores and living for years with his beloved mother. He never married and, except for work, evidenced few passions. While he grew famous, initially this was the result of his stores and tea; only much later in his life did Lipton become celebrated for his personality.

After his initial failure in America, Lipton later developed major financial interests in the country and traveled regularly across the Atlantic. He wrote, "My thoughts definitely and longingly [turned] to my boyhood passion—to the wind and waves and the salt spray lashing and a mast bending under a well-filled sail." In his forty-eighth year Lipton made a quantum shift: he purchased a two-year-old steam yacht named *Aegusa* for $300,000 and renamed her *Erin*.

2

"Only then did I realize that it is not good for any man to be tied, neck and heel, to his office desk. No matter how hard I worked there was always the complete change and pleasure of a week-end on the *Erin* to break the monotony and to give me fresh vitality. Besides, I found I could have much more companionship on my ship than I could possibly have ashore. By and by, the *Erin* became famous for her visitors . . . and here let me say that these people were not merely aristocrats—they were the men and woman who were pulling their weight in the Ship of Life in one form or another."

Lipton was not the type of man to do things in a small way, and once he became enthusiastic about yachting, he expanded his horizons and entered the 1899 America's Cup with his challenger *Shamrock; Erin* became a palatial escort. *Shamrock* lost the race to *Columbia*.

When Lipton returned to America in 1901 with *Shamrock II, Erin* was the most sought-after yacht in the country, famed for her parties, lunches, and dinners (seventy people at the on-deck dining table wasn't uncommon). Yet, Lipton lost again. Undaunted, he rebounded with *Shamrock III* in 1903, entertained royally once more aboard *Erin* . . . and lost a third time. When he later traveled to America with *Shamrock IV*, war intervened; *Shamrock* was laid up and *Erin* turned into a hospital ship. Even though Lipton continued lavishly entertaining, many of the guests now wore nurse's uniforms. And while *Shamrock* would remain safe, *Erin* was torpedoed in the Mediterranean in 1915, with the loss of six lives. After the war Lipton returned, yet again, to America and entered the 1920 America's Cup. He lost again. To accompany him during his fifth challenge to the Cup in

1930, Lipton commissioned *Shamrock V*; for an escort vessel the steam yacht *Albion* was purchased and renamed *Erin*. Lipton lost, the Susan Lucci of his day.

Lipton's good cheer in the face of adversity made him beloved by Americans, even if it took the Brits a while to warm to him. Although Lipton was a friend of Edward VII (and entertained Mrs. Keppel, the king's mistress, aboard *Erin*), the Royal Yacht Club bitterly opposed his becoming a member, as they objected to his using the "sport" of yachting to promote Lipton's Tea. Even the crowned heads of Europe took a dislike to him; Kaiser Wilhelm II (see page 33) was reported to have acidly commented that the king of England had taken to sailing with his grocer. However, Lipton's indefatigable spirit eventually won the day and in his eighty-first year the Royal Yacht Squadron—which had forced Thomas Assheton-Smith's resignation a century before when he commissioned the first steam yacht—finally admitted him as a member in May of 1931. Lipton died the following November.

For all his fame and wealth, Lipton remained a curiously circumspect character. After his mother died in 1889 ("I lost my best friend"), he had no close friends or living relatives. His will contained but a few personal bequests, and his vast fortune was left to his native city of Glasgow to help support the "sick and poor," while his nondescript mansion, Osidge (outside London), was directed to be turned into a nursing home.

Erin (II) was broken up in 1936.

Shamrock V has been restored and plies the waters of Narragansett Bay, Rhode Island (for charter information, see Sources).

The tea lives on.

Scott's Shipbuilding & Engine Company, of Greenock, Scotland, which built *Erin* (launched as *Aegusa*), began in 1711 and had a continuous line of family directors until its merger with Lithgows Ltd., of Port Glasgow, in 1968—a remarkable achievement. The company developed a reputation for innovation and opened the first graving dock in 1767, launched the first vessel already fully masted and rigged (the *John Campbell* of 1806), two paddle steamers (*Active* and *Despatch* of 1815), the first vessel with feathering floats (PS *Talbot* of 1819), the first vessel for the Royal Navy built of iron and with a screw propeller (the frigate *Pegasus* of 1845), the first submarine depot ship (HMS *Maidstone* of 1906), and the largest diesel-electric vessel built at the time, the tanker *Brunswick* of 1928. During both world wars Scott's devoted 100 percent of their resources to the respective efforts. Their postwar work has included cargo vessels, submarines, bulk carriers, tankers, frigates, and passenger/cargo liners intended for use in the Far East. In 1966 a merger was affected with Greenock Drydock Company that created a continuous yard from Cartsburn to Cartsdyke East. Today, Scott-Lithgow is nearing its third century of operation.

It's understandable why *Erin* was so popular in her day, and parties aboard must have been comfortable in the extreme. The main saloon (1) also typifies the period and offers every Victorian bric-a-brac imaginable; it's hard to believe this is a yacht. Yet who would not have been delighted to receive an invitation while *Erin* was at Cowes, the Clyde, Trouville, New York, or Newport, Rhode Island? However, I'd have hated to be one of the crew, because the majority of these trappings—the ones not screwed in place—would have had to be placed in specially fitted boxes and stored below before every cruise.

A grand yacht wasn't properly equipped without a piano. *Erin*'s music saloon (2) featured one, as well as an embossed overhead and silken straps for pulling the windows closed.

Erin's library (1) on the main deck, a cabin so lush, opulent, and enveloping that its improbably being suspended above water must have contributed to its appeal.

Erin's dining saloon in the hull (2) appears to have been topped by a material resembling whipped cream. Note also the exposed carbon filament light bulbs.

A stateroom aboard Erin featured a brass bed plushly surrounded by hangings (3). Again, note the exposed carbon filament light bulbs with pointy tips, in an age when electricity was new and, thus, great fun to show off. Who wanted to cover this innovation? (Such bulbs were quite different from their modern counterparts, being rather dim and casting a flattering golden glow.)

The second *Erin* and her tender in 1930.

The Royal Yacht Squadron, which admitted Sir Thomas Lipton as a member in 1931, was founded in 1815 as The Yacht Club, and meetings were held at the Thatched House Tavern in London. From these humble beginnings the club rose to become one of the most well-known and prestigious such organizations in the world. In 1829 it became The Royal Yacht Club before assuming its current name in 1833. Its majestic clubhouse, Cowes Castle, was originally part of Britain's chain of coastal defenses and was built in 1538–39 under the reign of Henry VIII. The club leased the castle and began renovations, which were completed in 1858. When the Prince of Wales (later King Edward VII) became commodore, the club was the epicenter for glittering social and yachting events. This royal association began with George IV and has continued unbroken since.

KANAWHA

1 8 9 9

Kanawha, like *Erin*, was a typical design for her day, only her triple pole masts offered a distinction, as did her other extraordinary feature: speed. She won the 1903 and 1904 Lysistrata Cup doing 20 knots. During the 1903 race one of the competitors, *Noma* (see page 125), had thick, black smoke pouring from her stack, while *Kanawha*'s funnel left a pale brown trace behind, the result of her hand-picked coal. It was no small consideration that *Kanawha* was owned by Henry Huttleston Rogers ... who also happened to own the Virginian Railway ... which just happened to haul coal from the Kanawha mines.

After easily winning the 1904 race against *Hauoli*, no other yacht, as author Erik Hofman writes, "wished to challenge *Kanawha* for the Lysistrata Cup."

Rogers had purchased *Kanahwa* in 1901 (she'd been commissioned by John. P. Duncan in 1899) to be used as a commuter between his eighty-five-room mansion in Fairhaven, Massachusetts, and New York. Erik Hofman, in *The Steam Yachts*, writes that "as the route between these ports was almost identical to that followed by the Fall River and New Bedford passenger steamers, Mr. Rogers obtained the services of Capt. E. R. Geer, probably the most skillful (or daring) of that superb group of ship handlers. Rain or fog, clear or stormy, *Kanahwa* ran between these ports on a clock-like schedule, through such treacherous waters as Buzzards Bay, Block Island and Long Island Sounds, and the Race. She bucked heavy traffic, strong tidal currents, and frequent fogs, without any electrical aids to navigation, even radio, but only compass, rev. counters, and foghorn or whistle."

Rogers (1840-1909) began a remarkable career in Fairhaven as a grocery clerk; he later delivered newspapers and worked for the Old Colony Railroad as a baggage master (at $3 a week). After huge oil fields were discovered in Pennsylvania, Rogers gathered $600 in savings and departed his hometown to seek fortune. He was twenty.

During the next fourteen years Rogers became a leader in the fledgling oil business and invented a way to separate naphtha from crude oil—"an epochal invention for the industry." Rogers also worked with Charles Pratt, who had an oil refinery business in Brooklyn; their company was acquired by the Standard Oil Company in 1874, and Rogers rose to become its vice president. Diversifying into other interests, Rogers became infamous for his dealings in gas, copper, and steel, becoming one of the directors of United States Steel in 1901, as well as of numerous railroads and mines. He was also the transportation magnate of Staten Island.

While his contemporaries, such as J. P. Morgan and Jay Gould, were rather unimpressive in their physical stature, awkward in manner, and shy, Rogers was tall, lithe, handsome, and had a commanding yet graceful presence. Even business enemies reported on his almost hypnotic charm.

In 1862 Rogers had married his childhood sweetheart, Abbie Palmer Gifford, who was the daughter of a whaling captain; the couple went on to have six children. When their daughter Millicent died at seventeen, the couple donated to the town of Fairhaven an Italian Renaissance-style library in her honor. Several years before, in 1885, the Rogers Grammar School had been donated to the town. These gifts to the community were soon expanded with the French Gothic-style Town Hall in 1894 (Abbie died three months after its dedication), the Masonic Building (1900), the Unitarian Memorial Church (1902), Cushman Park (1905), Tabitha Inn (1905), the Elizabethan-style Fairhaven High School in 1906, and Fairhaven's water supply.

Rogers gained renown for helping his close friend, author Mark Twain, avert bankruptcy and save his copyrights, and, as

227 feet and built in 1899 for John P. Duncan. Designed by Charles L. Seabury. Built by Gas Engine & Power and Charles. L. Seabury, Consolidated. Powered by a pair of steam engines that drove her at 20 knots.

Twain wrote, "his commercial wisdom has protected my pocketbook ever since." Twain also suggested that Rogers financially assist Helen Keller.

When Rogers died in 1909 he left a second wife, the former Amelle Augusta Randel, four surviving children, and an estate valued at $100 million (estimated at $5.5 billion, in today's dollars). All the buildings he donated to his beloved Fairhaven are extant and many are open to the public. A daughter, Mai, married William R. Coe, and their splendid estate at Oyster Bay, Long Island (Coe Hall), is now open to the public (see Sources). A son, Henry, bequeathed 108 ship models dating from 1650 to 1850 to the Untied States Naval Academy Museum. The Rogers Ship Models Collection includes scale models built for the British Admiralty and display cabinets from the seventeenth century (see Sources). Rogers's granddaughter, Millicent Rogers (1902–53), was a celebrated fashion icon and amassed a notable collection of Native American jewelry and textiles. This collection can be seen today in the Millicent Rogers Museum in Taos, New Mexico (see Sources).

Kanawha was sold by the Rogers estate in 1911; she went on to numerous owners, including Morton F. Plant (see page 72) and the U.S. Navy, during World War I (as the USS *Pique*, one of four vessels—*Noma*, *Aphrodite*, and *Corsair*—that served as the Brenton Patrol, operating far out at sea). After the war the aging vessel went into commercial service before being scrapped in 1922, bringing an end to one of the fastest and most well-known steam yachts of her day.

This—one of my favorite images—is an extremely rare photograph of numerous steam yachts under way, *Kanawha* being the foreground vessel. Her triple pole masts are elegantly raked, although only the foremast carried any sail. Standing on deck is a part of *Kanawha*'s complement of forty-two crew members.

My favorite quote of Mark Twain's, a good friend of Henry Rogers and a frequent guest aboard *Kanawha*, is: "When we remember that we are all mad, the mysteries disappear and life stands explained."

4

1

2

3

The open-air bridge (1), typical of early steam yachts and a feature that would last until the late 1920s. One wouldn't have envied the captain and crew on a cold, wet, windy day.

This image, and the remaining of *Kanawha*, have not been published since 1902.

Kanawha's engines room (2 and 3) consisted of two triple-expansion Seabury engines and four Seabury water tube boilers, unusual in a day of single-engine yachts.

Early steam engines, as Erik Hofman details in *The Steam Yachts*, "were largely hand built and finished. They were masterpieces of craftsmanship, hand turned, hand fitted, hand polished. Cylinder jackets were often made of polished and varnished woods. The whole engine-room staff took great pride in the spotless appearance of their engine rooms and spent a goodly part of their time polishing, shining, and painting their machinery. [And], there was apparently little standardization of parts of steam engines. Each one seems to have been individually built. Stresses pressures, and loads were comparatively low. Weight was not a limiting factor. Thus maintenance and repairs could be, or had to be, made aboard by simple machine tooling. Total breakdowns were practically unheard of."

Male bonding, circa 1901 (4). These seven men, it's believed, are on *Kanawha*'s aft deck and include, from left to right: Augustus G. Paine (a New York businessman), Henry H. Rogers, Thomas B. Reed (a former Speaker of the House), Mark Twain, Laurence Hutton (an editor at *Harper's* magazine and a lecturer at Princeton), W. T. Foote (lawyer and congressman), and Clarence C. Rice (a doctor who introduced Rogers and Twain).

These two images at right, of the music saloon in one of *Kanawha*'s narrow deck cabins, offer a window into the height of Victorian yacht decor, with wicker chairs so animated as to seem almost life forms, and a piano hiding under a shawl ubiquitous for the era. Note also the mirror-like finish on the varnished overhead.

While these photographs, as well as the remaining beautiful black-and-white images that grace this book, have—thankfully—captured moments in time, one must remember that settings such as this saloon actually looked quite different. For example, the Auditorium The-ater in Chicago was designed by Louis Sullivan and Dankmar Adler in 1889. Although I'd admired this im-portant space for years in black-and-white images, I was nonetheless startled upon visiting the restored au-ditorium in the late 1980s (see Sources). I wasn't pre-pared for the riot of color covering every surface, the intricate stencil work, the dazzle of gold leaf, and, in par-ticular, the seemingly magical glow created by ten thou-sand exposed carbon filament light bulbs, an integral part of the original design. What had appeared impres-sive, even intimidating, in old photographs, was in fact surprisingly intimate, and the many disparate elements worked together to create a harmonious space quite un-like anything I'd ever experienced.

So, to modern eyes brainwashed into a "less is more" sensibility, this music saloon is a strange beast. Yet why should this be so?

The narrow width of *Kanawha*'s deck cabins signif-icantly contributed to their intimate charm, a feature overlooked by modern designers who equate bigger with better.

The main saloon in *Kanawha*'s hull offered an extraordinary, even thrilling, feature: a pole mast piercing the cabin. It's exactly this type of detail that makes classic yachts so delightful. The otherwise plush saloon could have been mistaken for a room in a London townhouse. But the raked mast covered in highly varnished teak gave the illusion away.

Will heaven look like this?

The dining saloon in the forward deck cabin, connected to the galley below by a dumbwaiter, was an orgasm of fine mahogany woodwork. It's hoped that the design engineers, while calculating *Kanawha*'s weights, took into account the heavy tablecloth and fringe.

These images of *Kanawha* are duplicated from an old *Rudder* magazine, as I was unable to find the original negatives or even to ascertain who the photographer was. Was this a man named Lazarnick? He took many extraordinary images of palatial steam yachts in the late nineteenth century (including the pictures of *Erin* beginning on page 40), yet I've been unable, even after a decade, to locate a single such original negative or print. (Lazarnick photographed a wide variety of subjects—such as automobiles—and many of these images are extant.) Any reader who might offer assistance in this quest is requested to contact the author (see page 277).

LYSISTRATA

As a designer, I know it takes time and practice to create a successful design. Early Frank Lloyd Wright houses—for example, the Tomek House—were interesting experiments but not wholly successful designs. Yet the ideas embodied in Tomek show up a few years later in his Robie House—an acknowledged masterpiece of early modernism.

So, too, with yacht designers. George L. Watson designed a steady stream of yachts, including some of the most beautiful ever created. Yet, as with Wright, it took a while to get the proportions and details right, and even then, there were some design sidesteps, such as his design for *Lysistrata*, a vessel that appeared more naval vessel than yacht, more formidable than attractive.

Large early yachts often had upper decks that looked like they were encased in scaffolding, *Lysistrata* being a prime example. She also had several other features that were unique, to my knowledge, such as turtlebacks (steel plates covering an open deck) fore and aft. Under her aft turtleback was a house for cows (necessary for fresh milk), as well as an armory. And, while not unique, *Lysistrata*'s foredeck was reserved for the owner and his guests, while the aft deck was for crew, a reversal of the usual order of things.

Perhaps the most peculiar feature of *Lysistrata* was her bow figurehead: an owl. This nocturnal bird was a totem of sorts for her owner, James Gordon Bennett (1841–1918), although he never adequately explained why (reports differ). Bennett had the famed architects McKim, Mead, and White install twenty-six

286 feet and built in 1900 for James Gordon Bennett. Designed by G. L. Watson. Built by William Denny & Son. Powered by a pair of steam engines that drove her at 17 knots.

bronze owls along the cornice of his new Herald Building, which occupied a trapezoidal lot across from Macy's, in New York. Their fifty-two eyes "eerily blinked on and off throughout the night." Bennett also asked that Stanford White design an enormous owl (either sixty feet tall or two hundred; reports differ) to be used as the family mausoleum, a concept that, perhaps thankfully, was never executed.

Bennett was, as one might assume, as unusual as his yacht. The son of one of the founders of American journalism, Bennett inherited both his father's newspaper (*The New York Herald*) and an estimated $40 million fortune. This legacy allowed him to indulge in his passion for racing (he owned the schooners *Henrietta* and *Dauntless*), steam yachting (*Polynia*, *Namouna*, and *Lysistrata*), polo (he introduced the sport to America), and lawn tennis (he built the elegant Newport Casino in Newport, Rhode Island, across from his now demolished estate, Stone Villa). He was a notorious ladies' man, practical joker, all-around eccentric, and "controlled alcoholic sociopath."

Commodore of the New York Yacht Club for two terms, Bennett was also a canny newsman, when sober. He is the one who sent Stanley to look for Livingstone ("Dr. Livingstone, I presume?"), and his paper's coverage of the Spanish-American War boosted circulation 500 percent to an all-time high. Ben-

nett also founded a Paris edition of the *Herald* in 1887. During World War I he personally ran the edition. It was the only newspaper in Paris that remained in operation throughout the war, bringing Bennett unaccustomed respect. These career high notes were in contrast to his relentless (and inaccurate) attacks upon financier Jay Gould (page 22), who, for reasons unexplained, was one of the few people Bennett evidenced an intense hatred for.

Bennett married for the first time in his seventy-third year. His wife was the former Maud Potter of Philadelphia, the widow of Baron George de Reuter. To the surprise of everyone, the couple appeared quite happy together (Bennett had reportedly stopped drinking), although their union ended upon the death of Bennett just four years later. Bennett left no heirs and little money, his fortune having been almost completely dissipated.

During World War I *Lysistrata* was purchased by the Imperial Russian Navy and used as an Arctic patrol vessel, the *Yaroslavna*. In 1920 the Soviet Navy took over the yacht and renamed her *Vorovsky*. Four years later she was transferred to use as a fishery protection vessel with a pair of 4-inch guns mounted on deck and lighter weapons. She was "discarded" after 1945 (J. Meister, *The Soviet Navy*, Volume II) but remained listed in *Jane's* until 1966. Could she be extant?

William Denny & Brothers, which built *Lysistrata*, had its beginnings in 1818, when William Denny (1779–1833) started a shipbuilding business after having created the first steam vessel on the River Thames, the PS *Margery*. The company prospered and developed a reputation for innovation, producing small ships driven by battery; welding (as opposed to riveting); installing stabilizers on their vessels; developing hovercraft; and building a ship model test tank in 1883. Denny & Brothers created standards for excellence accepted throughout the shipbuilding world and enjoyed a reputation as one of the best recorded shipbuilders. Their demise in the 1960s after a century of building nearly 1,500 ships seemed to many to mark the end of the United Kingdom's domination of world shipbuilding.

In this remarkable image *Lysistrata*'s figurehead is up on blocks at the builder's yard previous to installation. One can fully appreciate Bennett's peculiar fascination with owls, as well as the impressive craftsmanship required to create such a unique work of art. The eyes were reportedly fitted with small lights that blinked on and off.

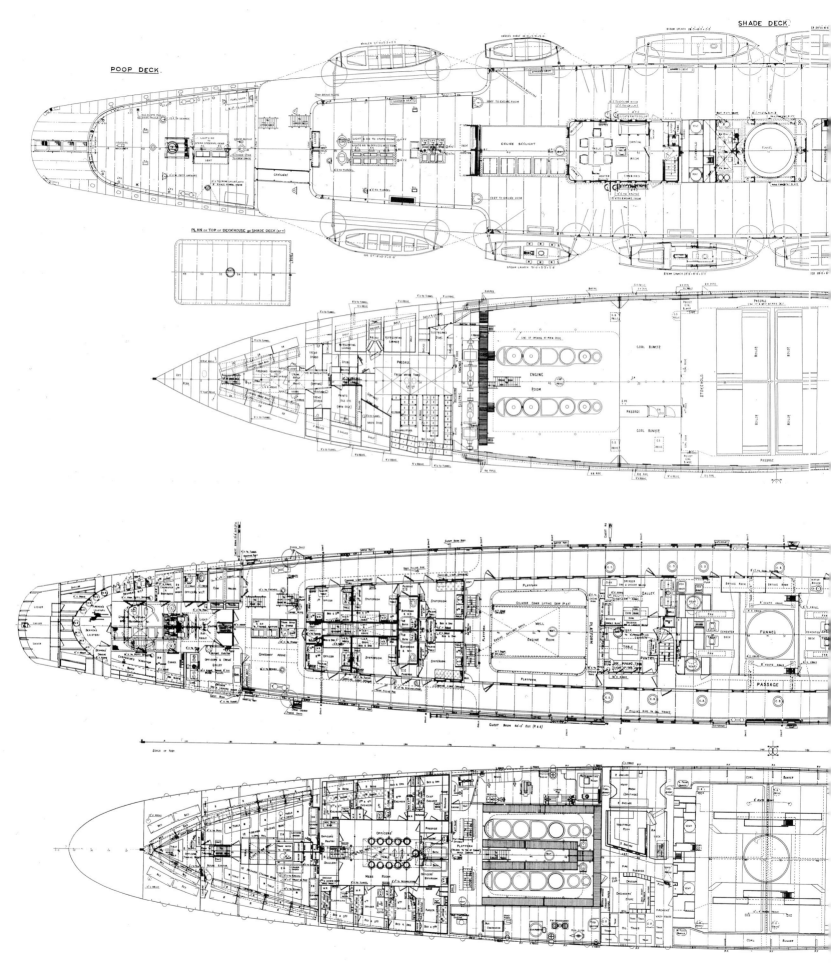

POOP DECK.

SHADE DECK.

PLAN OF TOP OF DECKHOUSE OR SHADE DECK (AFT)

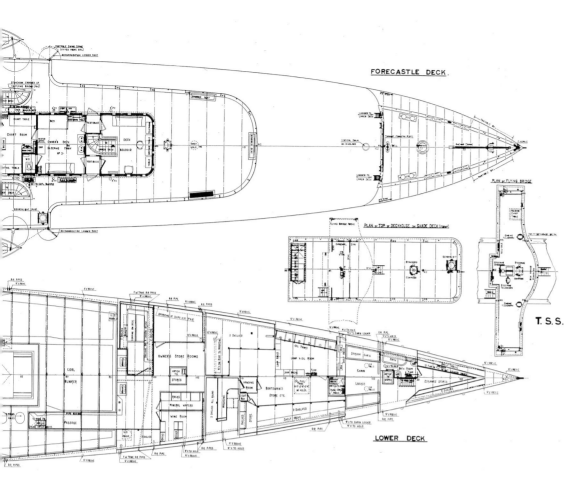

FORECASTLE DECK.

PLAN OF FLYING BRIDGE

PLAN OF TOP OF DECKHOUSE OR SHADE DECK (rear)

T. S. S.

LOWER DECK

Lysistrata had five decks, three owner's staterooms (Bennett, for reasons never fully explained, maintained a private suite on each main deck), a vast engine compartment, and crew quarters aft. A cow house, with two stalls, was on the port side, upper deck, opposite the Officers and Crew Galley.

George L. Watson (1851–1904) was one of the leading yacht designers of the nineteenth century, with over 400 vessels to his name, including the America's Cup contenders *Thistle*, *Valkyrie II* and *III*, and *Shamrock II*, as well as Edward VII's *Britannia*. Watson's office also designed forty-seven steam yachts by 1900. He began his career at sixteen as an apprentice draftsman for Robert Napier & Son in Glasgow (see page 14) and later worked for J & A Inglis, another Glasgow shipyard. At twenty-two, Watson set out on his own as a naval architect and within two years produced his first significant design, *Clothilde*, for the 5-ton class. The yacht bested a Fife design, *Pearl*, for a substantial purse. Other winning designs included *Vril*, *Vanduara*, *May*, and *Marjorie*. By the end of his first decade as a naval architect, Watson's reputation was far-reaching. Known as a workaholic, he supervised all the work in his office "with a meticulous eye for detail," yet he was uninterested in yachting as a sport, never owning a yacht and rarely taking time to sail or cruise. When he was fifty-one, Watson startled his friends by announcing his impending marriage to the heretofore unknown Miss Lovibond, a woman, as it later turned out, with whom he had carried on a relationship for two decades (largely by letter). The couple went on to have a daughter, although Watson died a few months later. His death was attributed to overwork, the price he paid for a successful career as the "father of scientific yacht architecture." His firm was still extant in the 1990s.

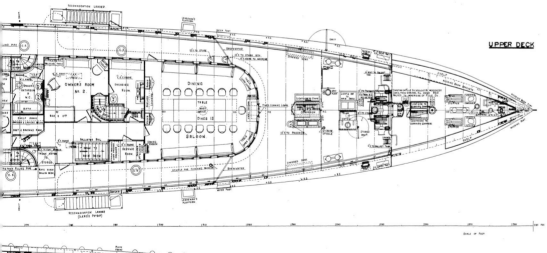

UPPER DECK

SCALE OF FEET

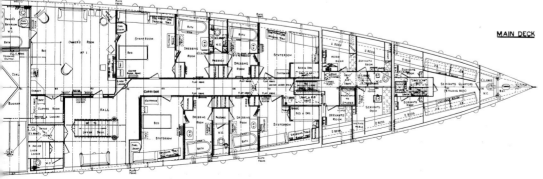

MAIN DECK

Bennett's two previous steam yachts, *Polynia* and *Namouna*, had interiors by a young Stanford White, who, besides being a brilliant architect, had a particularly fine eye for the subtleties of interior decoration. His rooms for the New York State Capitol are a marvel of rich textures and materials, creating one of the most extraordinay nineteenth-century interiors ever devised (extant).

White's work for *Polynia* was minor, a mere $500 billed. The bill for *Namouna* came to $20,837. Although Bennett enjoyed *Namouna* for eighteen years, the ex-tant records do not indicate that he commissioned White for his new yacht, instead turning to Messrs. Waring of London. Nonetheless, the design quality of *Lysistrata* is so extraordinary, and so similar to the work of White, that the author wonders: is it White's?

In an age of dark, highly polished woodwork and rich, colorful fabrics, *Lysistrata*'s interior decor was as unusual as her outboard design and owner, featuring brilliant white saloons and discreet, small-scale prints in pale colors. Her outstanding decorative feature was one not usually associated with the art of fine decoration: the owl. Waring (or White) incorporated Bennett's totem into a startling variety of objects, fabrics, and joinerwork. In the image above (marked Owner's Room No. 2 on the upper deck plans), there are at least nineteen owls evident, although this feature did not overwhelm the small cabin—a testament to the creative talents of Messrs. Waring. Or Standford White. (There are thirteen owls in the frieze, one incorporated into each of the three wall sconces, two sitting on the dresser, and one attached to the shelf on the bulkhead.)

Lysistrata's forecastle deck featured another private cabin for Bennett (marked Owner's Deck Sleeping Cabin No. 3 on the plans) and owls again dominated—subtly so. One was above the beveled mirror, two held lampshades aloft on the dressing table, another (reflected in the mirror) held another shade, and numerous others were woven into the chair and drape fabric.

The "Deck Boudoir" on the forecastle deck, forward of Bennett's sleeping cabin number three, featured still more owls. In this image, four appear to be holding up the center table (the top of the exposed table leg looks like the back of an owl), one is holding a lampshade (above the center window), and numerous additional birds are scattered across the desks.

The stair (extreme lower right of photograph) led directly down to Bennett's stateroom number two on the upper deck.

These interior images convey another appealing aspect of *Lysistrata:* she was well used by Bennett. It's rare to observe such a wealth of personal objects, note-cards, books, mementos, and photographs.

Lysistrata's dining saloon—another inviting cabin—was watched by an owl on each table (one with a hinged head), a pair perched on the wall sconce, and a flock in the joinerwork over the windows. It is possible that additional birds nested in the overhead light, the pillow fabric (upper right corner), and the chair fabric.

DREAMER

1899

This vessel, and the three that follow, offers instruction about the evolution of steam yachts at the turn of the century. *Dreamer* was an extremely advanced design and represented one of the last gasps for sail/steam hybrids. There could have been no mistake—this *was* a steam yacht. The continuous deckhouse was a significant advance, as was the stack rising high above. The twin masts retained vestigial sails, which could have been used in emergencies for propulsion but, more often, would have helped steady such early, narrow yachts, which rolled easily at the slightest wave or breeze.

Thomas William Lawson (1857–1925), who commissioned *Dreamer* in his forty-second year, is remembered by yachting enthusiasts for *The Lawson History of the America's Cup*, a lavishly produced, 402-page tome critiquing the New York Yacht Club's methods of selecting defenders for the America's Cup. Lawson (and Winfield M. Thompson) wrote the book after he was prevented from entering the 1901 Cup race because he wasn't an NYYC member.

Dreamer, her name later changed to *Rambler*, wasn't listed in *Lloyd's Register of American Yachts* after World War I.

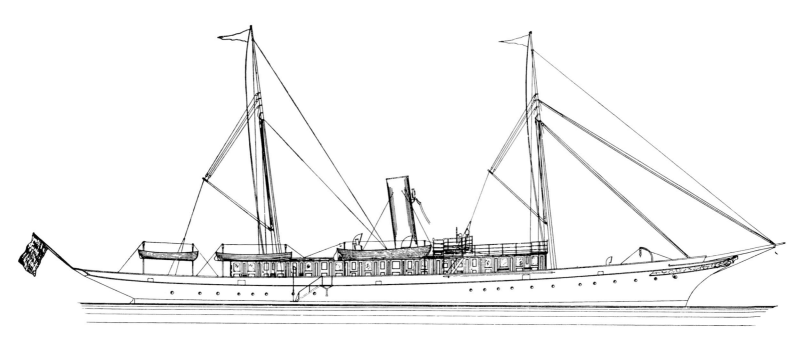

170 feet and built in 1899 for Thomas W. Lawson. Designed by Tams, Lemoine & Crane. Built by Crescent Shipyard. A triple-expansion steam engine drove her at 15 knots.

VALDA

1900

Where *Dreamer* was a quantum advance in motor yacht design, *Valda* was retrograde. Note her tiny, single cabin house, the slender stack not much taller than the deck cabin, and the open pilot station, features that would soon give way to more advanced designs.

She may not look it, but *Valda* was designed as a 13-knot commuter for the run between Marblehead and Boston. And, while in this day and age a 116-foot yacht would be considered quite large, note how little was offered in the way of accommodations aboard *Valda*. She had just one stateroom, although more guests could be accommodated on the settees in the main saloon. *Valda* also said a lot about her era because it took a crew of *nine* to operate a vessel designed to transport *one*, though her owner wasn't rich on a Vanderbilt scale. Another interesting aspect was the spaciousness of the engine room; the large steam engine seems almost tiny by comparison.

Interestingly, *Valda*'s original owner, Frank McQuesten, repurchased the yacht two decades after selling her.

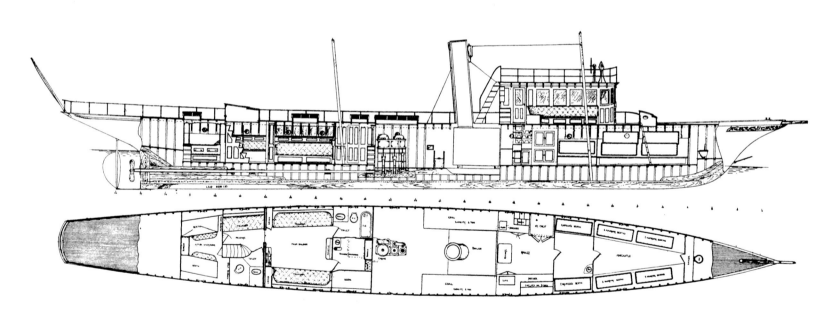

116 feet and built in 1900 for Frank B. McQuesten. Designed and built by George Lawley & Son. Powered by a triple-expansion Lawley engine, which drove her at 13 knots.

George Lawley & Son, the builder of *Valda*, began in 1866 in Scituate, Massachusetts. The company was catapulted into world renown when they built an Edward Burgess design for the 1885 America's Cup, the wooden sloop *Puritan* (which beat *Genesta*). The following year they launched another Cup winner, the Burgess-designed *Mayflower* (which bested *Galatea*). The demand for yachts built of iron and steel necessitated a move across Dorchester Bay to Neponset. At the same time the elder Lawley retired and his son, George Frederick Lawley (1848–1928), took over the company. Lawley & Son continued to grow and became one of the most prolific yacht builders in the United States. Although George Lawley retired in 1925, he maintained an active interest in a yard started by his son, Frederick Damon, in Quincy, Massachusetts.

CALUMET

140 feet and built in 1903 for Charles G. Emery. Designed by George Lawley & Son. Built by A. S. Chesebrough. Powered by a Lawley steam engine.

1 9 0 3

Calumet was more advanced than *Valda*—sporting a pair of deck-houses and pronounced stack—but less than *Dreamer*. The open pilot station remained an age-old fixture (as did the masts), and her aft deck lacked the expansive lounging area that would come to grace yachts in the decades to come. *Calumet*'s narrow beam was also typical of motor yachts until the 1930s.

As a ship's plan aficionado, I enjoy studying finely detailed plans such as this. Note that the deck-level pantry and galley below were not directly connected by stair or ladder, only by dumbwaiter. I also like the skylight over the icebox. In the main saloon (labeled Drawing Room) there was the ubiquitous piano (before radio, stereos, and CDs, if one wanted to hear music, one had to *play*—or hire players). Access to the hull staterooms wasn't from the deck saloon but aft, on deck (another feature that would soon disappear). Imagine the delight of walking under the two aft launches (the two amidships would have been hidden by the canvas awning).

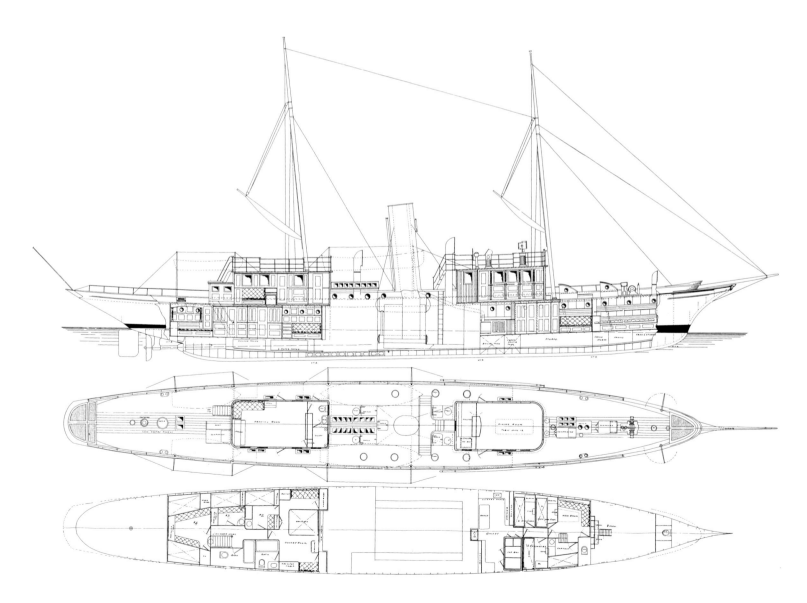

MEDEA

1904

140 feet and built in 1904 for William Macallister Hall (image dates from 1938). Designed and built by Alexander Stephen & Sons. Powered by a 254-hp compound steam engine, which drove her at 11.5 knots.

A survivor from a lost age, *Medea* today plies the waters off the California coast, thanks to the efforts of Paul Whittier and the San Diego Maritime Museum. Whittier, an oilman, yachtsman, and philanthropist whose family name adorns both a city and a university in Southern California, first spotted *Medea* locked in ice at Oskarshamn, Sweden, in 1967. The once elegant vessel was obscured by peeling paint, rusted hull plates, and peeling varnish. Whittier tried to purchase *Medea* and was rebuffed. Later, realizing just how rare the vessel was, he returned with an offer that could not be refused.

Whittier then enlisted the help of an old friend and trustee of the San Diego Maritime Museum, Joe Jessop, the museum agreeing to accept and maintain the restored *Medea*. After an eighteen-month restoration, the sixty-nine-year-old vessel was once again the elegant beauty she'd been upon her launch in 1904.

Medea was commissioned by William Macallister Hall, who gave the builder, Alexander Stephen & Sons, a ninety-day deadline (just in time for the grouse season). The builder, obviously up to such a challenge, completed *Medea* (to be used as a floating lodge) in a remarkable fifty-one days.

Over her lifetime *Medea* has had a variety of owners, including two members of the Stephen family, and served in both world wars (as a French submarine chaser in World War I and in the "little ships" evacuation of Dunkirk during World War II) before being rescued by Paul Whittier and offered a safe harbor by the San Diego Maritime Museum, where she has been for almost three decades now.

During a cruise in 1910, an amateur photographer snapped the image (opposite) of *Medea*'s owner, William Macallister Hall, and his guest, Mrs. Gauntlett, as they rested under the protective bulkheads and overhang of the "shelter," an area intended to insulate one from brisk winds and spray.

Above, the *Medea* was brought from Europe to California aboard the *Riederstein* in 1971.

Alexander Stephen & Sons, which designed and built *Medea*, began in 1750 and went on to achieve extraordinary longevity. Initially the company moved several times before settling in Kelvinhaugh, Glasgow; in 1870 Stephen moved again, to Linthouse. Known for their "unimpeachable quality," Stephen built a wide range of ships, including *Emerald* (owned by Christopher Furness), the first steam yacht across the Atlantic using turbines; numerous passenger liners (such as the *Marathon* of 1903 and the *Koninlijke* of 1913); cargo and passenger vessels for the

Imperial Direct West Indian Line and Elders & Fyffes; ships for the Royal Navy (including the mine-layer *Manxman* and aircraft carrier *Ocean*); and even a famous sloop that "made the famous dash from the River Yangtse in 1949"—the *Amethyst*. After launching close to a thousand vessels, the company ceased to exist in 1968 after 218 years of shipbuilding, becoming part of Upper Clyde Shipbuilders (UCS), a new entity, which also absorbed John Brown & Company (see page 81), Connell & Company, Fairfields, Ltd., and Yarrow, Ltd. (see page 140).

IOLANDA

In time designers piled decks upon decks upon decks. Such was the case on the impressive, nearly overwhelming, *Iolanda*, which had three deckhouses. Note also the pair of immense cowl vents (supplying air to the engine room and exhausting it) adjacent to the imposing stack.

This vessel—distinctive even in her day—was commissioned by Morton Freeman Plant (1852–1918), son of Henry Bradley Plant (1819–99). The elder Plant, among other endeavors, took over numerous southern rail lines ruined by the Civil War and extended service to a sleepy town named Tampa, building an extraordinary, 511-room hotel topped with thirteen silver minarets—the Tampa Bay Hotel (extant as the University of Tampa). He also developed the Port Tampa Inn, on a pier extending a mile out on Tampa Bay, which advertised that honeymooners could fish from their rooms. Finally, he was responsible for bringing the Cuban cigar industry to Tampa's Ybor City, resulting in its reputation as the "Cigar Capital of the World."

In stark contrast to his creative, workaholic father, Morton Plant divested himself of his business interests after 1902 and became a part owner of the Philadelphia baseball club and owner of the New London club. He also became a yachting enthusiast and owned a number of yachts, including the fast Herreshoff schooners *Elena* and *Ingomar*. Other vessels included the steam yachts *Venetia*, *Kanawha* (page 48), and *Vanadis* (page 119), as well as *Iolanda*. Plant sold *Iolanda* in 1911, after which she was owned by Mme. E. Terestchenko (1912–19), the British Navy in both world wars (renamed the HMS *White Bear*), Camper & Nicholson (1920–27), Mr. and Mrs. Moses Taylor (1928–39), and then commercial interests after 1947.

318 feet and built in 1908 for Morton F. Plant. Designed by Cox & King. Built by Ramage & Ferguson. Powered by a pair of steam engines that drove her at 19 knots.

ALOHA (II)

After the turn of the century, rigged masts had largely disappeared as a steam yacht feature, except for notable exceptions. The famed auxiliary bark *Aloha (II)* was one.

Once, while twilight of an evening in late June lingered and glimmered over the wake churned by the paddles of the Fall River Line steamer Priscilla *as she steamed eastward on Long Island Sound, [I saw], ahead of us, a splotch of white flickered against the gathering darkness. Coastal schooners were still thick along that route, and it was a common sight to come up on them as they plodded their way through the evening calm, grayish sails hanging slack in the zephyrs. This splotch diffused and grew bigger, however, spreading higher and whiter against the wall of night, until a pattern of square-rigged sails loomed higher, and suddenly her black hull and rigging pattern firmed in the pale light. We left her on the port hand, and she fell sharp back on the quarter, the ghostly white of her sails changed to sharp silhouettes. There, against the glow remaining in the northwest sky, was the starkly outlined tracery of the rigging and sails of a graceful bark. For a moment she stood bold against the horizon, and towered into the night, a dramatic reminder of an era that had already gone by. Fire from the departed sun tipped her upper yards and glinted off some glossy patch of paint on her topsides, and then, with* Priscilla *steadily chunk-chunking her way eastward, the vision faded astern into the murk of descending night and became nothing more than the wink of running lights dimming rapidly.*

Someone along the rail murmured "Aloha" as the ship stood against the sunset, for that's what she was, the beautiful 202-foot bark Arthur Curtis James had built as flagship for the New York Yacht Club in 1910. She was one of the most romantic yachts ever built, a bridge between the age of square-riggers and the luxurious floating palaces of the early twentieth century. No one who saw her will ever forget her.

This tale was told by well-known yachtsman Bill Robinson in his book *Legendary Yachts.*

Arthur Curtis James (1867–1941) had been an only child, born into comfort and wealth, attending private schools, and, at thirty-three, assuming leadership of the company his grandfather and father had built: Phelps, Dodge & Company, with diversified interests including manufacturing, copper mining, and railroads. Upon his father's death in 1907, James became Phelps, Dodge's largest stockholder. By the early 1930s, James controlled 40,000 miles of rail lines, "far surpassing the empires of earlier railroad magnates."

Unlike many wealthy and influential personalities of the era—such as Jay Gould, J. Pierpont Morgan, and James Bennett—James was not widely known. He married Harriet Eddy Parsons in 1890; the couple had no children. Although the Jameses lived lavishly, with elegant homes in New York City, Newport, Rhode Island, and Miami, Florida, they maintained a low profile, making substantial philanthropic contributions unaccompanied by fanfare. During his lifetime, James gave away an estimated $20 million. His will established the James Foundation, with $25 million in assets, stipulating that the income be distributed and, after twenty-five years, the principal as well. At the time of its closure in 1965, the foundation had disbursed more than $144 million to a variety of institutions.

James had learned about navigation and seamanship aboard

216 feet and built in 1910 for Arthur Curtis James. Designed by Tams, Lemoine & Crane. Built by Fore River SB and Engine Company. Powered by acres of canvas and one steam engine.

James is shown here boarding his launch at Glen Cove, Long Island, ready to speed toward his Manhattan office and *Aloha*, whose home berth was the East River.

Images such as this are interesting because they've captured a moment in time. Who, for example, was the woman standing on the bulkhead with four children? Mrs. James? A bystander? And, whoever she was, what was on her mind that morning? Was she having a good day? What was James thinking? Had he had a pleasant weekend? How was his business doing?

And, what about the officers and crew? Did they like Mr. James? What about *their* private lives, foibles, and dreams? Did anyone appreciate the moment?

(Like many old prints, this is damaged)

Coronet, a 125-foot schooner his father had given him, eventually cruising 60,000 miles and enjoying a voyage to Japan. In 1899 James had a 130-foot brigantine built and named her *Aloha* ("a splendid little vessel"), traveling 152,560 miles over the next ten years and making at least twelve transatlantic crossings. Although quite happy with *Aloha*, James longed for a world cruise and realized that a larger vessel was required for such an adventure. So he commissioned a successive yacht and did what you and I would have: had more of the same, from the same designers, and to great effect. The bark-rigged *Aloha (II)* was the result.

As a tender for *Aloha (II)* James commissioned *Lanai*, a 76-foot Trumpy house-yacht. (James ordered a successive 85-foot Mathis-Trumpy in 1927. For more on Trumpy house-yachts, see page 176.)

Aloha (II) was specially fitted for a world cruise, but World War I interrupted such plans. The elegant yacht was used by the navy for patrol duty until being returned to James after a refit. Still, it wasn't until September 1921 that *Aloha* realized the long-held dreams of her owner.

For her epic cruise *Aloha* had a complement, as Erik Hofman notes in *The Steam Yachts*, consisting of "her captain, two mates, a boatswain, a carpenter, a radio man, and 16 hands. Her engine room staff comprised a chief engineer, two assistants, two oilers, and two firemen. There were nine in the stewards department including a stewardess. A doctor was part of the after-guard on all extensive voyages."

It was also a good thing she was an auxiliary bark.

Aloha encountered remarkably few winds and during one 10,000-mile segment only managed to sail 250 miles. Her owner and guests amused themselves by reading to one another, playing countless games of bridge, and gazing long hours out upon seas sometimes so lonely that they'd not see another vessel, or even birds and fish, for weeks on end.

Of course, there were many lively moments, such as hiring camels to see the pyramids in Egypt, visiting temples and shrines in Tokyo, sightseeing pineapple plantations and a leper colony in Hawaii, enjoying comfortable trains and hotels in Seoul and Mukden, and being awed by the Taj Mahal and impressed by the ruins at Baalbek in Beirut.

Except for her stint in World War I, *Aloha (II)* was blessed with one owner before being scrapped in 1938 after twenty-eight years of service.

The schooner *Coronet* is now being restored by the International Yacht Restoration School in Newport, Rhode Island. It is the oldest and most original grand vessel remaining from a lost century of yachting (see Sources).

Lanai, the Trumpy tender for *Aloha (II)*, is extant as *Argo* in New York City.

Aloha was designed by Clinton Crane (1873–1958). After graduating from Harvard in 1894 Crane worked for the Cramp & Sons shipyard in Philadelphia, which built the first *Corsair* and *Atalanta*. Crane continued his education at Columbia University and in Scotland before joining the brokerage firm of Tams and Lemoine in 1899, later becoming a partner. *Challenger*, Crane's candidate for the Harmsworth Trophy (an international speedboat competition), caught fire during trail runs on the Harlem River. Crane, on board, pulled off his heavy clothes and dived overboard. Luckily, a nearby ferry boat pulled him to safety, except, much to Crane's annoyance, the boat was loaded with women, who crowded around the naked man, making it difficult for him to get into a stateroom to renew his modesty through borrowed clothes. Crane fared better when he was commissioned to design the first *Aloha* and, later, her successor. Other highlights were his schooners *Endymion* and *Deverish* and the enormous steam yacht *Vanadis* in 1908 (see page 119). In 1912 Crane left yacht designing to help his father's failing mining company, remaining until his 1947 retirement. Crane had returned to designing yachts on an amateur basis in the 1920s, and his J-boat *Weetamoe* was a close contender for the America's Cup, losing to *Enterprise* in late trials. Crane's own 12-meter, *Gleam*, influenced a later generation of 12-meters and today plies the waters of Narragansett Bay in Rhode Island under the care of Bob and Elizabeth Tiedeman (see Sources).

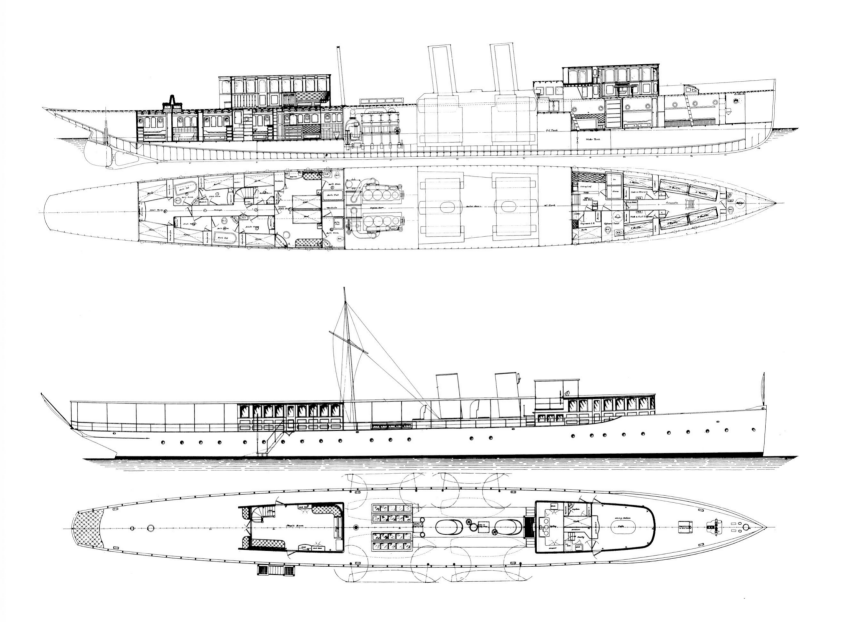

The outboard profile and main deck of *Gem* clearly show the separate deckhouses as well as the narrow beam typical of yachts before the 1930s. Note the "Music Room" and its upright piano, as well as the built-in settees.

The inboard profile and lower deck of *Gem* show the elaborate paneling and leaded glass cabinets in the "Music Room," and the seat on the aft deck, which had built-in glass panels to help light cabins below. *Gem* was also graced with twin heads for the owner's stateroom and two others for guests. Yet the "Maid's Room" had no direct access to these necessities; one feels for her discomfort in the event that all staterooms were occupied.

Gem's steam engines and formidable boilers were fueled by oil, an advance over coal, which took a considerable amount of time to load and, in the process, created a film of black dust that could coat an entire vessel, forcing the crew to spend hours wiping down everything. The shift to oil eliminated this unpleasant task.

GEM

164 feet and built in 1913 for William Ziegler, Jr. Designed by Cox & Stevens. Built by George Lawley & Son. Powered by a pair of steam engines that drove her at 15 knots.

Unlike the majority of power yachts built previously, *Gem* could not have been mistaken for a converted clipper ship. She was, unmistakably, a steam yacht, and must have been quite extraordinary in her day.

After a very difficult week, you're lying in a chaise on the aft deck of your 50-foot yacht. The stress you've felt all week is slowly draining from your body. Suddenly, a shadow blocks the warm, invigorating sun from your face. Opening your eyes, you see your wife blocking the sun; she asks you a question. Before answering, you note a sudden and dramatic change in her face. Gone is the casual and familiar look, its replacement one of wonder, even apprehension, as her eyes stare, seemingly riveted, at something off the stern. Worried, you get up and . . . gasp. Coming toward you is an apparition both elegant and dangerous looking. As it glides by, you stare openmouthed at the vessel, long and low to the water, with her 18-foot beam an extraordinary contrast to the 164-foot length—like a huge pencil, you think. The twin stacks puff a greeting while the captain waves from the raised pilot station. Dumbly, you wave back as the plumb bow before you knifes through the waves. Your eyes wander up to the long, carved scrollwork, and as the apparition cruises by, your stare remains fixed—like watching a long train go by—as foot after foot after foot of Gem *steams past. Putting your arm around your wife, you both remain speechless as the modified counterstern of* Gem *finally appears, only to slowly disappear. A few moments pass before your wife pinches you and asks, "Was that real?"*

During World War I, *Gem* performed harbor entrance patrol at New Haven, Connecticut, and she was later used by the Submarine Defense Association for experimental work (such as camouflage defense and testing submarine detection devices, course and speed indicators, and the efficiency of pulverized coal).

The war interrupted the yacht building industry shortly after *Gem* was commissioned, and few private yachts were launched until the early 1920s.

Gem was ordered by William Ziegler, Jr. (1891–1958), whose father was known as the "Baking Powder King." Ziegler, Jr., attended Harvard and Columbia universities, and in his twenty-first year became a director of the family business, the Royal Baking Powder Company; he was president from 1922 to 1929. When Royal merged with Standard Brands, Ziegler became a director of the successor company from 1929 to 1948. He was also active in real estate and devoted considerable time to numerous organizations assisting the blind.

Ziegler married Gladys Virginia Watson in 1912, and the couple had two children, Elizabeth and Barbara; they later divorced. A second marriage took place in 1927 to Helen Martin Murphy and produced two children, William and Helen.

Ziegler sold *Gem* in 1922. She went on to a variety of owners and did not appear in *Lloyd's* after World War II. Ziegler appears not to have owned another yacht until after the war when he concurrently sailed *Bounding Home*, a 52-foot auxiliary schooner (ex-*Savannah*); *Sea Frolic*, a 34-foot auxiliary sloop; and *Spookie*, a 45-foot auxiliary cutter. Today, the family yachting tradition continues with William Ziegler III and his sailing racer, *Gem*.

NAHLIN

1930

300 feet and built in 1930 for Lady Yule. Designed by G. L. Watson. Built by John Brown & Company, Ltd. Powered by a pair of steam-geared turbines that drove her at 17 knots.

One of the last great steam yachts ever built, and the last designed by the firm of George L. Watson, *Nahlin* had four distinguishing features. First, she was tinged with scandal. Second, she's still around. Third, she was steam powered in an age when diesels had revolutionized yachting. And, fourth, she was one of the few yachts commissioned by a woman—Lady Yule, a jute millionairess.

The scandal part of *Nahlin*'s history involved a certain Duke of Lancaster, who chartered the yacht in 1936 for a cruise. This seemingly innocuous event erupted into a celebrated international scandal due to the fact that the duke was, in fact, a king—one Edward VIII. Also on board was a Mrs. Wallis Simpson. They were photographed holding hands. And we all know the rest.

The historic records concerning Lady Yule (Annie Henrietta) are scant. What is known is that she married Sir David Yule in 1900 and, after his death in 1928, commissioned *Nahlin*. At 300 feet the yacht was impressive even in her day. What possessed the new widow to undertake such an adventure? Research to date has been unable to answer this intriguing question.

After several years of being chartered by Lady Yule, *Nahlin* became the Romanian royal yacht (the *Luceafarul*), and later a floating restaurant moored on the Danube at Galati, before being placed in the "Heritage" category by the Romanian Ministry of Culture in 1998. The author, after laborious negotiations, had finally arranged to have current images taken of this fascinating vessel, one of the last remaining steam yachts and one of the largest ever built. But, in a breathtaking turn of events, *Nahlin* suddenly left Romania and returned to Britain after an absence of six decades for a planned restoration. Once complete, she will be one of the most extraordinary yachts in the world.

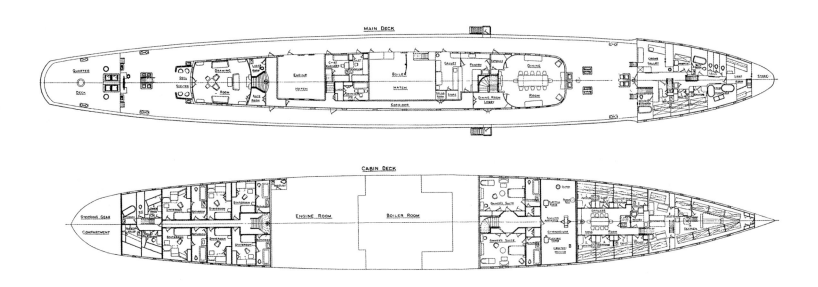

Nahlin's plans were both state-of-the-art in 1930 and antiquated. Her general arrangement plan was quite sophisticated, with every inch being used sensibly (note the owners apartment forward and adjacent gymnasium). Yet, because she was steam powered in a diesel age, space was taken up by machinery and fittings unnecessary on a diesel vessel.

John Brown & Company, Ltd., which built *Nahlin*, endured for almost a century (1899–1968) and launched some of the most famous vessels ever created, such as the elegant *Aquitania*, the royal yacht *Britannia*, the *Queen Mary*, and the *QE2*. The yard produced almost 400 vessels during its history and had its beginnings in 1856, when John Brown, a former Sheffield apprentice steel merchant, opened his own business at the Atlas Works. In a little over a decade Brown was to provide the armour for 75 percent of the ironclads built in the U.K. Later, control of the company passed from Brown, although the name lives on as John Brown Engineering, Ltd. (although unrelated to marine engineering).

AVALON

1930

180 feet and built in 1930 for Ogden L. Mills. Designed by Cox & Stevens. Built by Pusey and Jones. Powered by a pair of Winton diesels that drove her at 16 knots.

This yacht and the three that follow offer instruction about shifting design aesthetics during the late 1920s. On *Avalon*, the classic clipper-type bow was modernized and the pole, figurehead, and gilded trailboards were gone; the stack was scaled so as to no longer be a prominent feature (a full-circle shift), and an unusual military-type latticed mast was installed. Yet, *Avalon*'s stern was still recognizable from yachts a century old.

Avalon was commissioned by Ogden Livingston Mills, who was born into wealth and prestige and a was U.S. Secretary of the Treasury during the Hoover administration. His father, Darius Ogden Mills, had made a fortune during the Gold Rush era in California investing in railroads, banks, and silver and gold mines. His mother, Ruth Livingston Mills, was descended from Hudson Valley property owners prominent since the seventeenth century. The family mansion, built on property owned by the Livingston family since 1792, in Staatsburg, New York, is a McKim, Mead and White–designed home now open to the public (see Sources).

ALVA (II)

1930

264 feet and built in 1930 for W. K. Vanderbilt II. Designed by Cox & Stevens. Built by Krupp-Germaniawerft. Powered by a pair of 8-cylinder Krupp diesels.

Alva, like *Avalon*, opened a brand-new design book, one that disdained the past and reached forward. She looked, in short, very little like any yacht built before. Her bow was no longer plumb, clipper, or even *Maine*-type battleship, but slightly curved; and her topsides extended above the main deck (a startling detail that yacht designer Jon Bannenberg would bring to an extreme five decades later on *Oceanfast 3000,* a floating spaceship). Also note the $57,000 seaplane over the aft deck, and deckhouses that were no longer brilliantly varnished mahogany or teak but white painted steel. Yet, all said, *Alva* was more formidable looking than attractive.

William K. Vanderbilt II (1878–1944), who commissioned *Alva*, was a member of a family that owned more yachts than any other, including the prolific Goulds. And, while many Vanderbilt homes are today splendidly restored and open to the public (the Breakers, Marble House, Biltmore, Hyde Park), their dozens of equally impressive yachts have vanished entirely; few are even remembered in histories of this unique family. And W. K. II (a great-grandson of "Commodore" Vanderbilt) owned more yachts than any other member of his extended family; at least fifteen between 1878 and 1944. While his brother, Harold Stirling (see page 95), was a famed sailing aficionado, William enjoyed long exploratory cruises, particularly aboard the *Ara* and her successor, *Alva (II),* named after his father's ill-fated yacht, which had sunk in Martha's Vineyard twenty-eight years earlier. A man with a wide variety of interests—architecture, ichthyology, aviation, sailing, anthropology, ornithology, art, and automotive technology and racing—William filled Eagle's Nest, his mansion on Long Island, New York, with animal, marine, and ethnic specimens from his numerous world cruises (Eagle's Nest is now open to the public; see Sources).

Alva carried Vanderbilt and his second wife, Rosamond, on a world tour of 37,952 miles, a voyage that began on March 5, 1931, in Kiel, Germany (*Alva* was built by Krupp-Germaniawerft), and ended a year later. It was also a voyage that ended in a different time and place, which even a Vanderbilt could not ignore: the Depression.

In 1941 Vanderbilt loaned *Alva* to the U.S. Navy for a war he thought was imminent. The yacht was converted into a patrol boat, the USS *Plymouth*. Two years later she was struck by a torpedo from the German submarine U-566 while part of a convoy escort; she went down in under two minutes, with just eighty-five of her 183-man crew rescued. In the late 1980s she was discovered, in 2,200 feet of water, off the coast of New Jersey.

Above, a giant clam posing with William Vanderbilt aboard *Ara* in 1928.

Reproducing yacht plans is a difficult process. Original drawings are quite large, often six feet long. In reducing these images for a book, once crisp lines and lettering become indistinct. Therefore, old yachting magazines are the best source for reproducing these drawings; the plans they contain were usually drawn specifically for such publications, although they lack the wealth of detail that can distinguish the original, as well as the observable hand of brilliant drafting. The original plans of *Alva (II)* were untraceable. The plans shown here were copied from a book, although the amidships section was not reproducible. It was decided that, even with this loss, the remaining details were informative.

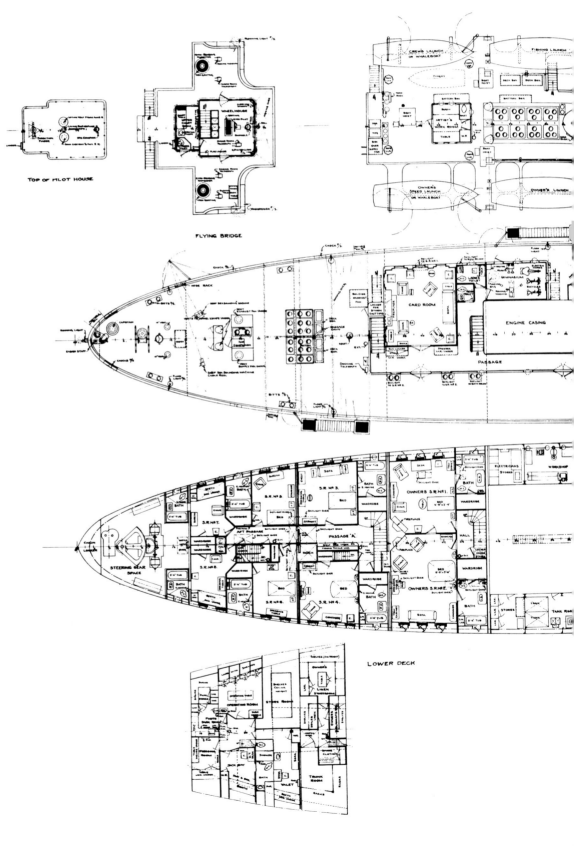

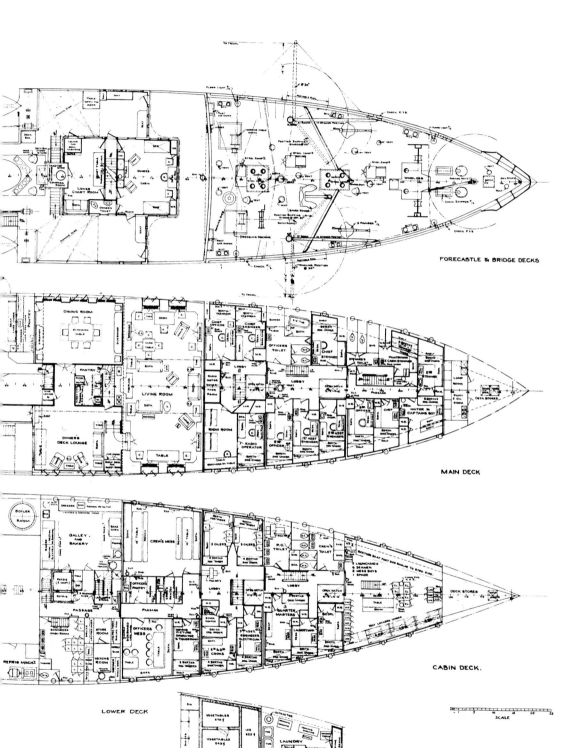

FORECASTLE & BRIDGE DECKS

MAIN DECK

CABIN DECK.

LOWER DECK

SCALE

Alva's plans (left) were as unique as her profile. Her beam was quite ample as compared with those of vessels built just a few years previous, and entirely different than that of *Atalanta* (see page 22). This afforded *Alva* a heretofore unsurpassed level of interior comforts; indeed, this plan appears more ocean liner than yacht. But, as *Alva* was designed for extensive world cruising and research, such accommodations were understandable.

Alva (II) was built by Krupp-Germaniawerft, in Kiel, Germany. Germaniawerft had been taken over by the Krupp company (armaments and steel) in 1902, and production refocused on U-boats and ships of war. Still, the company developed a reputation for building yachts of the highest quality, including Friedrich Krupp's personal yacht and two successive racing yachts named *Meteor* for Kaiser Wilhelm II (see page 33). With specialized knowledge of diesel-electric motors, Krupp garnered a significant corner of the large luxury yacht-building business, launching twenty-two such yachts from 1923 to 1931—almost all destined for American waters—and including several vessels depicted in these pages, such as *Hussar*, *Happy Days*, *Vanadis*, and *Haida*.

HAPPY DAYS

1927

While *Avalon* and *Alva* represented advances in naval architecture, nothing can convince me that the elements that made up *Happy Days* were improvable: the thrilling clipper bow with figurehead and gilded trailboards, the two decks upon a single sweeping sheer, all ending in a fine modified counterstern. And, her masts were just right; while the stack was large enough to be noticed but not overwhelming. *Happy Days* culminated a century of motor yacht design. Ira C. Copley (1864–1947), who commissioned *Happy Days*, was a man born into a poor farming family who went on to transform a failing utility company into a giant corporation, served twelve years in the U.S. Congress, owned twenty-four newspapers (many in his home state of Illinois), and was a member of the New York Yacht Club. The Copley Memorial Hospital, in Aurora, Ill., and the Copley Press endure as part of his legacy.

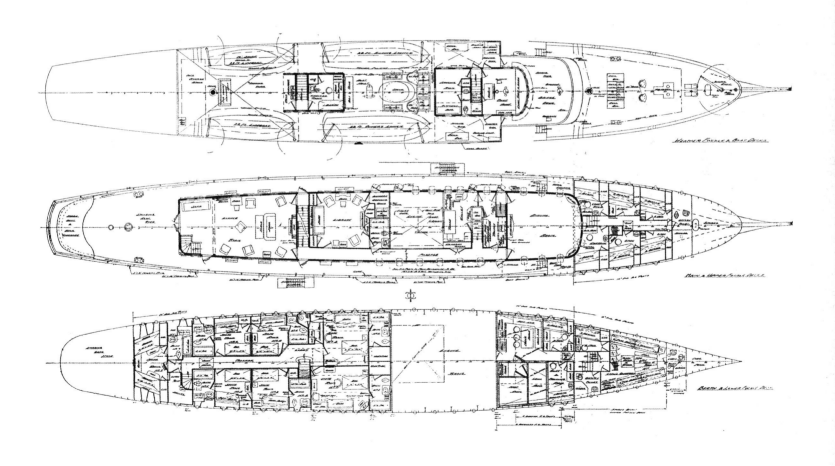

195 feet and built in 1927 for Ira C. Copley, of Aurora, Illinois. Designed by Cox & Stevens. Built by Krupp-Germaniawerft, Kiel, Germany. Powered by a pair of 6-cylinder Krupp diesels.

The deck plans of *Happy Days* show the sophistication evident in yachts in the latter 1920s.

AVALANCHE (IV)

1929

154 feet and built in 1929 for Anson W. Hard. Designed by Tams & King. Built by Consolidated Shipbuilding. Powered by a pair of 6-cylinder Winton diesel air injection-type engines.

If *Happy Days* represented a high mark in a century of motor yachts (her design lineage dating back centuries), and if *Avalon* and *Alva* represented breaks with this tradition (reaching toward the future and disdaining the past), than *Avalanche* was like an alien intruder.

At a glance, it's obvious that she was radically different, strikingly original and rakish. In contrast, *Avalon*'s attempts at being Moderne related only to her bow and pole mast; her general lines weren't much different from those of *Happy Days*.

Avalanche, however, represented a breathtaking shift. Yet her long, low features didn't catch on. Instead, *Alva* was the true mother of modern yachts, and what she represented can easily be linked to the most advanced designs today.

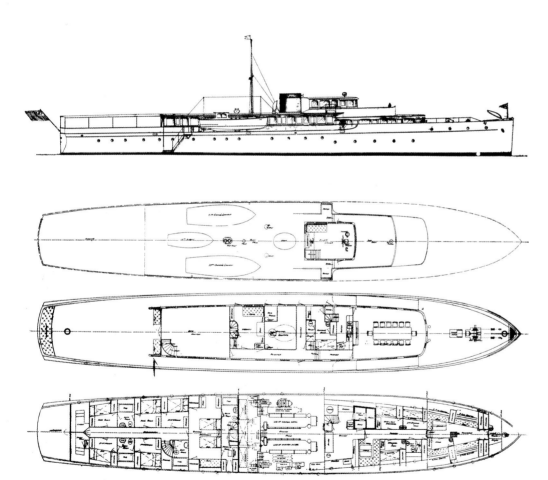

Consolidated Shipbuilding, the builder of *Avalanche*, had its beginnings in 1879, when Charles L. Seabury left the employ of the Herreshoff Manufacturing Company (see page 98) and opened his own firm at Nyack, New York, building steam launches. Nearby, the Gas Engine and Power Company, located on the Harlem River, at 131st Street and Brook Avenue, was developing an enviable reputation for their success with naptha-powered launches. Based on the same principal as steam engines, which boiled and vaporized water, the Gas Engine launches boiled and vaporized naptha vapor and were an improvement over steam in that naptha engines hardly ever exploded. In 1896 the two companies joined forces with the unwieldy name of Gas Engine and Power Company and Charles L. Seabury Company, Consolidated. In 1893 the company began production of its first gasoline engine, the Consolidated Speedway. During the ensuing decades the company (its name condensed to Consolidated Shipbuilding) became possibly the largest manufacturer of custom yachts in existence, having no fewer than thirteen launching ways and, like Herreshoff, the ability to produce virtually everything that went aboard a Consolidated vessel.

STERNS

VIDOR

LAUNCHED AS SIVAD

171 feet and built in 1926 for D. P. Davis . Designed by H. J. Gielow. Built by Todd Shipyard. Powered by a pair of Bessemer diesel engines. Capable of extended ocean cruising.

This photograph documents a high-mark of naval architecture: a counter (the overhanging stern) with fantail (an elliptical bulwark). Movie buffs will recognize this same feature, dramatically increased in scale, as the one Leonardo DiCaprio and Kate Winslet clung to as the *Titanic* took her icy plunge into the Atlantic. Yet this extraordinary stern type—a sweeping combination of complex curves that appear effortless in their creation—disappeared as a yacht feature in the early 1930s. Moreover, the "clutter" evident on the upper decks of *Vidor*, anathema to modern naval architects, was a charming aspect of classic motor yachts. Is less *really* more?

Victor Emanuel, who purchased *Vidor* shortly after her launching, was born in 1898 in Dayton, Ohio. He attended St. Mary's College (later the University of Dayton) and Cornell University before assuming the presidency of his father's firm, the Albert Emanuel Company (a Midwest interurban rail company), in 1924. Over the ensuing decades Emanuel diversified into an impressive variety of holdings, including utilities, an investment house, airlines, shipbuilding, appliances, farm implements, kitchen cabinets, and radio stations. Emanuel also gave $300,000 to the University of Dayton, contributed to the Wil-

liam Wordsworth Collection at Cornell University Library, and was a member of numerous clubs and civic organizations. He was married in 1920 to the former Dorothy Elizabeth Woodruff and the couple had two sons, Albert and Barton.

There is some confusion as to *Vidor*'s original name. The *Lloyd's Register* lists it as *Sivad*, yet contemporary accounts state it was *Vidor*. She was commissioned by David P. Davis (Davis spelled backward is Sivad), a flamboyant Florida real estate developer who made $18 million in a single year (on paper) from his Tampa success story, Davis Islands. He then overextended himself creating another development, and lost his fortune as quickly as it had been gained. In October, 1926, the same year *Sivad* was launched, Davis booked a cruise on the elegant Cunard liner *Majestic*; he was never seen again, either falling overboard or faking his disappearance (a $300,000 insurance claim was paid). It appears that Victor Emanuel purchased *Sivad* early in the 1926 season, although he didn't own the renamed *Vidor* for long, selling her in late 1927 or early 1928. By 1930 *Vidor* had gone through two more changes of name (*Hi-Esmaro* and *Hilda*), and in 1938 she became *Velda*. A decade later the yacht was no longer listed in *Lloyd's*. It appears that *Vidor* was the only yacht Emanuel owned in America.

NOURMAHAL (II)

160 feet and built in 1921 for Vincent Astor, of New York. Designed by Cox & Stevens. Built by Robert Jacob, City Island, New York. Powered by a pair of 6-cylinder Winton diesels.

This image highlights the fine counterstern gracing *Nourmahal* (shown here with *Advance*). Vincent Astor (1891–1959), who commissioned *Nourmahal*, was a member of a family, like the Goulds and Vanderbilts, prominent in yachting. He owned numerous palatial vessels. When Astor (whose fortune was based on real estate) took possession of the second *Nourmahal* in 1921, she was the "last word in comfort" (or so said *Yachting*), and the largest full-powered diesel-engined yacht built in America at the time. Astor commissioned a third *Nourmahal* seven years later, and at 263 feet, it may be presumed that she was considerably more comfortable than her 160-foot predecessor.

Astor's father, John Jacob IV, died aboard the *Titanic*, leaving the young Astor with a reported $100 million, the bulk in real estate. He was twenty-one. In the 1920s he sold about half of his real estate holdings and, later, most of the remaining properties. In 1948 he founded the Vincent Astor Foundation, which proceeded to give away enormous sums of money to a wide variety of causes. Upon Astor's death in 1959 (he left a $123 million estate), his third wife, Brooke Russell Marshall Astor (born 1902), became legendary for distributing nearly $195 million until she closed the foundation in 1997, its funds spent. It's extremely rare for an endowed foundation to touch, much less exhaust, its capital. Such an effort should be applauded—loudly.

When the elder Astor died aboard the *Titanic*, he owned *Noma* (see page 125); the 262-foot yacht was bequeathed to Vincent, who sold her in 1921. *Nourmahal (II)* was lost during war service in 1941.

VIRGINIA

While *Vidor* and *Nourmahal (II)* had sterns with a counter and fantail (which I simply call countersterns), *Virginia* offered a variation: a counter with a transom section (which I call a modified counterstern).

Virginia was commissioned by Sir Stephen Courtauld (1883–1967), who inherited a fortune from his family's textile company (rayon). The youngest of six children, Courtauld studied natural science at Cambridge University and was also interested in climbing mountains, raising orchids, collecting old masters (such as Turner), architecture, and yachting. When he was forty Courtauld married a woman at least a decade his senior, Virginia Peirano (whom their yacht was named after). The dynamic Virginia Courtauld had, among other distinc-

tions, a snake tattoo on her ankle and was of Italian and Hungarian descent.

In 1933 the Courtaulds began construction of Eltham Palace, a dramatic Art Deco mansion attached to a medieval banquet hall—all that remained of a former royal palace. After being bombed in 1944 (Courtauld managed to keep the flames under control until the fire brigade arrived), the couple gave up their ninety-nine-year lease and later moved to Mutari, Zimbabwe, where they built another grand house, LaRochelle.

Today, after a slavish restoration, Eltham Palace is open to the public (see Sources), and LaRochelle is now a hotel. Many of the painting and prints collected by Courtauld can be seen at the Yale Center for British Arts in New Haven, Connecticut (see Sources).

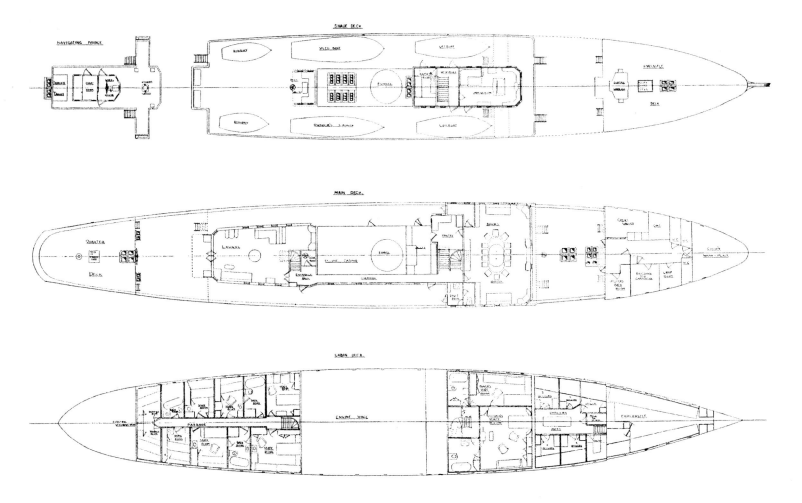

Opposite, the deck plans of *Virginia*, like those of *Happy Days* (see page 87), offered state-of-the-art spatial design for the late 1920s. Note also the unusual full-beam dining saloon and the owner's suite forward.

William Beardmore & Company, Ltd., which built *Virginia*, was the heir and successor to Robert Napier & Sons (see page 14). After taking over the famed Napier company in 1900, Beardmore later moved to an expansive site just west of their rival, John Brown of Clydebank, in 1905. For the next quarter-century Beardmore produced an impressive variety of items,

such as sixty contracts for the Royal Navy (including seaplanes), airships, steel products, machinery, armour plating, and even the taxicabs that prowled the streets of Glasgow and London. Of particular note was Beardmore's vital contribution to World War I. After overextending itself postwar, the company fell on hard times and closed in 1930.

G L A D Y S

128 feet and built in 1883 for Neil Mathieson. Designed by John Reid. Built by John Reid & Company, of Glasgow. Powered by a steam engine.

Another modified counterstern, shown here gracing *Gladys*, her bottom being scraped and repainted at East Cowes in 1885. Three years later *Gladys* provided a special service, when, for his daughter's wedding, owner C. M. Burt dressed the yacht with bunting fluttering from the masts and stays. With dozens of owners over a long life, *Gladys* was serving as a houseboat when records cease in 1951.

The company that designed and built *Gladys* got its start in 1847, when John Reid received a commission to build a floating church for use in Loch Sunart, in Scotland, district of Morvern. His son James later joined the company, located in the Port of Glasgow, and as an enthusiastic yachtsman, he promoted the construction of yachts in iron and then steel, such as their 1886 America's Cup challenger, *Galatea*. The company also launched the largest fully rigged ship built of steel in the 1880s, *British Isles*, and, later, the 198-foot steam yacht *White Heather* (also known as *Apache*). Reid & Company continued, through various corporate incarnations (and a move to Whiteinch, Glasgow), until 1909.

VARA

150 feet and built in 1928 for Harold. S. Vanderbilt. Designed by the Purdy Boat Company. Built by Herreshoff Manufacturing Company. Powered by a pair of 12-cylinder Trieber diesels.

With this comparison image of *Vara*, one can fully appreciate just how seductive a counterstern is. *Vara* (shown here at the Harvard races) was the last of the big Vanderbuilt yachts and one of the least attractive of her era, in part because her transom stern was highly unusual for a large yacht. The Purdy Boat Company, which designed *Vara*, often featured transom sterns hung with attractive, cast bronze, single rudders, yet rarely to this scale.

A few years after her completion the exterior of *Vara* was redesigned and her pilot house was moved forward and lowered, while the white painted steel deckhouse was either painted black or covered by dark stained wood. It's not known if these alterations resulted from any dissatisfaction with the original design.

Vara was commissioned by an experienced yachtsman, Harold Stirling Vanderbilt (known as Mike), perhaps the only Vanderbilt still remembered for his yachting activities and the dominant figure of the J-boat era during the 1930s—a rich man's sport superimposed over a depressed age. Vanderbilt skippered *Enterprise* and *Rainbow* to victory and then, as owner and skipper, sailed *Ranger*; becoming the only triple winner of the America's Cup. Besides *Vara*, Vanderbilt owned motor yachts such as *Magistrate*, a 63-foot Herreshoff-designed and-built vessel launched in 1916; *Maintenon*, a 46-foot Consolidated built in 1924; and *Bystander*, a 42-foot shuttle built in 1930, which he owned for several decades (*Bystander* was built as the tender for *Enterprise* and was initially owned by a syndicate, which included Winthrop Aldrich—see page 96).

The Purdy Boat Company, which designed *Vara*, had a unique beginning: a garage on the infield of the Indianapolis Speedway. Carl Graham Fisher, who built the speedway, had made a fortune producing carbide headlights for automobiles. Fisher later developed a sandy stretch of land, home to coconut trees, snakes, alligators, and cockroaches, that later become famed for its Art Deco hotels and fashion models—Miami Beach. By the time Fisher decided to order a yacht from Consolidated (see page 88), he had become impressed with two brothers who worked in the design department, Edward D. (Ned) and Gilbert (Gil) Purdy; he set the men up in his Speedway garage in 1916. The Purdys built their first two yachts for Fisher—*Raven I* and *II*—before the millionaire moved the new company to Miami Beach. The brothers specialized in developing fast, elegant commuters with distinctive lines. The company relocated yet again, this time in Michigan, until finally settling in Port Washington on Manhasset Bay, Long Island, in 1925. The brothers prospered until their bank failed in 1932, wiping out their capital and hastening the death of Gil Purdy. The boat works lingered on until World War II, when it received contracts from the U.S. Navy for eighty-eight vessels. Postwar, Purdy had trouble downsizing (like many yacht builders), and by 1950 the once formidable Purdy Boat Company was simply a service and repair facility, its days of launching sleek, high-powered yachts long over.

WAYFARER

Before the 1930s, a transom stern was atypical for large yachts such as *Vara* but ubiquitous on smaller vessels. This type of stern was, and is, relatively easy to design and inexpensive to build.

Winthrop Williams Aldrich (1885–1974), who commissioned *Wayfarer*, had a personal and professional life intertwined with Rockefeller interests. The son of a U.S. senator (Nelson Wilmarth Aldrich), and a graduate of Harvard University and Harvard Law School, Aldrich became a junior partner in the law firm of Byrne, Cutcheon & Taylor in 1916. In the same year he married Harriet Alexander; the couple had six children.

Aldrich was a yachting enthusiast, joined the U.S. Naval Reserve, and later enrolled at Uttmark's Nautical Academy in Brooklyn, New York. During World War I, he served aboard the USS *New Orleans* as assistant navigation and communications officer.

In 1918 he joined the law firm of Murray, Prentice & Howland, becoming a partner in 1921. His sister, Abby Aldrich, had married John D. Rockefeller, Jr., and Winthrop devoted his later career to Rockefeller family interests. He was a key player in the Williamsburg Restoration (1927); the development of the Rockefeller Foundation (1929); the merger of the Equitable Trust Company and the Chase National Bank, which created the world's largest bank (Aldrich became its president in 1930); and Rockefeller Center (1932).

An early critic of Adolf Hitler (Chase had $35 million loaned in Germany in 1933), Aldrich developed the British-American Ambulance Corps in 1940 and led the Allied Relief Fund, which provided vital supplies and food during the Battle of Britain. He also chaired the National War Fund, which disbursed over $100 million to help America's allies. During the Eisenhower administration Aldrich was appointed an ambassador to Great Britain (1952–57). After his 1957 retirement, he devoted himself to yachting and numerous charitable causes, particularly the Columbia Medical Fund, for which he served as a trustee.

Aldrich's passion for yachting is evidenced by the number of vessels he owned, such as *Flying Cloud*, a 90-foot schooner built by Lawley in 1913, and *Nokomis*, a 58-foot auxiliary schooner designed by Cox & Stevens in 1925. For the 1930 America's Cup, Aldrich was part of the syndicate that owned *Enterprise* (the defender against Sir Thomas Lipton's *Shamrock V*) and her tender, *Bystander* (a 42-foot motor yacht built in 1930). Aldrich also owned *Valiant* (an 80-foot sloop built in 1928) and, for close to forty years, *Little Wayfarer*, a 39-foot Consolidated motor yacht built in 1935. For a brief period he flirted with fiberglass when he concurrently owned *White Dolphin*, a 37-foot Bertram motor yacht built in 1963, but he returned to wood construction upon his purchase of a successive *Wayfarer* in the early 1970s, a 1960 Trumpy motor yacht (launched as *Claybeth*). Aldrich was a New York Yacht Club vice-commodore from 1920–30 and commodore from 1931 to 1932.

104 feet and built in 1929 for Winthrop W. Aldrich. Designed by Henry. J. Gielow. Built by George Lawley & Son. Powered by a pair of gas 6-cylinder Wintons.

SCOUT

The canoe stern was rarely seen on yachts over 50 feet, more often it was a feature of small launches and, well, canoes. The one shown here graced *Scout*, commissioned in 1899 by August Belmont II (1853–1924), a financier, sportsman, and son of a wealthy banker. Among other achievements, Belmont introduced spiked track shoes while a collegiate sprinter at Harvard University, and he was a leader in the development of the New York City subway system (owning the only private subway car in existence), the Cape Cod Canal, and—an avid horseman—Belmont Park in New York. He married Elizabeth Hamilton Morgan in 1881; the couple had three children.

Belmont used *Scout* as a tender for his 70-foot racing sloop, *Miniola*. Her builder and designer, the Herreshoff Manufacturing Company, later built seven nearly identical vessels for a variety of experienced yachtsmen, including Cornelius Vanderbilt (as tender for *Rainbow*), Howard Gould *(Niagara II)*, and Morton Plant *(Express*, later owned by J. P. Morgan, Jr.).

Scout was designed by Nathanael "Capt. Nat" Herreshoff (1848–1938), who, after a three-year stint at the Massachusetts Institute of Technology and nine years with the Corliss Steam Engine Company, of Providence, Rhode Island (the leading engine builder in the United States), joined the family boat-building business located in Bristol, Rhode Island, and run by his brother John. The two proved a good team, with John focused on business and Nat on the art of design and engineering. As Bill Robinson writes in *The World of Yachting*, "Yacht designers have never been a dime a dozen. Not enough of them can make money to keep many in full-time operation in any one generation. Hundreds of men have doodled over drawing boards and turned out workable boat designs, but the ones who have left their mark on a generation have been few."

Capt. Nat, with unrivaled engineering and design skills, has left his mark on several generations, and the Herreshoff Manufacturing Company was extraordinarily successful, employing 300 people at its height and occupying dozens of buildings. The company had two huge construction sheds (one for wooden vessels, the other for steel) and its own forge, drafting room, pattern shop, sail loft, mill and cabinet shop, machine shop, foundry, model making facilities, and boiler shop, all heated by Herreshoff-designed and-built boilers.

While known today for his sailing vessels, as well as his intense involvement in the America's Cup races (he defended the Cup six times as a designer, helmsman, and engineer), Capt. Nat was fascinated by marine engines and developed significant improvements. For twenty years, beginning in 1870, he devoted his attention principally to the design and creation of steam launches and steam yachts. It was said that his expertise with high-speed engines was unsurpassed; by 1900 he had designed more types and sizes of steam engines than anyone, although a freak 1888 boiler explosion aboard a Herreshoff vessel during speed trials killed a man and cost Capt. Nat his steam engineer's license.

Many employees worked decades for the two brothers, and the company, with its well-paid workforce, high morale, and ability to produce virtually every component of its in-house–designed vessels, was highly esteemed among boat builders. In its heyday, the intense atmosphere of the Herreshoff Manufacturing Company must have been remarkable.

While John Brown (J. B.) Herreshoff isn't as well remembered as his famed younger brother, he was an extraordinary character, and it could be argued that, without him, Capt. Nat might never have attained the heights he did. Even though afflicted with blindness at the age of fourteen, J. B. went on to found a boat building and sawmill business, and early on showed a great capacity for business. He was also blessed with an often overlooked asset: people skills. As detailed by L. Francis Herreshoff (son of Capt. Nat) in his book *Capt. Nat Herreshoff, The Wizard of Bristol*, J. B. was the one who heard the workmen's grievances, knew the value of keeping a good crew together, could tell a good story, and stimulated good feeling thoughout the plant. These talents cannot be underestimated in helping to build and manage a successful company. Capt. Nat, like many engineers, distinctly lacked interpersonal skills.

81 feet and built in 1899 for August Belmont. Designed by N. G. Herreshoff. Built by the Herreshoff Manufacturing Company, Bristol, Rhode Island. Powered by a Herreshoff steam engine, which drove her at 20 mph.

APHRODITE (II)

72 feet and built in 1928 for John Hay Whitney. Designed and built by Albany Boat Corporation. Powered by a pair of gas Wright-Typhoon engines.

Another canoe stern, gracing *Aphrodite (II)*.

When Oliver Hazard Payne died in 1917, the owner of an immense steam yacht named *Aphrodite*, he left a vast estate to his nephew, Payne Whitney, who, upon his death a decade later, left a $179 million estate (the largest that had ever been appraised in the United States) to his son, John Hay Whitney, known as Jock. Jock was twenty-two.

Aphrodite (II) was used by Jock as a commuter between his Long Island estate, Wall Street, and Albany, New York (for the Saratoga horse racing season). Later, Jock would commission a third *Aphrodite* from the Purdy Boat Works, in Port Washington, New York. This elegant vessel (extant) looked similar to the previous *Aphrodite*, yet her lines were remarkably streamlined, and

the canoe stern of the second *Aphrodite* was transformed into a dashing torpedo stern. Few yachts as spectacular have ever been launched. (In the 1990s a replica was commissioned.)

Whitney built a palatial boathouse on his estate (garnering a twelve-page story in *The American Architect*), was an investor in the movie *Gone With the Wind*, and served as a colonel in World War II (escaping capture by the Germans) before becoming, in 1958, the American ambassador to the Court of St. James. He later served as publisher of the New York *Herald Tribune*.

Phil Moore, in his book *Yachts in a Hurry*, writes that "while cruising in the summer of 1961, we found the forlorn remains of *Aphrodite (II)* in the mud of a backwater off the Connecticut River."

RAMNA

Walter B. Lasher transformed—with dashing results—the transom stern on his year-old *Ramna* into a modified counter with a hard knuckle below the waterline. It was claimed he did this to keep the stern from settling in the water (that's what the knuckle is for), but he could have just been overly fond of countersterns.

91 feet and built in 1926 for Walter B. Lasher. Designed and built by Luders Marine Construction, which also did the modifications. Powered by a pair of 150-hp Winton diesels.

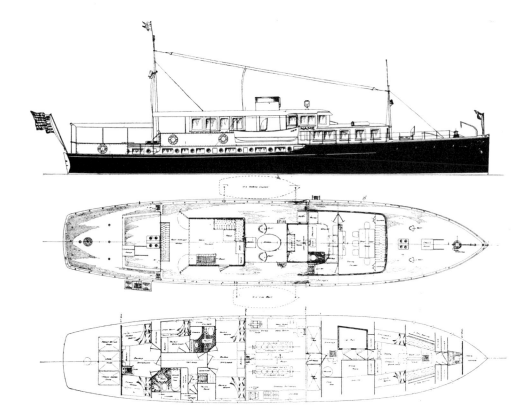

The Luders Marine Construction Company, which built *Ramna*, was located on the west branch of the harbor in Stamford, Connecticut. Founded by Alfred E. Luders in 1908, the company became one of the premier builders of yachts during the 1920s and 1930s and made something of a specialty of building fast, sleek commuters with a pronounced rakish quality that, along with distinctive bow scrollwork, announced LUDERS.

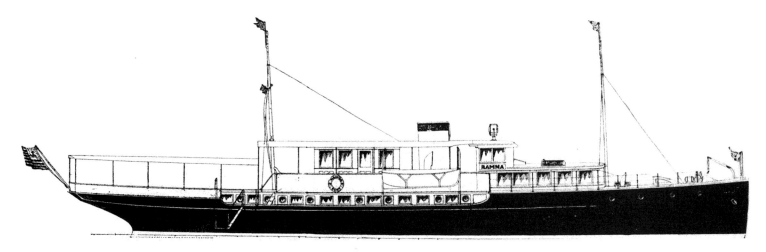

BOWS

EDAMENA IV

The inboard profile and accommodation plan for *Edamena IV* highlight some unusual features. For a vessel 99 feet long, it was surprising that Lawley didn't include a deck-level main saloon, instead incorporating a "Lounge" in the aft of the trunk cabin. The crew shower tucked under the forward cockpit was a clever spatial design. And the galley had impressive headroom and plenty of ventilation.

A plumb bow graced *Edamena IV,* gripped by her launching cradle in this fine image. *Edamena IV* was commissioned by Earle P. Charlton (1863–1930) who transformed a Fall River, Massachusetts, five-and-dime into a retail empire. Charlton started with $50 worth of goods in 1890 and within a quarter century owned fifty-three stores across the United States and Canada, becoming a co-founder of the F. W. Woolworth Company. He also founded the Charlton Mills in Fall River, which by 1930 had 1,500 looms and 60,000 spindles and employed 700 people. Later in his life Charlton became a noted philanthropist and underwrote the surgery building at Truesdale Hospital in Fall River; helped raise $2 million for the Clarke School for the Deaf at Northampton, Massachusetts; endowed a fund to help support the Harriet Lane Home Department of Johns Hopkins University and the Fall River Nursing Association; and bequeathed $1.5 million to various Fall River institutions and Tufts College. Continuing this family tradition, Charlton's grandson and namesake recently donated $3 million to the University of Massachusetts (UMass), Dartmouth, for a school of business and industry in honor of his grandfather.

Charlton, a member of the New York Yacht Club, married the former Ida Stein in 1889, and the couple had three children, Ruth, Earle Perry, and Virginia. Besides *Edamena IV*, Charlton owned a number of other yachts, including *Edamena*, a 75-foot gas engined yacht built in 1910; *Edamena II*, a 45-foot Lawley gas launch built in 1916; *Watch Your Step*, a 37-foot William Hand, Jr., gas launch built in 1915; and *Edamena III*, a 55-foot Hand-designed motor yacht built in 1920.

99 feet and built in 1926 for Earle P. Charlton. Designed by Walter. J. McInnis. Built by George Lawley & Son. Powered by a pair of 300-hp Speedway gas engines.

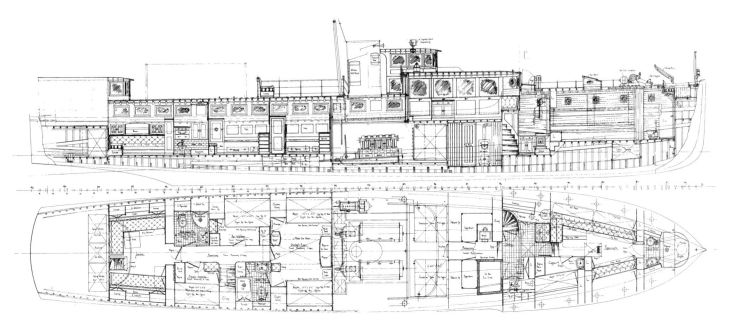

ROAMER

This vessel was designed by Capt. Nat Herreshoff as his family's personal yacht. While Herreshoff's skills as an engineer were legendary, he seemed wholly unable to design an attractive motor yacht, a marked contrast from his brilliance in designing sailing vessels. *Roamer*'s unusual spoon bow is just one of her features that isn't quite right. Others were the tall skinny funnel and the twin masts a bit too close; one mast would have been better.

93 feet and built in 1902 for N. G. Herreshoff. Designed by Nathanael Herreshoff. Built by the Herreshoff Manufacturing Company, of Bristol, Rhode Island. Powered by a single steam engine.

DELPHINE

258 feet and built in 1921 for Horace C. Dodge. Designed by H. J. Gielow. Built by Great Lakes Engineering Company. Powered by a pair of quadruple-expansion steam engines (extant) that drove her at 14 mph.

This image highlights a rare battleship-type bow, gracing a yacht that has led a life both damned and charmed. *Delphine* has suffered a disastrous fire, was sunk and submerged for several months, and had four separate careers. Today, nearing her eighth decade—with her original steam engines intact—she is being restored.

Delphine began life as the realization of a childhood dream. Automobile magnate Horace Elgin Dodge had long wished to own the world's largest yacht. With the success of his business, he was able in indulge in his passion for yachting and speed, ordering a succession of faster and faster vessels until his *Hornet II* attained a record of 41 miles per hour. Trading speed for comfort, he commissioned the 180-foot *Nokomis* in 1914, a graceful Gielow & Orr–designed steam yacht. The Dodge family enjoyed *Nokomis* for many years, until she was called for war service. Dodge then

commissioned *Nokomis (II)* in 1917; this 243-foot vessel was also purchased by the navy after her completion. Later, the first *Nokomis* became well known as *Saelmo* (the official welcoming yacht for New York City and State) and was later owned by the state of Maryland as the *Dupont*.

But Dodge's childhood dream had still not been realized. So, he retained Henry J. Gielow to design a vessel reportedly exceeding the gross tonnage of J. P. Morgan's 1,136-ton *Corsair (III)*. Built at the Great Lakes Engineering Works in Michigan, the 1,286-ton *Delphine* had as her distinctive feature a battleship-type bow, a departure from the more usual clipper bow then in fashion. This unusual touch was necessitated by Dodge's request for the absolute maximum of interior accommodation, while taking into account the length limitations imposed by the locks

of the Welland Canal and on the Saint Laurence River, enabling *Delphine* to travel from the Great Lakes out to the open sea.

Dodge's dream would remain, technically, unrealized. *Delphine* was easily outstripped by dozens of yachts with greater bulk, such as the 1,830-ton *Margarita (III)* and the 1,942-ton *Lysistrata*. These dozen yachts were, at the time *Delphine* was commissioned, in service as naval vessels to various countries and thus no longer private yachts. While some were lost during such service, many returned to snatch the "world's largest" title from *Delphine*.

Dodge didn't live to see this, as he died before *Delphine* was completed. His widow, Anna Dodge, took over and personally saw to the completion of the vessel, named after their daughter.

The completed yacht wasn't as striking as many of her contemporaries. In particular, her awkward stern would have been better served by a cruiser-type design, while both masts and the stack had very little rake to them. The battleship-type bow, however, was formidable.

Anna Dodge enjoyed life aboard *Delphine*, sometimes cruising in the winter to Florida and the Caribbean, with summers usually spent along the coast of Maine. Becoming a fixture at Bar Harbor and Camden, *Delphine* was an impressive presence. Camden Harbor, as yacht historian Fred Crockett observed, "glowed like Broadway when *Delphine* turned on her 3,000 electric lights at night."

Anna Dodge married Hugh Dillman in 1926 (they divorced in 1947), and while the two were attending the New York Opera in 1926, *Delphine* caught fire and sank in the Hudson River, where she remained for sixty-seven days. While Mrs. Dillman must have weighed the expense of refloating and refitting against the cost of a new yacht, it was decided to restore *Delphine*, at a reported cost of $350,000. It took a little over four months to restore the yacht, considerably less time than it would have taken to build a new vessel. During her refit, *Delphine*'s exterior remained unaltered, while the interior decor would change dramatically. The dark and elaborately carved mahogany paneling was ripped out and the renewed *Delphine* was decorated throughout in an understated, modern, and more feminine manner. Beamed overheads were covered with flat white painted panels, and everything was made simpler and less ornate. Most of the main saloons featured white painted paneling and simple furnishings, often covered in a gay chintz. The reborn *Delphine* presented a subdued but comfortably elegant appearance, not dissimilar to the look of many English royal yachts.

Jay Ottinger, who joined the crew of *Delphine* in 1931, reminds us that, in an age of jeans and T-shirts, modern clothing designed for yachting is more relaxed than the regimented standards he was familiar with. Ottinger, in his book *The Steam Yacht Delphine and Other Stories*, writes, "Each man aboard *Delphine* was furnished with a complete set of clothing except underwear. Sailors were issued a suit of dress blues, three suits of dress whites, two suits of un-dress whites, two suits of dungarees, and a wool sweater—all with '*Delphine*' embroidered across the chest. Two dress white hats, two dungaree hats, and a watch cap. Black leather shoes, white sneakers, and denim-blue sneakers, with matching sox. We also received a pea jacket and a large, blunt-ended folding knife [as well as] a full set of oilskins, sou'wester, and knee boots." Ottinger concluded that if a "man finished the season and completed the lay-up, the outfit was his."

Anna Dodge Dillman managed to keep *Delphine* in commission through the 1930s, but when war was declared, she offered the yacht to the United States Navy. Renamed the USS *Dauntless*, she became the flagship of Admiral E. J. King, commander in chief of the United States Fleet and chief of naval operations.

After the war, Anna Dillman was persistent in her efforts to have the *Dauntless* returned. However, as with all yachts used for naval service, the *Dauntless* was no longer the elegant vessel she once had been. Few millionaires, realizing this, to say nothing of the cost of refurbishment, *wanted* their former yachts back. Yet Anna Dillman spent a reported $300,000 to transform the USS *Dauntless* back into the luxurious *Delphine*. Thereafter, she enjoyed a Grosse Pointe mansion, Rose Terrace (unnecessarily demolished in 1976), but she spent most of her time from spring until fall aboard her beloved yacht, cruising and enjoying a favored pastime: fishing.

Author William K. Anderson once told a story attesting to Anna Dillman's qualities as a yachtswomen. One night, while sixty-mile-an-hour winds raged, Dillman boarded *Delphine* at midnight as she lay at anchor in Buffalo Harbor, in itself a formidable task. Informing the captain of her desire to be in Detroit by morning, she retired to her stateroom below. The next morning, when informed about the details of the a harrowing night voyage across a storm-tossed Lake Erie (a fierceness I can attest to), she replied, like an old salt, with a curt "Didn't know a thing about it."

After forty-one years of service to the Dodge family, the grand old yacht was offered for sale. That there were no immediate takers was understandable considering the $500,000-a-year maintenance costs. With *Delphine* falling into disrepair, the Seafarer's Harry Lundeberg School of Seamanship, of Piney

Point, Maryland, took possession of the vessel in 1968 and re-renamed her the *Dauntless*.

Under her new owners the quiet elegance that defined *Delphine* was replaced by shipshape function and practicality. Gone apparently forever were the days of leisurely cruises to the sun, midnight strolls around the deck with a cocktail replenished by an attentive steward in a starched white uniform, and restful sleep made possible by mounds of down and white, crisp linens.

Well maintained by the school, *Dauntless* aged gracefully for the next two decades. In the late 1980s, the school offered *Delphine* for sale, and her future looked bleak. After all, how many people wanted or could afford a seventy-year-old yacht? In the early 1990s Delphine was auctioned for a reported $50,000, a stunning figure considering that a survey revealed a hull in surprisingly sound condition. This would not have surprised Horace Dodge, for he'd requested that *Delphine*'s steel plates be 20 percent thicker than necessary, knowing that, over time, they'd deteriorate. By the late 1980s these plates had eroded, on average, about . . . 20 percent. Moreover, *Delphine* retained her original engines and steamed across the Pacific Ocean, where she was to undergo an extensive refit in Singapore. These plans unraveled, and *Delphine* spent the next few years being bounced between numerous owners and unrealized schemes. Purchased by a Belgian textile magnate living in Tunisia, Jacques Bruynooghe, the yacht was brought to Belgium to begin a long-awaited restoration and conversion into a small cruise ship. Today, *Delphine* is the oldest and largest power yacht in such original condition (see Sources for more information).

Delphine's first interior was typical of the era and featured rich, dark paneling, carved furnishings, and sensuous embroidered fabrics.

After *Delphine*'s disastrous 1926 fire and sinking, she underwent a total refit and her interior was gutted. The new interior was a radical departure from its previous incarnation and featured smooth overheads, simple white painted paneling, and fully upholstered chairs covered with a gay chintz. In short, the masculine interiors specified by Horace Dodge were replaced with distinctly feminine saloons by Anna Dodge Dillman.

Great Lakes Engineering Company, which built *Delphine*, got its start in 1902 after having purchased the Riverside Iron Works; by 1910 the builder had three plants. The first was located in Detroit, Michigan; a much larger yard was seven miles south of Detroit (River Rouge); while the third was located in Ashtabula, Ohio. The company specialized in large cargo vessels, passenger steamers, canal barges, and scows, but principally the large freighters that traveled the Great Lakes, such as the ill-fated *Edmund Fitzgerald*, which mysteriously sank during a Lake Erie storm with 30-foot waves in 1975—the *Titanic* of the Lakes. Interestingly, *Delphine* appears to be the only yacht the company launched. After building more than 300 vessels, Great Lakes Engineering was dissolved in 1961, the Detroit area's last remaining major shipyard (Defoe was located in Bay City).

Fast-forward seven decades and observe the foredeck of *Delphine* as she awaits rebirth (1). While she looks grim, *Delphine* has managed to retain almost all her original features.

Delphine's pilot house (2) has miraculously managed to survive the ravages of eight decades. The main stair (3) awaits restoration.

In 1998 *Delphine* was hauled out of the water in Belgium to begin her restoration (4). Observers had assumed her arrival meant another kind of project was under way. Urbain Ureel, who took this photograph, comments, "The *Delphine* was towed cautiously from Brugge to Ostend (via Zeebrugge and a stretch of 15 miles of sea). [She] was handled as a dead ship, with her masts and funnel removed, [and] looked very much like a hulk bound for the scrapyard." Ureel was surprised that, on closer inspection, the seemingly derelict vessel was in excellent overall condition.

CANGARDA

In the remarkable image below (see also pages 18–19), the sophisticated beauty of a clipper bow is highlighted by a varnished pole surmounting brilliant gilded trailboards. This type of bow, a holdover from the age when sails ruled the waves, is hard to design, for while it may look beautiful from one angle, it can seem awkward from another; getting it right takes talent and practice. Such a bow design has been out of fashion for seventy years (at least regarding motor yachts), proof that civilization is experiencing a steady decline.

Four years after her launching, *Cangarda* was purchased by George Fulford, of Brockville, Ontario, for a reported $10,000. Fulford had made a fortune in pharmaceuticals, particularly from Dr. William's Pink Pills for Pale People. The Fulford family enjoyed *Magedoma* (ex. *Cangarda*) for thirty-four years and maintained a crew of ten at all times—a testament to the power of Pink Pills. After many more owners and no maintenance for twenty-nine years, Richard Reedy purchased the decaying vessel in 1983 with the hopes of completing a full restoration. The yacht was gutted and her main steam engine and six auxiliary engines (for the heating system, winches, etc.) were sent to England, completely torn down, and rebuilt by the Kew Bridge Steam Museum. Her forward deck house was 70 percent rebuilt, while the 130-foot hull was totally replated to ABS standards, at which point, after an expenditure of $850,000, Reedy's funds ran out. During the 1990s *Cangarda*'s empty hull bobbed along the waters just south of Boston airport, and after breaking from her lines, she partly sank in the murky water. In 1999 she was threatened with being scrapped by the Massachusetts Port Authority until being purchased, quite near the last minute, by J-Class Events, Newport, Rhode Island (see Sources). *Cangarda*'s disparate parts will be brought together, her hull raised, repaired, and cleaned, and she will then be reoffered for sale. As of this writing, the future of this remarkable vessel remains hopeful.

*130 feet and built in 1901 for Charles J. Canfield, of Chicago.
Designed by Henry C. Wintringham. Built by Pusey & Jones.
Powered by a Sullivan triple-expansion steam engine.*

Cangarda is listed by the U.S. Park Service as being one of fifty-seven vessels in the United States that are of national significance, the USS *Constitution* being another. Her plans, construction records, photographs, and final tests are available from the Hagley Museum and Library (see Sources); all are invaluable restoration materials. In this image the brand-new vessel is tied up along the wharf at the Pusey & Jones Shipyard in Wilmington, Delaware.

Cangarda was built by Pusey & Jones, founded by Joshua L. Pusey (1820–91) and John Jones (1818–97) in 1848. Early projects included the construction of steam engines, miscellaneous machinery, and repair work. The company launched its first vessel in 1853, the iron side-wheeler *Mahlon Betts*. After the Civil War Pusey & Jones launched 110 steam vessels for use in South American waters; other commissions included a variety of vessels for the U.S. government. Their steel *Volunteer*, designed by Edward Burgess, won the 1887 America's Cup. The company also built numerous fine motor yachts (such as *Avalon*, depicted in these pages). Pusey & Jones was diverse and produced the iron work for the famed Crystal Palace in New York City, built for the Exhibit of the Industry of All Nations in 1853 (on the site now occupied by the New York Public Library). Other profitable enterprises included machines that made paper, making Pusey & Jones one of the largest such manufacturers with sales internationally. The company, located in Wilmington, Delaware, closed in 1960 after more than a century of production.

MAID OF HONOR (II)

LATER KNOWN AS SYLVANA

Another striking clipper bow, further graced by a carved wooden figurehead (note the protective canvas overhead). *Maid of Honor (II)* lived a long life, serving in World War I as an auxiliary patrol vessel (fitted with 12-pounder guns), resuming a postwar career as a private yacht, and enjoying numerous owners until records cease in 1952. She was commissioned by William Millar, who had previously owned another vessel of the same name (ordered by the Earl of Cawdor in 1891).

175 feet and built in 1907 for William. K. Millar. Designed and built by Ailsa Shipbuilding Company, Troon. Powered by a pair of steam engines.

Maid of Honor II was built by the Ailsa Shipbuilding Company, which was founded in the early 1870s by the Marquis of Ailsa (1847–1938) under the looming presence of Scotland's great showpiece, Culzean Castle in Ayrshire. The Marquis also designed many of the vessels launched from the yard and was known as a fine seaman. In 1885 the company moved to the Troon shipyard (in operation since 1811), and the noted yacht designer William Fife managed the yard for a time. While the company was never noted for technical innovations (as Robert Napier & Sons were), Ailsa enjoyed a reputation as a place for excellent craftsmanship and good customer relations, which led to a significant number of repeat orders. After the marquis died in 1938, the company continued under the ownership of the Hutchison family until being threatened in the late 1970s, as were a number of shipyards. British Shipbuilders took over the company, and today, in its second century, and after launching over 500 vessels, Ailsa is vital to the economy of Troon.

Maid of Honor (II) in good company at Cowes.
  After World War I an annual user's tax was imposed in the United States on the overall length of yachts and designers turned to plumb bows as a yacht feature. When the tax was repealed, clipper bows reemerged on larger vessels in the late 1920s.

WAKIVA

239 feet and built in 1907 for L. V. Harkness and H. S. Harkness. Designed by Cox & King. Built by Ramage & Ferguson. Powered by a pair of steam engines.

I've ostensibly included this fine image of *Wakiva* because it highlights the drama of a clipper bow. It also reveals a fascinating and seldom photographed scene: a steam yacht under a protective winter cover. Note the rough wooden planks covering the pilot station and wing bridge—like a barn dropped on an elegant yacht—and the canvas protecting her shelter deck, various pieces of hardware, and mummified figurehead.

Wakiva was turned over to the U.S. Navy by the Harkness family during World War I and was lost in 1918 while on convoy duty off Brest.

VANADIS (II)

The reason for the unusual bow of *Vanadis*—a truncated clipper—is unknown, but the overall design of this Cox & Stevens yacht was also peculiar. Her features seem an attempt at creating something bold and original, an effort more fully developed by Cox & Stevens on their design for *Alva* (see page 83).

Designed for extensive world cruises, *Vanadis* was the largest diesel yacht ever built at the time and came equipped with one 37-foot Speedway sedan launch, one 33-foot Speedway-powered owner's launch, a pair of 28-foot raised deck cruisers with Scripps engines, and another pair of 28-foot sail and power lifeboats with 10-hp engines.

Vanadis was commissioned by Cornelius Kingsley Garrison Billings (known as C. K. G. Billings), who owned a number of vessels, including *Surf,* from 1901 to 1908 (200 feet and built in 1898), a previous *Vanadis,* from 1908 to 1915 (277 feet and built in 1908), and the second *Winchester* (see page 218), from 1916 to 1920. Until commissioning the second *Vanadis* in 1924, it appears that Billings, a member of the New York Yacht Club, was without a yacht during the intervening years.

The first *Vanadis* offers a lesson in how easily history can be distorted. An often repeated story was of her harrowing maiden voyage from Scotland to the United States, when, after her coal supply was unexpectedly exhausted, her elegantly appointed paneling was ripped out of her saloons and staterooms to feed the stokehold fires. Yet, while a great story, it isn't true. Clinton Crane, who designed the first *Vanadis,* was aboard for her maiden voy-

240 feet and built in 1924 for C. K. G. Billings, of New York.
Designed by Cox & Stevens. Built by Krupp-Germaniawerft.
Powered by a pair of 900-hp Krupp diesels.

Billings's love for horses was a particular passion, dramatically displayed in 1903 when he hosted a party at the elegant Louis XV-style ballroom—protected by painted tarps—of Sherry's restaurant for thirty-six guests … all on horseback.

age and detailed an accurate version in *Clinton Crane's Yachting Memories*. Due to a workers' strike, *Vanadis*'s joinerwork hadn't yet been installed. Billings, impatient, ordered all the woodwork stored aboard, to be later installed in America. As such, *Vanadis* departed. On the third day out, Crane was informed by an ashen-faced engineer that they were running out of coal. It developed that scaffolding had been left in the main cross bunker; while appearing full from the top, it was thirty tons short. Crane's solution was to drop speed from 13 knots to 10 knots (less coal was required for slower speeds), while shifting course from New York to New London. They arrived with "not a pound of coal in the bunkers." As New London wasn't used to having yachts arrive from abroad, it took a while to arrange for a customs officer to clear them. The officer, upon seeing the unfinished interior with joinery piled high, "took no interest in the trunks, the rugs, or the tires, and let us all come in free of duty."

Billings (1861–1937) inherited a fortune from his father, Albert, the presidency of Peoples Gas, Light, & Coke Company in Chicago, and a love for "trotter" horses. Clinton Crane observed, "Unlike so many millionaires who seemed to have no friends, only sycophants and toadies, Billings had a group of friends, almost as rich as he was, who usually worked together in promoting new enterprises." Billings was a founder of Union Carbide (and its chairman), and had interests in a variety of enterprises and corporations. Although rated at one point as one of the richest men in America, Billings loathed publicity and today is largely forgotten (as compared to J. P. Morgan, Jay Gould, or any number of Vanderbilts); finding biographical information is difficult. While owning a variety of splendid homes over the years, including Farnsworth, at Matinecock, Long Island (demolished), Billings eventually settled in Santa Barbara, California.

Billings owned *Vanadis* for just a short period before she was purchased by Harrison Williams, who had made a fortune in public utilities; he recommissioned Cox & Stevens to make some drastic changes, most notably the raising of her aft topsides to further enclose the main deck. While this alteration markedly improved the yacht's appearance (renamed *Warrior*), the stunted bow and blocky upper cabins negated the beauty typical of Cox & Stevens designs. Today, *Vanadis*, rechristened *Lady Hutton*—with a clipper bow added—is the Malardrottningen Hotel on Lake Malaren, located in Stockholm, Sweden, and perhaps the only grand classic motor yacht that one can experience for the price of dinner or hotel room (see Sources).

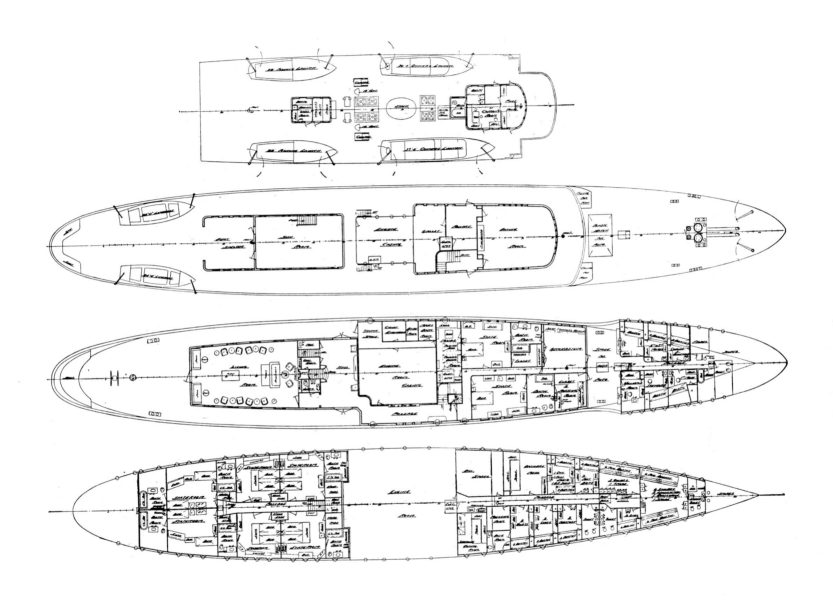

Vanadis's unusual outboard profile was matched by her peculiar interior layout. Certainly, the full beam accommodations on the main deck were unique for 1924 (*Alva* would match this feature in 1930), while the starboard passage had an awkward "crook" connecting to the aft saloons. The discontinuous deckhouse on the upper deck was another ungainly feature.

SHEER LINES

NOMA

This image highlights a basic, classic sheer: one unbroken line from stem to stern (and a nice modified counterstern it was). A distinctive feature of *Noma* was her twin stacks, unusual for a yacht. The second one was added (for reasons unknown) when John Jacob Astor IV and, later, his son Vincent owned her (1910–21).

Noma was commissioned by William B. Leeds, who proved a most difficult client. Clinton Crane, her designer, detailed his tribulations with the millionaire who micro-managed *Noma*'s construction. After the drawings were complete Leeds decided that a larger yacht was more in order, and Crane went back to the drafting board. Then Leeds insisted on a number of items—such as heavy fresh-water tanks high up to assist with pressure, heavy, carved paneling, and massive porcelain bathtubs—that Crane felt would make the vessel top-heavy. Eventually, the yacht was "lengthened, re-boiled, and re-engineered." When *Noma* was ready for inspection, Leeds was still unsatisfied. He carried a walking stick cut to exactly three feet and, holding it sideways, proceeded down a long companionway—which he'd demanded be three feet wide—scratching and gouging the paneling in every place less than the specified dimension.

Leeds (1861–1908), an entrepreneur and financier who made a fortune when his American Tin Plate Company was sold to United States Steel, owned *Noma* until his death in 1908. His estate sold the yacht two years later to Astor. In World War I, *Noma* served, along with *Aphrodite*, *Kanawha*, and *Corsair*, as the Brenton patrol reaching far out to sea. Postwar, *Noma* was laid up until being purchased by Rodman Wanamaker, who later commissioned a Mathis Trumpy house-yacht, *Nirvana* (see page 189), in 1925. Nelson B. Warden of Philadelphia purchased the yacht in 1927 and owned her until 1933, at which point she went into commercial service and disappears from the records.

262 feet and built in 1902 for William B. Leeds. Designed by Tams, Lemoine & Crane. Built by Burlee Dry Dock Company, Port Richmond, Staten Island. Powered by a pair of steam engines that drove her at 19 knots.

FROLIC II

On *Frolic II*, the foredeck toerail swept down to the lower deck, a popular detail gracing the majority of yachts in the 1920s.

Frolic II was commissioned by Walter P. Chrysler (1875–1940), who founded the automotive giant of the same name in 1925. Chrysler, born in Wamego, Kansas, skipped college and began his career as a machinist apprentice in the railroad industry. In 1908 he became the youngest superintendent (at thirty-three) for the Chicago Great Western railway, with an annual salary of $4,100. In 1912 he shifted his attention from railroads to the fledgling automotive industry, joining the Buick Motor Car Company in Flint, Michigan, at an annual salary of $6,000. Three years later, after doubling Buick's output and reducing payroll by a quarter, Chrysler demanded a salary increase to $25,000; quite sensibly, this request was granted. When Buick became a part of General Motors in 1916 Chrysler was named the division's president and general manager and, later, vice president in charge of manufacturing. His new salary? A stunning $500,000 a year. Chrysler's success enabled him to retire at forty-five (a shift perhaps motivated by his dislike for the erratic management style of his boss, William C. Durant, the founder of General Motors).

In 1920 Chrysler went back to work to help the ailing Willys-Overland and Maxwell Motor Car companies—enticed by a $1 million annual salary. Chrysler proved his value with the development of the Chrysler Six, which set an industry sales record after selling 32,000 units. This success led to the formation of the Chrysler Motor Car Company (the successor to Maxwell), which rose from fifty-seventh to fifth place in industry sales within the year. By 1929, Chrysler Motor Car was part of what would become the fabled Big Three and by the mid-1930s was the number two automobile manufacturer in the United States.

Another enduring legacy of Chrysler is the New York City skyscraper of the same name, its remarkable Art Deco spire both stunningly original and an architectural icon.

While Chrysler was a man who had no trouble thinking big and could obviously have afforded any yacht he pleased, the relatively small scale of *Frolic II* would seem to indicate that his yachting dreams were modest. Perhaps confirming this theory, when Chrysler commissioned a larger commuter, *Frolic III* (see page 229), in 1928, she was a mere five feet longer than her predecessor, while the first *Frolic*, built in 1923, was a 62-foot Consolidated.

Frolic II was designed by John H. Wells (1879–1962), who was a rarity among naval architects in that he specialized in the design of motor yachts, including four in these pages (*Acania,* the 1928 *Cigarette, Frolic III*, and *Margaret F III*). Wells graduated with a marine engineering degree from Cornell University in 1903 and went to work for the Matthews Boat Company (see page 190). Later employers included the prolific firm of Henry J. Gielow and the Elco Company. During World War I Wells managed a feat that seems miraculous: supervising eleven shipyards. After the war, and in his forty-fourth year, Wells opened his own office and produced some of the most elegant and stylish yachts ever launched. Upon his retirement in 1960 he had designed approximately 150 vessels, including motor sailers and large sailing yachts based on Gloucester fishing schooners. The South Street Seaport (see Sources) has a significant Wells archive.

70 feet and built in 1925 for Walter P. Chrysler. Designed by John H. Wells. Built by George Lawley & Son. Powered by a pair of 6-cylinder gas Winton engines.

METTAMAR

The topsides of *Mettamar* sported several unusual features. First, there were a pair of toerail "sweeps" fore and aft, the former unique, to my knowledge, in terms of the extremity of its curve. And, second, like Thomas Jefferson, who designed his home, Monticello, to look like a one-story edifice even though it's three, the dark strip between the pair of toerail sweeps almost hid a varnished mahogany row of windows for the hull cabins, a teak companionway above.

Mettamar, like *Frolic II*, was commissioned by a fabled automobile maker—Ransom E. Olds (1864–1950), of Oldsmobile fame. Olds was the son of a blacksmith, machinist, and farmer who opened a machine shop in Lansing, Michigan, in 1880. In his twenty-second year, Olds took over the business and garnered his first success with the invention of a steam engine with a gasoline burner, enabling pressure to be achieved much faster than typical steam engines. The invention sold well, about 2,000 units between the years 1887 and 1892, the Olds company increased its earning six times from 1885 to 1896. Olds was convinced, however, that steam engines were impractical for use in road vehicles. While attending the 1893 World's Columbian Exposition in Chicago, Olds learned about the internal combustion engine and, upon his return to Lansing, set to work developing such a type. Its introduction in 1897 boosted the company's sales by 50 percent. Encouraged, Olds decided to build his first automobile, a one-cylinder, five-horsepower model. Yet the success of Olds engines made it difficult to divert resources to produce entire automobiles. Help came in 1899, when Samuel L. Smith, who had made a fortune from copper mines and real estate, invested $200,000 into the new Olds Motor Works. He also controlled the stock. Early Olds models were received unenthusiastically by the public until a small, curved-dash, $650 car was introduced in 1900, the first to carry the Oldsmobile label.

The Olds Motor Works was the number one auto company in the world by 1905 (the first Ford automobile wasn't introduced until 1903). To keep up with such unprecedented demand Olds, well in advance of Henry Ford, introduced a technique now known as mass production.

Even though Olds was clearly the genius behind the company that carried his name, he didn't control it—Smith, and his son, Fred, did. Disagreements regarding policy led Olds to sell his stock and resign his board position in 1904. He founded a new company, the Reo Motor Works (after his initials), and produced a $1,250 car. Although twice the price of the Olds runabouts, it sold well, and by 1907 the Reo company was among the top five U.S. automobile companies. In the meantime, the Olds Motor Company experienced a significant decline and was acquired by William C. Durant (who created General Motors) in 1909. The Reo Motor Works prospered; its Lansing plant produced trucks until the 1970s. Olds left the company in the mid-1930s after disagreements with fellow board members.

Olds married Metta Woodward in 1889, and two of their children survived infancy.

Besides his yacht *Mettamar*, Olds owned a number of vessels, including *Reomar*, a 90-foot auxiliary schooner built in 1909; *Reomar II*, a 98-foot auxiliary schooner built in 1911; *Reola II*, an 80-foot gas-engined Cox & Stevens design built in 1915; *Reomar III* (unnecessarily scrapped in 1998), a 100-foot Cox & Stevens–designed motor yacht built in 1924; *Reomar IV*, a 125-foot John H. Wells designed motor yacht built in 1926 (launched as *Sylvia*); *Reometta*, a 67-foot New York Launch & Engine Company motor yacht built in 1929; *Joanbar*, an 84-foot Cox & Stevens-designed motor yacht built in 1930 (launched as *Lotowana III*); and *Mettamar II*, a 57-foot Burger motor yacht built in 1948.

93 feet and built in 1930 for Ransom E. Olds. Designed and built by The New York Yacht, Launch and Engine Company. Powered by a pair of 6-cylinder Hill diesels.

ZAPALA

124 feet and built in 1928 for Howard E. Coffin. De-signed and built by Luders Marine Construction. Powered by a pair of gas 8-cylinder Wintons.

Like *Mettamar*, *Zapala* featured a pair of toerail "sweeps" almost hiding the hull cabin windows between them. *Zapala*—one of the best-designed yachts of the period—was a lithe beauty.

She was commissioned by another auto tycoon, Howard E. Coffin, founder, chief engineer, and vice president of the Hudson Motorcar Company of Detroit. Coffin parlayed his fortune into a real estate empire that included his 1912 purchase of almost all of Sapelo Island, a twenty-thousand-acre barrier island off the coast of Georgia; and his purchase and development of nearby Sea Island into an exclusive resort (designed by noted Palm Beach architect Addison Mizner). Coffin ferried notables aboard *Zapala* between the mainland and his island resorts; his passengers included President Calvin Coolidge. Although Sea Island thrived (as it does today), the Depression ruined Coffin, who died a broken man in 1938.

Coffin had previously owned *Miramar* (ex-*Marigold*), a 1912, 95-foot Gielow & Orr design. *Zapala* was listed in *Lloyd's* until 1971; this, however, isn't a sure indication that she's no longer extant, leading one to wonder: Is this elegant yacht still out there?

RADIANT

Radiant featured an unusual sharp-angled break between her upper and lower decks, a detail uncommon for her designer John Alden and rarer still for her builder, Luders (known for their aerodynamic lines). Nonetheless, *Radiant* was a dashing yacht. Note the NYYC burgee at the bow and the owner's signal flying from the mast.

75 feet and built in 1926 for Clifford R. Hendrix, of Larchmont, New York. Designed by John Alden. Built by Luders Marine Construction. Powered by a pair of 6-cylinder gas Sterling engines.

Radiant's pilot house (surely the command station for the Emperor of the Universe?) featured gleaming engine controls (1). The center wheel had throttles on each side and gear shifts underneath. The rumpled leather cushion offered a more seductive invitation than its modern, tightly fitted, foam counterpart could.

Radiant's cozy aft cockpit (2) featured Moderne rattan, a canvas awning, and a wraparound glass windshield—the perfect setting for cocktails while at speed.

The main saloon aboard *Radiant* featured furnishings typical of yachts during the late 1920s and offered the type of relaxed comfort that we today would fondly associate with a visit to Grandma's house (3). Note the built-in settee; it rested on the raised sole of the pilot station just aft of the paneled bulkhead—a nice touch even if one had to step up to take a nap.

This delightful image of *Radiant* (opposite) offers a plethora of features that spell "classic": the varnished and highly detailed deckhouse; canvas awning with a nice stitching detail; a varnished handrail atop painted stanchions (with bulbous centers pierced by a cable); a teak boarding ladder; and, most important, the narrow and intimate scale.

Down below, *Radiant*'s dining saloon (1) featured both painted and varnished joinerwork and an inviting L-shaped banquette covered in a tapestry fabric.

Classic yacht galleys featured a device known as an annuciator, a small box usually attached to a bulkhead that worked in tandem with various strategically placed buttons—usually mother-of-pearl surmounted by a polished brass plate—scattered in various locations. When such a button was pressed, a number would "drop" in the annuciator (each area had a different number), alerting the crew that the owner, or guest, needed attending. Note *Radiant*'s annunciator just below the exposed lightbulb (2).

Aboard *Radiant,* my favored kind of cabin (3): snug, fitted with built-ins, topped with a repeating pattern of beams, and offering the handy feature of a folding sink (worth a fortune today in a maritime salvage shop). Note the photographer reflected in the mirror.

A pair of formidable gas Sterling Coast Guard engines (4) powered *Radiant.* Note the checked linoleum floor and knife-edge electrical panel above a work table.

John Alden (1885–1962), who designed *Radiant*, was "laconic in the best New England tradition, with an economy of phrasing that got to the point quickly, and [he] never stood on ceremony very much," as Bill Robinson observed in *The Great American Yacht Designers*. Alden's passion for yachting was evident at an early age, when he took a solo, and unauthorized, cruise in his sister's rowboat; he was six. He later eschewed a formal education and entered the Boston office of B. B. Crowninshield, supplementing this work with a course in naval architecture at M.I.T. In his twenty-third year he survived a harrowing adventure in a fishing schooner during a winter blizzard. The vessel's hull had deeply impressed Alden as to its seaworthy quality, a realization that profoundly influenced his later designs. His full-bodied hulls and short overhangs, distinctive spoon bows, and modified countersterns became Alden trademarks. For his personal boats Alden used the stock name Malabar, and he produced thirteen yachts thus named before his retirement in 1955. He would sail each *Malabar* for a season before selling to prospective buyers "literally waiting at the dock" upon each final cruise. Other popular designs included the Malabar Jr. class, the 36-foot Coastwise Cruiser, and the 42-foot Off Soundings yawl. During his career Alden produced about a thousand designs, used to build perhaps five thousand yachts—an extraordinary achievement.

CANVAS

Classic yachts owe their appearance to myriad details, such as majestic clipper bows and countersterns. However, these main features are just part of an overall composition. Canvas, for example, has largely disappeared as a yacht feature, having been replaced by the virus of yachting: fiberglass—two materials radically different in not just their construction but their look and sensual appeal.

The joy of canvas awnings is varied. They ripple slightly in the wind as their edges mimic the waves below. The sun can penetrate some types, offering a highly diffused and most attractive light. Canvas awnings also have a delicacy that's in pleasing contrast to the robust and solid hull below. Such contrasts are the stuff of art. Of course, the sun and wind conspire to rot canvas, which is why fiberglass was readily seized upon as an alternative.

SACANDO

This canvas awning was typical for the period. *Sacando* was a stock 54-foot model designed and built by American Car & Foundry (a.c.f.), detailed later in these pages.

54 feet and built in 1929 for Samuel C. Dobbs, Jr. and Sr. Designed and built by American Car & Foundry. Powered by a pair of 6-cylinder 5 x 7 Hall-Scott gas engines.

AVALANCHE (III)

99 feet and built in 1926 for Anson W. Hard. Designed and built by Consolidated. Powered by a pair of gas 6-cylinder Speedway engines.

In this image, the cozy aft deck of *Avalanche (III)* highlights another lost-in-time feature: not only have canvas awnings almost entirely disappeared but so, too, the custom of Oriental rugs on teak decks.

Most of the images depicted in these pages are devoid of people, yet a few clues are on occasion scattered about to offer proof as to their existence. In this image (one of my favorites),

note the record player atop the wicker table with an unprotected record resting on the shelf below, the books casually strewn on the ottoman, and the smoking stand between the chairs.

This was the third *Avalanche* owned by Anson W. Hard. Her successor was of an extremely advanced design and is depicted on pages 88 and 89.

ARAS

In contrast to the intimate aft deck of *Avalanche III* was the immense scale of *Aras* (additional views of *Aras* begin on page 142), her deck protected by a massive awning. In this image (taken at Bath Iron Works), *Aras* hadn't yet left the builder's yard, and the many details that make a space inviting (such as Oriental rugs and cushions) were not in place, while the wicker furnishings were still randomly placed.

A QUESTION OF COLOR

In the days of numerous lines, full harbors, and floating debris of oil and excrement, it was difficult to keep a white hull clean. And while black hulls solved this problem, the sun heats up black more than white and, so, causes additional stress on a hull, while water and salt show up clearly on black, requiring extra maintenance to keep one's pride looking bristol. Such considerations are outweighed by what I consider the overarching reason for black: it's damn dashing.

Yarrow, the company that built *Winchester (III)* and her predecessor, was founded by twenty-three-year-old Alfred Fernandez Yarrow (1842–1932) in 1865. The young man had an extremely inventive mind and at the age of eight developed his first mechanical device: an automatic wool-winder, which freed him of the tedious task of assisting an elderly aunt in winding her wool. A few years later Yarrow developed a self-acting candle extinguisher for the same aunt, who, scared by the device, scolded the youngster. When he later became intrigued by the new study of electricity, he electrocuted (mildly) an elderly and unsuspecting cook; fearing reprisal, he hid in the coal cellar. At the age of fifteen, these talents, constructive and dubious, were better channeled when he apprenticed to the firm of Messrs. Ravenhill, marine engineers. During the next five years the young man spent time in the drafting office, pattern shop, foundry, and machine shop, experiences he would build a career on. When

his father had to declare bankruptcy (through an investment gone bad), the young man was offered employment by Ravenhill for the paltry annual salary of 100 pounds sterling. Yarrow, feeling taken advantage of as a result of his family's distress, left the company. With more confidence than prospects, he was startled by help from an aunt, who gave him 200 pounds sterling, from an old acquaintance of his father's who sent the same amount, and from a man who had been impressed with the young man's talents and offered an impressive 1,000 pounds sterling with the promise of another 1,000. Thus buttressed, both financially and in spirit, Yarrow spent the next two years in charge of the London office of Messrs. Coleman, agricultural engineers, and, among other duties, promoted a steam plow (patented by Yarrow and designed in conjunction with an old friend, James Hilditch) and the Yarrow-Hilditch steam carriage. When Parliament later banned this latter contrivance from

common roads, the invention—what would later be called an automobile—was pursued no further. Finally, Yarrow decided to launch his own engineering company. With a Mr. Hedley, he opened Yarrow & Hedley on the Isle of Dogs in east London. Yarrow hit upon the idea of building small steam launches, which were repetitive, easily costed-out projects. This idea proved a boon to the struggling company, and after dissolving his partnership with Hedley in 1875, Yarrow formed Yarrow & Company, Ltd., which shifted its attention to two types of vessels that would bring the company renown: a knock-down shallow draft ship intended for use in the tropics, and the torpedo boat destroyer. By the turn of the century Yarrow & Company was thriving. In 1906 it moved from London to Scotstoun, on the north bank of the river Clyde near Glasgow. Specializing in naval vessels, the firm enjoyed continued growth and is today in its second century (as part of Upper Clyde Shipbuilders).

WINCHESTER (III)

This famous and formidable yacht was known for her speed, but I like her enormous length painted a wicked black, the Darth Vadar of her day. Note also the cruiser stern. (There is more on *Winchester* and her sister ships on pages 214–227.)

225 feet and built in 1915 for P. W. Rouss. Designed by Cox & Stevens. Built by Yarrow. Powered by a pair of Yarrow turbines.

ARAS

243 feet and built in 1930 for Hugh J. Chisholm. Designed and built by Bath Iron Works. Powered by a pair of 2,000-hp Winton diesel engines.

This dark-hulled beauty is better known as the presidential yacht *Williamsburg*, although her long-delayed restoration doesn't include returning the hull to its original glory: black (note the man on the boarding ladder, opposite).

Aras (see also page 139) was commissioned by Hugh J. Chisholm, head of the Oxford Paper Company, and this impressive and elegant vessel served as a private yacht until being taken over by the U.S. Navy in 1941 for use as a command/headquarters, transport, and VIP escort ship. After the war the renamed USS *Williamsburg* became the presidential yacht for Harry Truman, replacing FDR's *Potomac* (now restored and open to the public; see Sources). In 1953 the USS *Williamsburg* was decommissioned, then laid up until 1962, and later served a variety of uses over the ensuing decades until being sent to Genoa, Italy, in 1993 for conversion into a cruise ship—plans that never materialized. As the years have passed, this dashing vessel continues to decline, and repeated attempts to save her have remained unrealized. An Italian scrapyard, awarded the vessel in lieu of unpaid fees, stated its intention to sell the yacht (instead of destroying her). Mr. Kim Nielsen, director of the U.S. Navy Museum, monitors the current status of the *Williamsburg* and maintains extensive files (see Sources). The Hagley Museum and Library, in Wilmington, Delaware (see Sources), has a remarkable set of photographs that extensively detail almost every aspect of this history-laden vessel; they are also an invaluable asset for restoration.

Chisholm owned two previous vessels of the same name, the first, 127-foot vessel being designed and built by Bath Iron Works, in 1924, while the second, 162-foot vessel was designed by Bath but built by Newport News Shipbuilding, in 1926.

Another view of *Aras,* her black hull and varnished superstructure giving her a distinction she lacked when these elements were later painted white.

Bath Iron Works (BIW), which built *Aras,* is now in its second century as an engineering and shipbuilding company, having been founded in 1884. While today specializing in naval vessels, such as guided missile destroyers, before the mid-1930s BIW launched a diversified array of vessels, including sixteen wooden Seawanhaka-class schooners. During its first forty-four years of operation BIW launched thirteen large power yachts. During an eighteen-month period beginning with the launch of *Corsair (IV)*, in June 1929, the company built thirteen more grand yachts, all but one having its keel laid after the October 1929 stock market crash—a testament to poor timing. One of these vessels, the spec-built *Aletes* (see page 17), was laid-up incomplete in 1932 and remained as such until being sold to the U.S. Navy in 1941.

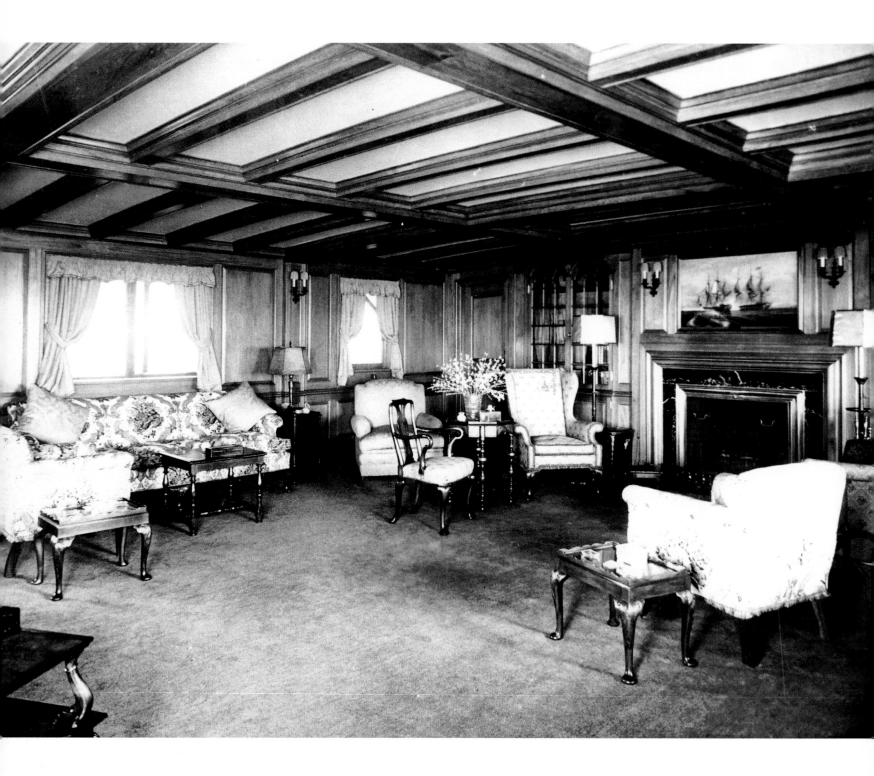

Aras's main saloon was typical of the understated elegance aboard large yachts in the late 1920s and early 1930s. There was nothing fussy, the furnishings were a comfortable mix, but, except for the painting over the fireplace, there was no evidence that such a setting ... floated.

Yachts from the turn of the century, even large ones, were very narrow, which resulted in a sense of interior intimacy difficult to achieve on later vessels—such as in the dining saloon aboard *Aras*—and impossible to replicate on modern, much wider vessels.

This saloon was also secretive about the fact that such elegance was suspended above water. After being purchased by the U.S. Navy, the entire interior of *Aras* was replaced. For safety reasons (the yacht was converted to a patrol gunboat), teak and mahogany

joinerwork was ruthlessly ripped out, thrown overboard into a waiting dump truck, and deposited in a dump. In its place, panels of fireproof asbestos were installed, creating a resolutely plain interior. In the dining saloon, only the marble mantel survived.

CORSAIR (III)

John Pierpont Morgan and his son owned four successive black-hulled yachts named *Corsair*, which were the most famous of their day, and of the four, *Corsair (III)* achieved the most fame, respect, and longevity, serving the U.S. Navy in both world wars and remaining in service for forty-five years. One of her designers, J. Beavor-Webb, became good friends with Morgan Sr.

Morgan (1837–1913), remembered as the most powerful banker in the world, was, like Jay Gould, a man quite different than depicted. Wisconsin Senator Robert W. La Follette proclaimed that Morgan was "a beefy, red-faced, thick-necked financial bully, drunk with wealth and power, [who] bawls his orders to stock markets, Directors, courts, Governments, and Nations." To those close to Morgan and to those who had business dealings with him, this characterization was comically inaccurate.

Morgan spent the bulk of his life dominated by his banker father, Junius Spencer Morgan, and was remarkably inarticulate and surprisingly shy. Trusted business associates were granted an unusual level of freedom, and many people found the banker open to new ideas and quick to make decisions, a man of few words and scrupulously fair.

Junius Morgan had impressed upon his son the importance of steady markets, honesty, and a good reputation. The younger Morgan absorbed these lessons, and they became the mainstay of his transactions. Later in life, when the late nineteenth- and early twentieth-century press painted him as a financial monster, he was baffled. As detailed by Jean Strouse in *Morgan, American Financier*, the banker "organized giant railroad systems and corporate 'trusts,' presided over a massive transfer of wealth from Europe to the United States, and, at a time when America had no central bank, acted as a monitor of its capital markets and lender of last resort." Morgan's ingrained belief in the importance of steady markets to the health of the United States was the driving force behind many of his business dealings, not, as the press stridently insisted, simply a desire to make as much money as possible. (Morgan left an estate valued at a quarter that of "Commodore" Vanderbilt and about half that of Jay Gould; of this, a substantial portion had been inherited from his father.)

Morgan vacillated between periods of intense work and, because he faced periodic breakdowns, extensive travel. In 1882, after chartering the British Royal Squadron's *Pandora* for an extended Mediterranean cruise, Morgan observed that "there is no limit to the gymnastics which a ship may go thro' and still be entirely safe." Upon his return he purchased the 185-foot *Corsair* from Charles J. Osborn (Jay Gould's private banker). An L-shaped dock was built to accommodate the elegant yacht at his Hudson River estate, Cragston.

Corsair proved a blessing to Morgan, freeing him of the tyranny of rail schedules, a prying public, and domestic matters; while married for almost fifty years to "Fanny," his second wife—his first died shortly after their marriage—the couple rarely saw each other and were usually on different sides of the Atlantic. During the warm months Morgan took to sleeping aboard *Corsair* as she lay at anchor off West Twenty-third Street, and he found the yacht conducive for business meetings, as well as a discreet place for entertaining several mistresses.

After his father died, doubling Morgan's fortune, a new *Corsair*

The New York Yacht Club had its beginnings in 1844, when John Cox Stevens and eight friends met aboard his yacht *Gimcrack;* a new club was the result, and Stevens was named its commodore. Even though a yacht may have seemed an appropriate meeting place, Stevens donated land on his estate at Elysian Fields, in Hoboken, New Jersey, where a Gothic revival clubhouse was erected (extant, now at Harbor Court, the NYYC station at Newport, Rhode Island). The first America's Cup was won by *America*, a yacht owned by NYYC members including Stevens, in 1851. The club retained the silver Cup trophy for 132 years, described as "the longest winning steak in sports." Over the years the NYYC has developed a reputation as one of the most recognized and prestigious yacht clubs around the globe. In 1987 the club acquired another impressive facility, Harbor Court, the former Newport, Rhode Island, summer home of club member John Nicholas Brown.

304 feet and built in 1899 for J. P. Morgan, Sr. Designed by J. Beavor-Webb. Built by T. S. Marvel, of Newburgh, New York. Powered by a pair of steam engines that drove her at 19 knots.

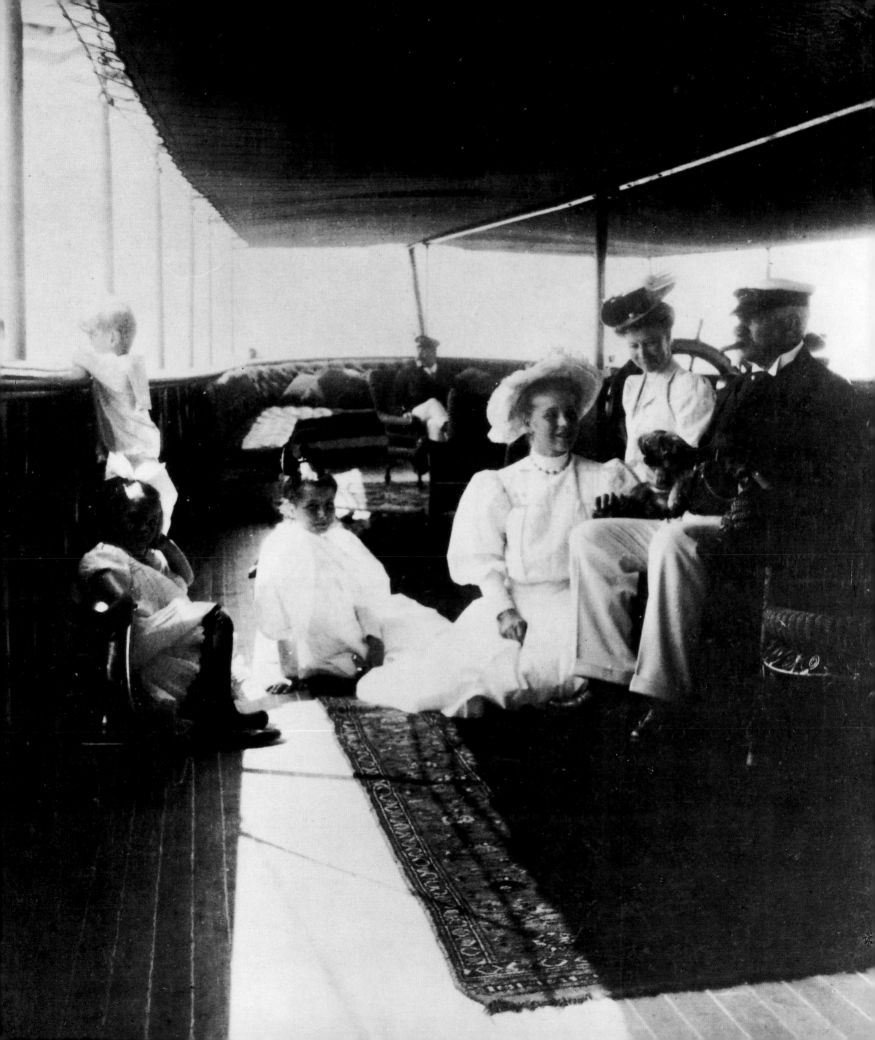

was ordered in 1890 (her predecessor was sold for $70,000). The commission to design the interiors and fittings of the new yacht was handed over to a young J. Frederick Tams (John Beavor-Webb designed the hull and engines), who discovered that his new client was not at all as expected. When Tams asked Morgan about particulars, Morgan replied that he liked the first *Corsair* and simply needed a larger vessel. Yet Tams, who was familiar with the inadequacies of *Corsair*, went on to critique numerous aspects of the yacht. "I shall never forget the expression that came over his face," Tams recalled. "He looked at me for some appreciable moments with those eyes of his and I suddenly became aghast at my temerity. I thought he might explode or order me out of the room."

To Tam's relief, Morgan said, "in the gentlest sort of voice, 'You are right; go ahead on that basis.'" Tams was further startled when Morgan handed over a blank checkbook, telling the designer to "draw until you are stopped." He never was.

Morgan enjoyed the 241-foot *Corsair (II)* for eight years until she was "requested" for service by the U.S. Navy to help with the Spanish-American War. *Corsair* was reluctantly sold—for $225,000—and went on to a distinguished career with the Navy as the USS *Gloucester*. (After the war, the vessel was sold to commercial interest but was lost in a hurricane off Pensacola, Florida.) Bereft of the vessel that gave him so much pleasure and solace, Morgan had immediately ordered a third vessel of the same name, lines, and hull color. When he was elected commodore of the New York Yacht Club in 1897, the third *Corsair* became an impressive flagship and presided over club races.

The following year Morgan donated $150,000 for land on West Forty-fourth Street in Manhattan to allow for a new clubhouse. The resulting design by the usually staid Warren & Wet-more featured voluptuous bay windows of limestone and glass shaped like the sterns of ancient galleons.

On many of Morgan's frequent trips abroad, he would take a White Star Liner (he owned the company) with *Corsair* following; upon his return to the United States, the yacht would precede him, Morgan making it a point of pride to have her escort the liner into New York's harbor.

During the 1890s Morgan was giving away over $40,000 annually (equivalent to $2.5 million today), and his purchases of rare art and manuscripts—he was known for rarely quibbling over prices—dramatically escalated with the passing years. To house them, he built a lavish library, designed by Charles Follen McKim, of McKim, Mead, and White (now the Pierpont Morgan Library and open to the public; see Sources).

After Morgan, Sr., died in 1913, *Corsair (III)* was inherited by his son and namesake (known as Jack), who enjoyed the vessel until she was turned over to the U.S. Navy during World War I; the stripped-down yacht traveled 49,984 miles during a distinguished naval career, once steamed 19,000 miles in a five-month period without shutting down her boilers, and later towed the mine-damaged SS *Californian* 300 miles to safety. After the war, the refitted *Corsair* once again became the flagship of the NYYC—twenty-three years after her original stint—when Jack was elected commodore in 1920.

Jack continued the family tradition by ordering a fourth *Corsair* in 1929. The third *Corsair* remained in service with the U.S. Coast Guard & Geodetic Survey (as *Oceanographer*) until being requested again by the U.S. Navy for World War II service. After the war, the forty-five-year-old vessel was deemed unworthy of a refit and so, in accordance with Jack Morgan's conditions, was scrapped in 1944.

It's been said that pictures tell many words; so, too, this well-dressed family gathering on the aft deck of *Corsair*. Stiffly sitting in the chair, like the family patriarch he was, is J. P. Morgan, Sr. To his right is daughter-in-law Jane Norton Grew Morgan (1868–1925). And, tellingly, in the distance is Jack Morgan on the aft settee, husband of Jane and son of Morgan, Sr.; father and son were never particularly close. Three of the children sitting on the Oriental rug are Jack and Jane's. The boy leaning over the starboard bulwark is Henry Sturgis (known as H. S., 1900–1982), the girl sitting on the deck is Frances Tracy (Mrs. Frances Tracy Pennoyer, 1897–1989); and the teenager sitting next to J. P. is Jane Norton (Mrs. Jane Norton Nichols, 1893–1981). Jack and Jane's forth child, Junius Spencer (1892–1960), is not present in this image. The girl sitting in the chair next to Henry Sturgis remains unidentified.

CORSAIR (IV)

Jack Morgan decided to replace the aging *Corsair (III)* in 1929 and commissioned a successor that looked quite similar to her famed predecessors except that, while only forty feet longer than *Corsair (III)*, the new, $1,455,190 yacht was more than double her tonnage. In the impressive image adjacent, the fourth *Corsair* is readied for her launch at Bath Iron Works.

The timing of Morgan's decision would prove unfortunate, as the Depression intervened. While Jack enjoyed a major cruise in 1934, *Corsair* was laid up the following season and in 1939 was sold to the British Navy for $1.

The Morgan *Corsair*s had blessed the yachting world for sixty-seven years. The Morgan firm is still going strong.

343 feet and built in 1930 for J. P. Morgan, Jr. Designed by H. J. Gielow. Built by Bath Iron Works. Powered by a pair of steam engines that drove her at 17 knots.

After World War II, *Corsair (IV)* was converted to a cruise ship, and in 1949 foundered on rocks near Acapulco (below). She later fell on her side and was declared a total loss. Her main turbo-generators were salvaged and used to provide electric power to Acapulco.

This is one of the rare images that exist of *Haida,* particularly with her original hull color. Finding such images is, as I have learned, an art form. For this book, I have tried to obtain prints from original negatives. This results, usually, in extremely crisp reproductions. When this ideal is not available, I order prints made from prints, such as this image of *Haida.* The museum holding the original, slightly blurred *Haida* print obtained it from a newspaper archive. Because newspapers cannot reproduce to the same level of halftone dots per inch that a book can, such images tend to be of lesser quality. The interior images of *Atalanta* (see pages 26–29) were also obtained from prints. Due to their extraordinary nature, great expense was incurred having them manipulated by a computer to increase their clarity and contrast. (It was a thrill first seeing these never published images, long encased in the Gould family albums.)

HAIDA

KNOWN AS ROSENKAVALIER

Like *Hussar* (next page), *Haida* is another rare survivor from a lost century of power yachts, and, also like *Hussar*, her once gleaming black hull, as well as her teak deck cabins, have been long diminished by white paint.

Haida was commissioned by Max Fleischmann in 1929, and for such a well-known vessel in commission now for seven decades, obtaining original images of her is surprisingly difficult. Perhaps the fact that Fleischmann used her extensively on the West Coast of America—which wasn't blessed with the plethora of photographers who prowled the East Coast (Rosenfeld, Levick, Stebbins, and others)—accounts for this scarcity of images.

Having already owned an extraordinary twenty-two yachts, Fleischmann used *Haida* for big game fishing and numerous trips along the West Coast. She was designed by Cox & Stevens (and built by Krupp-Germaniawerft) to withstand much heavier seas than East Coast yachts would normally encounter.

In 1940 *Haida* was purchased by the U.S. Navy and used for coastal patrol duty (as the USS *Argus/PY14*) until being decommissioned six years later. (Fleischmann ordered another *Haida* from Bath Iron Works in 1946; the 167-foot vessel was extant in the late 1980s as *Astarte*.)

After the war, Maurice Adda, an Egyptian cotton tycoon, purchased the vessel, and the renamed *Sarina* was sent across the globe to Alexandria, Egypt. After King Farouk (a friend of Adda's) was overthrown, Adda wisely relocated to the safety of Cannes, where *Sarina* was used as a home, office, and tax haven.

Sarina was sold in 1968, and her new owner kept her for just a year before reselling to Loel Guinness, a British member of Parliament, who embarked on a systematic restoration during his nine years of ownership, before poor health forced a sale of the vessel to film producer and Australian Robert Stigwood *(Saturday Night Fever)*. For the next three years *Sarina* traveled extensively, entertaining Hollywood celebrities, potential film investors, and friends. In 1981 the elegant yacht was sold again (Stigwood later purchased *Jezebel*, a 271-foot Cox & Stevens diesel yacht launched as *Reveler* in 1930, extant as *Talitha G*), this time to a mysterious recluse who used the renamed *Rosenkavalier* to explore the Greek islands and who lavished care on the original Krupp diesel engines and generators. Seven years later *Rosenkavalier* was sold to the Isaka family of Yokohama, and she embarked on a 9,000-mile voyage to her new home of Japan. Her next owner, Andreas Dion Liveras, a Greek Cypriot businessman, first saw *Rosenkavalier* in 1992, lying in Phuket, Thailand. "I looked at *Rosenkavalier*, fell in love with her, and bought her. The 6,000-mile journey back to Greece was completed in just twenty-five days, and I felt as though I was in heaven."

The seventy-year-old vessel was purchased by a German owner in the year 2000, and her original name restored: *Haida*. She is today one of the oldest and most original grand power yachts in existence (see Sources for charter information).

217 feet and built in 1929 for Max Fleischmann. Designed by Cox & Stevens. Built by Krupp-Germaniawerft. Powered by a pair of Krupp diesel engines (extant), which drive her at 12 knots, cruising.

HUSSAR

Perhaps the most famous grand motor yacht ever built is *Hussar,* better known as *Sea Cloud,* although few would recognize the four-masted barque with her hull painted its original color: black. Built in Germany at the Krupp-Germaniawerft in Kiel, *Hussar* was commissioned by Marjorie Merriweather Post and her second husband, Edward Francis (E. F.) Hutton. Post had inherited a vast fortune in her twenty-seventh year (the Postum Cereal Company), while Hutton was a successful Wall Street financier; the couple combined their respective talents/fortunes and transformed Postum into the General Foods Corporation.

After completing Mar-a-Lago, their enormous mansion in Palm Beach, Florida (converted to a private club by developer Donald Trump in the 1990s), the Huttons decided to commission *Hussar,* the fifth successive Ed Hutton yacht bearing that name. While initially Ed's dream, Marjorie devoted two years to the planning of their new yacht, even going so far as to have full-size plans drawn on the floor of an immense Brooklyn, New York, warehouse for her to study.

The Huttons and their daughter Nedenia (today known as the actress Dina Merrill) enjoyed the *Hussar,* cruising extensively. (Marjorie had two grown daughters, Adelaide and Eleanor, from her first marriage, to Edward B. Close.) When the couple divorced in 1935, Marjorie retained ownership of the huge yacht, which she renamed *Sea Cloud.* Later that year Marjorie married for the third time. When her husband, Joseph E. Davies, became the U.S. Ambassador to the USSR, the *Sea Cloud* served as a surreal floating diplomatic palace in Leningrad until World War II intervened. The yacht was later leased to the U.S. Navy in 1942 for the symbolic $1 a year (reportedly over the objection of FDR, who thought the vessel too beautiful for service), and the glorious ship was demasted, her bowsprit removed, hull and superstructure painted gray, and, the last indignity, named *IX-99.*

After the war, *IX-99* was returned to the Davies family, who promptly renamed her *Sea Cloud.* They spent $1.5 million to restore the vessel to its prewar elegance. Joseph Davies declined to spend much time aboard the yacht, and, in Marjorie's seventy-eighth year, the couple broke up.

In 1955 the aging *Sea Cloud* was purchased, for an undisclosed sum, by Rafael Leonidas Trujillo Molina, the feared dictator and president of the Dominican Republic, who renamed the vessel *Angelita.* Trujillo used the yacht infrequently, and she was taken over by his illegitimate son, Rafael Jr., who moved *Angelita* to berth #86 in Los Angeles harbor and used her as a glamorous bachelor pad. Soon, a bevy of stars and starlets, reportedly including Zsa Zsa Gabor and Kim Novak, were guests on board; *Angelita* quickly garnered notoriety, causing Rafael Sr. to order his son and yacht back to South America. A few years later, in May of 1961, Trujillo was assassinated after a thirty-year reign, and Rafael Jr. departed for Paris after ordering the *Angelita* to Cannes. This plan was thwarted when the new Dominican government sent a fleet of destroyers to retrieve the vessel, which they renamed *Patria.*

William Kooiman (who now works for the National Maritime Museum Library, in San Francisco, California) remembers his visit aboard *Patria* long ago. "I first laid eyes on her after the assassination of Trujillo. At the time I was chief purser of Grace Line's SS *Santa Monica* and had only a passing interest in sail. But, one look at this lovely vessel, docked just across from us, led me to realize that this was no ordinary ship. Being ignorant of her already long history, I expressed interest when port officials boarded her. To my surprise, they offered to give me a private tour.

"The vessel appeared to be spic and span both above and below deck, her main deck showing signs of recent holy-stoning by her naval crew of almost a hundred ratings. I was shown the late president's private quarters, his admiral's uniform still in the closet. The bathroom fixtures were pointed out to me as solid gold (whether this was factual, I cannot say). The furniture in the cabins and saloon was described as French provincial."

Patria remained idle, as the government had little use for her. In time, the immaculate ship remembered by William Kooiman declined. "The next time I saw *Patria* she was a sad sight, heeled over in the mud at Colon, Panama, her rigging in tatters. I was told her ownership was in doubt and that she had already been badly used as a party ship by local officials. I thought this was probably the end of the line for the old lady."

360 feet and built in 1930 for Marjorie and Edward F. Hutton. Designed by Gibbs & Cox. Built by Krupp-Germaniawerft, Kiel, Germany. Powered by a pair of 3,200-hp Krupp diesel engines that drove her at 14 knots.

Hussar was designed by Gibbs & Cox, which began in 1929 when William Francis Gibbs (1886–1967) took in a partner, Daniel Cox, of the prolific yacht design firm Cox & Stevens. Gibbs, a self-taught naval architect, abandoned a law career at twenty-eight, took a sabbatical, and developed plans for a 1,000-foot "super liner." J. P. Morgan hired him to develop the liner for International Mercantile Marine Company (IMMC). World War I interrupted these plans and Gibbs became IMMC's chief designer. After the war, Gibbs and his brother, Frederick, were hired to refit the *Leviathan,* the famed German liner seized by the United States. When her German builders demanded $1 million for her plans, Gibbs embarked on a unique effort to remeasure the entire vessel. Her successful rehabilitation brought the brothers world fame, and they remained a lifelong team. Other achievements included the liner *Malolo* (the first with sliding watertight bulkheads), four luxury liners for the Grace Line, numerous luxury yachts, *Fire Fighter* (the most powerful tugboat built at the time), and the liner SS *America* in 1938. Another notable effort was Gibbs's "Liberty Ships" design in World War II—vessels built in an astonishing forty-two days. It was also estimated that Gibbs & Cox designed 70 percent of all U.S. ships during the war. Finally, in 1951, Gibbs realized a dream four decades old when his "super ship," the SS *United States* (which could do 38.32 knots, the fastest liner ever built) was launched. Overall, Gibbs produced designs or specifications for over six thousand vessels.

The fate of *Patria* became international news, prompting the *Los Angeles Times* to report, "Tan, sleek and proud, the powerful *Patria* today lies amid the rubble of a Dominican Navy yard, like a faded, bejeweled dowager gone slumming."

In 1963 the government finally sold the yacht, for $725,000, to Operation Sea Cruises, who renamed the vessel *Antarna.* After a complete refurbishment and a new set of hand-sewn sails, *Antarna*'s elegance was restored.

However, over the next few year a series of bizarre financial and legal mishaps befell *Antarna,* until she was purchased by a group of German businessmen, who intended to restore not only the yacht but her name. In the summer of 1978 *Sea Cloud* sailed across the Atlantic with her plumbing out of order, no electricity, defective ventilation, and huge blocks of ice for refrigeration. After a harrowing passage and more legal wrangling, *Sea Cloud* returned—after forty-seven years—to the very yard where she'd been launched for a scheduled $7 million restoration and conversion to a cruise ship. Today, after a tumultuous few decades, *Sea Cloud* is again the elegant vessel that Marjorie Post and Ed Hutton intended (see Sources for charter information).

Recently, a sister ship was commissioned: *Sea Cloud II.*

MASTS

Although early motor yachts carried masts, which carried nominal sails (often used to help steady these narrow vessels), by the turn of the century this clipper ship vestige had been transformed into another lost-in-time feature: pole masts, a stripped-down mast that carried no sail.

Of course, pole masts had their utilitarian features (such as handling cargo, flags, wireless lines, and lights), but they offered two features essential to the design of classic yachts: they gave the illusion of speed even while standing still, and, like skyscrapers, they pointed to the heavens, their emphatic verticality offering a pleasing contrast to a horizontal hull and horizon.

Yet pole masts were a lot of work. As Jay Ottinger writes in his book *The Steam Yacht Delphine and Other Stories,* "refinishing the masts was a job for six men; four in the bos'n chairs and two tenders on deck. Dummy gantlines were kept rove to a block at the masthead. New lines were rove off with the dummies and chairs then attached. One went to the masthead and one halfway up. A nice quiet day was selected, and we were hoisted aloft with scrapers to scrape the spar down to bare wood. This was comparatively easy, as the brittle prime coat was shellac. The top men also reinstalled the trucks, which had been overhauled and gold-leafed, and rove off new signal halyards. After cleaning off the old varnish, we were again hoisted up to sandpaper the work. We were relieved by other sailors at noon, work continued, and a coat of shellac was applied, which dried in an hour or so. If we were lucky, a thin coat of varnish was on by three in the afternoon. The next day, a good coat was applied and finally a coat of Smith's Spar Coating—a heavy, slow-drying finish—went on. The masts sparkled."

AGAWA

KNOWN AS CYTHERA

215 feet and built in 1907 for Charles W. Harkness, of New York. Designed by Cox & Stevens. Built by Ramage & Ferguson. Powered by a single steam engine.

While we revisit *Agawa* (see cover), note the wonderful jumble of *things:* pole masts leaping into the air, lines running every which way, boarding ladders hanging off the hull, launches eager to speed away, davits awaiting their next mission, anchor chains resting over the forward bulwark, whistles anticipating their next occasion to shriek, canvas gently dancing to the rhythm of the wind, life preservers ready to save lives, and the majestic bowsprit pointing the way home. Modern vessels, in their maniacal drive for streamlining, have lost all this animation. Is this good?

Lawyer Charles W. Harkness (1860–1916), who commissioned *Agawa,* remains a wholly elusive figure. He owned a previous vessel, named *Peerless,* 166 feet and built in 1885 by Cramp & Sons (see page 22). Harkness owned *Agawa* until 1916, when she was taken over by the U.S. Navy and used out of Gibraltar; after the war she was returned to the Harkness family, who retained her until World War II, when she was used again by the Navy (as *PY-26*), until two torpedoes fired from the German U-402 blew her "to pieces." Her armed depth charges exploded upon contact with the water; two enlisted men survived out of a seventy-one-man crew.

One of the survivors, James M. Brown, wrote a graphic account of the sinking. "After the waves passed, I looked around and saw the last part of the ship, the bowsprit, sink from sight. A minute or so later I saw Carter [Charles Harold Carter, the other enlisted survivor]. . . . After a few minutes, we heard the submarine surface. We saw it slowly circle around and toward us. We attempted to hide in the water but the moon gave away our position and the submarine closed and picked us up." Brown and Carter were interned in Germany for the war's duration.

ARCADIA

This image highlights another important feature of pole masts: they enabled wireless lines to be strung high above a steel hull, which interfered with transmissions.

Moreover, this image always soothes me, as everything seems peaceful. Note the small dinghy to *Arcadia*'s port (one can assume the captain was making every effort to reduce wake), and the crew on the foredeck standing idle.

It's not known if Galen Luther Stone (1862–1926), who commissioned *Arcadia*, lived to enjoy her, as he died in December of the year she was launched. It's possible he had one season aboard.

Stone was, like many people depicted in these pages, a man with only a high school diploma who went on to earn a fortune. His first job was with the *Boston Commercial Bulletin*, and, as a journalist, he learned about conditions that affected the stock market. He left a second job as financial editor for the *Boston Advertiser* and became a stock trader at twenty-nine for Clark, Ward & Company (working as a customers' man). A fellow employee was Charles Hayden; the two opened Hayden, Stone & Company in 1892. The small firm prospered and by 1922 had $30 million in capital. Stone served on the boards and was a trustee of a variety of companies and contributed to several philanthropic causes.

Married in 1889 to the former Carrie Morton Gregg, the couple had four children: Katharine, Margaret, Barbara, and Robert Gregg.

Previous vessels included *Cossack*, a 64-foot Lawley gas engines motor yacht built in 1916, and *Makabaro II*, a 40-foot William Gardner–designed sloop built in 1916.

Arcadia was reported scrapped in 1969.

188 feet and built in 1926 for Galen L. Stone. Designed by Cox & Stevens. Built by Newport News Shipbuilding Corporation. Powered by a pair of Winton diesel engines totaling 1600 hp; they drove her at 16 knots.

HARDWARE

68 feet and built in 1927 for Hugh C. Creswell. Designed by Cox & Stevens. Built by Consolidated. Powered by a pair of 4-cylinder gas Sterling engines.

SAGA

Many classic yacht fittings are wholly different on modern yachts even though their functions remain the same; they've just lost their "fun" appeal. Take this revealing shot (opposite) of *Saga*, another of my favorite images. Up forward is a cowl vent, an imminently practical design for drawing/expelling air that has almost disappeared as a yacht feature; the fact that it could often be in the way only added to its charm, like a puppy underfoot. And note the long-handled polished brass engine controls. Today, these controls would be simple buttons adjacent to a bewildering array of other buttons, dials, and switches—perhaps more functional, but certainly less interesting. Instead, can you imagine having one hand on the varnished wheel of *Saga* while pulling the long bronze throttles and feeling the power of the engines vibrating under your feet as *Saga* takes on speed through choppy waters? What fun! I also like the portholes atop the deckhouse—an unusual but attractive detail—and adjacent leather cushions.

This image also highlights a feature prominent on many yachts before the late 1920s, and a standard the previous decades: an open-air pilot station. Although *Saga*'s captain was blessed with a windshield and wooden overhead, at the turn of the century such stations were wholly exposed or perhaps only graced with a small expanse of canvas overhead, such as aboard *Kanawha* (page 48).

Yet yacht designers weren't sadists. Open pilot stations reflected an era when being exposed to fresh air and bracing winds was considered good for one's health. The Fisher brothers (page 166), who produced automobile bodies, encountered this belief when they tried to produce closed bodies in the first decade of the twentieth century. Skepticism, primarily from auto manufacturers, persisted until the 1920s, when the brothers were finally able to produce closed car bodies; by 1927, such a type made up 85 percent of U.S.-produced cars. Interestingly, during this same period, open-air pilot stations largely disappeared as a motor yacht feature.

Saga's plans and inboard profile.

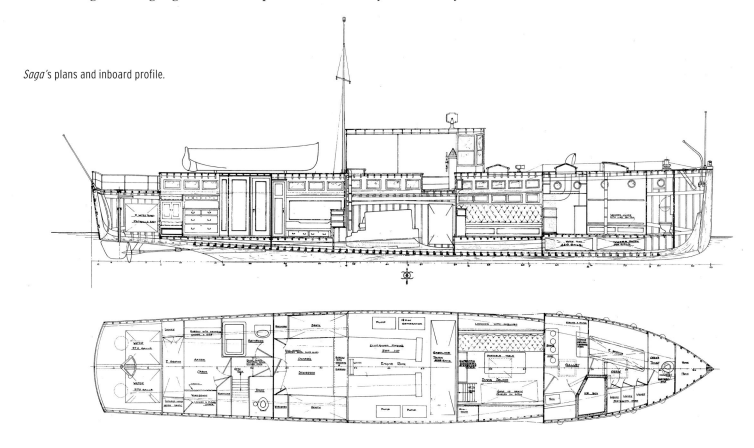

3

While *Saga*'s combined main/dining saloon was hardly spacious (1), it nonetheless excelled at civilized comfort.

The owner's stateroom (2) aboard *Saga* was simple, spacious, and cheerful. Note the photographer lurking in the mirror.

The bunks in *Saga*'s aft cabin (3) were unusual. A more typical arrangement can be seen aboard *Percianna,* on page 239; it's unknown why Cox & Stevens designed this arrangement. While the top berth must have offered a nice view through the windows, and benefited from a breeze, the lower berth must have been claustrophobic and stuffy.

ATHERO II

Raw power, the old-fashioned kind. Everything in this image works to express a singular feature: length. Observe the rhythm of the teak deck setting into motion rules the other players follow. The anchor chains and anchors? At attention. As are the storage boxes finished bright. And cleats. Handrails, too. Only the raised wall of the pilothouse, the delicate canvas as a gentle brake, arrests this march into the horizon.

Athero II was commissioned by Jesse Lauriston Livermore (1877–1940), the son of a farmer who, with little education, went on to amass—and lose—four separate fortunes. In his sixteenth year he began working with the Boston firm of Paine, Webber & Company, writing quotations on the customers' board for $6 a week. His first trade ($10) realized a $3 profit, but his employers ordered such trading stopped. Instead, Livermore resigned and over the ensuing years grew bolder in his speculations, making a $250,000 profit in one 1906 deal and reportedly amassing a $3 million fortune by 1907. In 1915, at thirty-eight, he was forced into bankruptcy with $2 million in liabilities. Undaunted, he resumed trading, paid off his debts in full, and in one deal made a reported $10 million profit. Twice more he was forced into bankruptcy and twice more paid his debts in full. The Depression, combined with more stringent market regulations as a result of the 1929 stock market collapse, prevented Livermore from being able to recover from his 1934 bankruptcy. A member of the New York Yacht Club, he wasn't listed in the 1932 *Lloyd's Register of American Yachts.*

Livermore's roller-coaster financial career was mirrored by his personal life. He was married three times: to Nettie Jordan in 1918 (divorced that same year); to Dorothea Wendt, also in 1918, a union which produced two children, Jesse Lauriston and Paul Alexander (divorced in 1931); and to Harriet Metz Noble, a widow, in 1933. Dorothea later shot their sixteen-year-old son, Jesse, Jr., in 1935; he survived, only to commit suicide—after a tumultuous adulthood—in 1975. Livermore, Sr., killed himself in the cloakroom of New York's Sherry Netherland Hotel in 1940.

Previous to *Athero II,* Livermore had owned a number of yachts, including *Sweetheart,* a 40-foot motor yacht built in 1916; *Athero,* a 153-foot commuter launched as *Gem* (see page 79); and *Gadfly,* a 107-foot Gielow & Orr design built in 1917.

171 feet and built in 1926 for Jesse L. Livermore. Designed by Henry J Gielow. Built by George Lawley & Son. Powered by a pair of 6-cylinder Bessemer diesels.

COMFORT

The yachts depicted in these pages reflect a time and place before computers, fax machines, call waiting, jet airplanes, and regular flights into space. As such, they reflect something we've largely lost: a sense of leisure and the ability to design for it.

Just *looking* at the adjacent image slows me down. Inexorably, I'm drawn in and can suddenly feel the afternoon sun upon my skin while my eyes become heavy. Overtaken, I want to stop writing this caption and lay down on one of those inviting tufted leather seats, my head cushioned by that large, oomphy-looking pillow, and nod away the remains of the day.

MARGARET F III

Forward cockpits, a relatively rare feature aboard yachts, often sat no more than a few people. John. H. Wells designed this supremely inviting cockpit aboard *Margaret F III*. (Note the image of the photographer and another man reflected in the rakish windshield; and, as proof that we are in an age far removed from these times, note also that both men are wearing hats and probably suits.)

Lawrence P. Fisher (1888–1961), who commissioned *Margaret F III* (named after his mother), was one of six remarkable brothers who expanded their father's blacksmith shop in Norwalk, Ohio, into a business creating fully enclosed car bodies ("Body by Fisher"). They sold the business twenty years after its being incorporated for a reported $208 million to General Motors. The Fishers also built the spectacular Art Deco Fisher Building in Detroit, designed by noted architect Albert Kahn.

The brothers were also yachting enthusiasts. William built a sister ship to *Margaret F III*, *Lura M* (the forth successive such-named vessel); Fred owned *Nakhoda*, a 234-foot Cox & Stevens design built in 1930; and Charles owned *Saramar* (the third successive such-named vessel), a 153-foot John H. Wells design built in 1930.

Lawrence, called the "most flamboyant" of the six brothers (a seventh brother wasn't involved in the automotive company, nor were four sisters), married Dolly Roach in his sixty-third year; the couple had no children.

The Lawrence Fisher mansion in Detroit is open to the public for tours (see Sources), and the Fisher Building at 3044 West Grand Boulevard in Detroit is open during normal office hours.

106 feet and built in 1928 for Lawrence P. Fisher, of Detroit. Designed by John H. Wells. Built by Robert Jacob. Powered by a pair of gas 8 x 10 Winton engines.

ZAPALA

We revisit this fine vessel (see page 130) to observe her wonderfully snug shelter seat amidships (forward is the pilothouse and just aft is the main saloon). This type of leftover space was typical for the period, in an age before maximizing every inch for interior accommodations became de rigueur, an age before we became uneasy with the weather, an age before we became prisoners to air conditioning.

It's a late fall afternoon and Zapala *is at speed after a long weekend. The day, while cloudy with a brisk wind, has a majestic quality, a quiet dignity. Amidships aboard* Zapala, *you're settled on the comfortable shelter seat, wrapped tight in your favorite coat—the one with the frayed collar that your spouse hates—and further protected by the glass windshield. The steward has brought a hot brandy and you take leisurely sips, pulling the wool blanket close to your neck, as your mind wanders. A smile slowly reveals itself as you remember the previous few days, the grand time everybody had and, in particular, making love on the shelter seat after everybody had gone below to sleep, with only the stars above as witness.*

As Zapala *speeds through the choppy waves, your smile broadens.*

MIRAMAR

Of the over 500 yachts I have on file, none offers such an inviting enclosed lounging area; surely the universal epicenter for romance?

In my files, this image is marked *Nirvana,* but she is clearly not either of the two such-named vessels therein. I believe that she's *Miramar,* 100 feet and built in 1926 for E. M. Statler. Designed by H. J. Gielow.

A PERSONAL ODYSSEY

AN EARLY INFLUENCE

When I was eight a great opportunity arose: my parents purchased a German-built fiberglass sailboat and proudly named her *Astart*. It was the early 1960s, and from then on our VW departed every Friday night from our new suburban development and went past the hundreds of other identical houses, the gleaming and geometrically precise shopping centers, movie houses, and libraries before we reached the highway. After an hour and a half drive this world of crisp perfection and relentless newness was suddenly, thrillingly, replaced by old houses, derelict warehouses, ancient gas stations, and a particular maritime perfume—seaweed, oil, and rotting fish.

The home for *Astart* was North Star Sail Club, fronting the Clinton River, which branched west from Lake Saint Clair (nestled under Michigan's thumb). About a mile upriver from the club was an immense, ancient, wooden storage shed. Unpainted, surrounded by weeds and gray with age, it had fascinated me for years whenever we drove by. What, I wondered, could be contained within such a vast, unkempt structure, which no one seemed to enter? It beckoned for years, but, while only about a mile from North Star, to a child on foot, this seemed a great distance, greater then I had ever traveled on my own.

The years passed, and as my body developed in size I also developed a compelling curiosity. I *had* to mount an expedition to the Great Gray Shed. The perfect summer day arrived, and as my family raced the Saint Clair, a friend and I set off. Our first stop was a favored little grocery store, layered by time. Hanging from the turn-of-the-century tin ceiling were 1950s fluorescent lights, which were reflected upon the polished 1940s checkerboard linoleum floor. The shelves, streamlined white enamel in the 1930s, were now chipped and dented, the faded remains of red 'racing stripes' still along their edges. The whole store seemed to have no clear order; bread was piled alongside cans of outboard motor oil next to dog food jammed against cookies lying atop heavy rope. There was nothing like this in my suburban life of order and precision. I loved it.

After stocking up on lunch provisions, we continued our journey. Arriving at the marina, our primary mission was not to be discovered, and weeds as tall as we were provided vital camouflage. We reached the back of the shed. A missing board offered an opportunity and we squeezed through; inside, the only light came from a gritty skylight high above. As our eyes slowly adjusted to the enveloping darkness, our pounding hearts were the first indication that we'd happened upon the extraordinary.

Before us, sitting majestically in cradles on a dirt floor, were dozens of wooden boats layered with dust or covered with torn and decayed canvas. Curiously, most of the boats were larger than those on the river. The largest seemed to be about 45 feet, the biggest vessel I'd ever seen. She had brilliant white topsides, which even the faded light could not obscure, and canvas-covered decks with small tears here and there. Her mahogany trunk cabin was finished with layers of varnish, now cracked and yellowed.

My friend and I looked at each other, mouths agape, and laid claim to the great vessel before us. We unconsciously sensed that the beautiful relics surrounding us were sacred, and to honor this feeling we, over successive weekends, did what we could to make "our" yacht shipshape, secreting away cleaning supplies from our parents and putting everything in good order. We enjoyed many lunches aboard that summer, dining at her mahogany table surrounded by wood paneling, cabinets with stained glass inserts, and delicately arched mahogany beams overhead. We played for many hours with her switches and dials, overlooking the fact that nothing worked; our imaginations did. At her wheel, I was not surrounded by vessels becalmed by walls but on the high seas, battling great storms and always bringing her and the fleet back to port safely without even a scratch to her topsides.

I loved this vessel and walked her decks with pride. On occasion I'd wonder about her *other* owners. What would they think to find her shipshape after so many years? And, I wondered, how could anyone walk away from such a fine craft? My parents' little glass boat, *Astart,* suddenly seemed thin and cheap. Instead of being created from mysterious resins, fiberglass fabric, and molds, the vessels in the shed were built in a way I understood. Their intricate construction fascinated me; I could see the individual planks and reach into bilges to touch oak frames and copper bolts. They also smelled of wood and oil, so different from the plastic resins of *Astart,* which made one nauseated if cooped up inside too long. Moreover, the yacht my friend and I claimed had built-in mahogany cabinets and bunk cushions covered in faded green corduroy that enveloped the sitter. *Astart* had plastic laminate cabinets and perfectly fitted foam seats with tight avocado-colored vinyl covers. The yacht in the shed had her name emblazoned across a mahogany stern in brilliant gold leaf; *Astart* was spelled out in black stick-on letters.

My time aboard this beached creature in the darkened light would help me forget my other life, a suburban existence where everything was new, precise, and perfect. In the gray shed I was a proud captain; the canvas, mahogany, and bronze under my feet surely loved me, and I returned this love. Summer after summer I returned to the shed, never seeing an adult the whole time.

The summer of 1969 proved my last on the Clinton River when my family moved to Florida. The fate of the many wooden vessels bathed in shadowy light would remain a mystery, but their lines, craftsmanship, construction, and even smell made an indelible imprint.

It was a hot, oppressively humid evening that summer of 1986 when I found myself at the South Street Seaport in New York City, overlooking the East River and the Brooklyn Bridge. Trying to escape the heat with too many frozen daiquiris, my heavy-lid-ded eyes were gazing upon the river when a motor yacht cruised by, a large vessel with classic lines and proportions. She was strung with twinkling lights, and the many partygoers on board filled the stagnant air with music and laughter.

As the vessel slowly glided along I felt a tugging sensation somewhere deep inside myself, seemingly nourished by the yacht before me. But why? And why did the yacht itself look so familiar? I'd never seen her before. As I continued staring at the mirage gliding past me, a rusty steel door in my mind opened—to a youth long forgotten.

I *had* seen yachts such as this. During the countless bored hours that accompany childhood, I'd looked through copies of *Yachting* magazine, particularly the "For Sale" ads that occupied many pages at the end of each tattered issue. These small photographs were a window to another world and displayed a wide variety of vessels not seen on the Clinton River. Of particular interest to me were the big power yachts from the 1920s. I felt drawn to their lines, vertical bows, smokestacks, and an extraordinary feature called a counterstern, which jutted out over the water with a great seductive curve.

These features were a holdover from the time I had watched *A Night to Remember* on TV, experiencing a thrill I'd never known. My teachers were dismayed that, during drawing classes, while the other students were busily creating brightly colored depictions of houses, dogs, and flowers with smiles on them, I'd be drawing, one after another, dark-and-doom-filled images of a great liner going down fast by the bow, with dozens of people—albeit stick figures—jumping off the great counterstern in their futile attempt to save themselves.

I wanted all yachts to look like miniature *Titanic*s. Indeed, such facsimiles could be found in the back pages of *Yachting.* During my youth these vessels seemed unobtainable. But on that hot night in the summer of 1986 came a realization: the tiny images I'd gazed at long ago could now be brought to full scale.

THE HUNT BEGINS

Bringing a childhood dream to life entailed a lot of work. The many wooden vessels evidenced in the 1960s on the back pages of *Yachting* were in scant supply in the late 1980s. Broadening my search engine, I subscribed to *Soundings* and *WoodenBoat*. This shift proved fruitful. Noon—the time when the mail arrived—became my favorite time of day. When I heard mail drop through the door slot my heart would leap; this enticing sound promised treasures.

Grabbing the pile, I'd frantically shuffle through the envelopes to see if any response had favored me from the variety of yacht brokers I'd contacted. Finding one, my breath would quicken as I tore the manila envelope open and quickly scanned the spec sheet and the pictures often included. During the next several days this information would become dog-eared. I'd read and reread the tiny bits and pieces that attempted to convey a yacht. The pictures followed me into the bathroom, accompanied my lunch, and traveled the subway in my lap.

In time, the occasional treasure pushed through my mail slot became a river. A few months after my search began, the realization of an old dream finally awaited my inspection: a yacht on Long Island, full size.

The wind blew cold and strong, lashing out against empty, icy docks. It was winter, hardly an auspicious time for experiencing the joys of yachting, but I was too excited to notice. Mostly. Walking along the slippery dock was made all the more difficult as it was resting on flotation tanks and heaving up and down. Accompanying me was the yacht broker who'd sent the listing, perhaps sensibly not expecting any response until spring. She smiled, brave soul, and carefully stepped between chunks of ice in her high heels, her voice carried away by the wind. At the end of the dock, cruelly long, awaited the focus of this expedition, a 1962, 60-foot Chris-Craft. She'd been the only listing I'd received that was remotely close to my home; so, ice, wind, and cold be damned.

There would prove another problem. While the Chris-Craft was lovely, she did nothing for my heart. Standing on the dock as it conspired to toss us into the icy waters, I tried to explain this to the broker after our tour. She retained her smile (was it frozen into place?) while suggesting that I do a little research before contacting her or any other broker again. And, with her heels imitating grappling hooks in the ice, she disappeared into the snow-clouded wind.

I decided to follow her advice.

And so began my trips to the New York Public Library. Over the next few months as winter thawed, my search started with, yet again, an old friend: *Yachting* magazines from the 1960s. Of course, it wasn't the glossy images of the "new and improved" yachts gracing the middle of the magazines that got my attention (with long-legged blondes in bathing suits draped across fiber-glass foredecks) but the older, wooden vessels featured in the "For Sale" ads. I quickly went through all issues from the fifties, forties, and thirties, before slowing down in the 1920s. Making copies of everything that appealed to me, I soon had a burgeoning file at home (the beginnings of what would prove to be this book). This file represented yacht features influenced by a life-long fascination for the *Titanic,* and the indelible memory of a Great Gray Shed.

A year after looking at the 1962 Chris-Craft under arctic conditions, I finally felt ready to schedule a look at a second yacht. My many trips to the library had blessed me with a pile of information, and, surely, I was now an expert. I'd discovered a vessel, the same type I'd longingly gazed upon decades before in *Yachting*. Her name was *High Spirits*, and she was blessed with the Ross Requirements: a stack, plumb bow, and coun-terstern. In short, she was as close to the *Titanic* as I'd ever hoped to find.

Delving into my burgeoning files, I discovered information on *High Spirits*. She'd been launched as *Maemere* in 1929 and was 112 feet LOA. Moreover, she'd been built by the best, the Mathis-

Trumpy Company. With her images clutched close to my heart, I boarded a plane to Fort Lauderdale.

A few hours later, I walked down a dock toward *High Spirits*. She was regal and impressive; my heart quickened. Captain Eric greeted us, and for the next few hours (the yacht broker grew bored and left) I studied every nook and cranny, carefully noting where the actual differed from my 1929 photographs.

I was enthralled. Until Captain Eric had a talk with me.

"You know, while you may be able to afford her, have you con-sidered the operating expenses?" he asked as we stood in the sun-filled pilothouse.

My head nodded dumbly. I'd had no such thoughts.

"Well, I thought my business partner and I could do much of the work."

Captain Eric, as though dealing with a slow child, put his hand on my shoulder and shook his head. "Ross, this vessel has a full-time crew of five and even *we* can't keep ahead of all that needs to be done. Between the charters and maintenance, the latter always loses."

I tried to absorb this.

"So, do yourself a favor. Don't, I repeat, don't, buy anything over seventy feet."

My dream for owning this particular *Titanic* facsimile was dashed.

Johan Trumpy (1879–1963), a third-generation boat builder, left Norway in 1902 and later founded the Mathis Yacht Company, in Camden, New Jersey (Mathis was the principal investor in the new company and owned the land it was lo-cated on). The company later moved to Glouces-ter City, New Jersey, and changed its name to John Trumpy & Sons in 1943. Four years later the company moved once again when it purchased the Annapolis Yacht Yard, Maryland. From the beginning, Trumpy defined a particular breed: the house-yacht. The company prospered through the decades until it became increasingly difficult to find workers skilled in the art of creating finely detailed and stoutly constructed wooden yachts. As fiberglass became the dominant ma-terial of boat construction, the refined elegance of an oak, pine, mahogany, and teak Trumpy be-came an anachronism. Finally, John H. Trumpy & Sons closed in 1973, not for lack of orders but for lack of skilled workers.

MAEMERE

This Johan Trumpy design was unusual in that her Pullman windows (the large topside windows) were arched on top, a superfluous detail that appeared unique to *Maemere*. And, while her modified counterstern was attractive, the elliptical version offered more grace.

DeWitt Page (1869–1940), who commissioned *Maemere*, was another of those late-nineteenth-century personalities (like Thomas Lawson and Walter Chrysler) who came from humble beginnings, had little schooling, and yet rose to prominence and fortune. Page began his rise with, of all things, a bicycle bell. While employed by New Departure Bell Company, of Bristol, Connecticut (he later married the sister of one of its founders), Page benefited from the company's success with its introduction of a bicycle bell actuated by a thumb lever and later innovations, which included improved braking devices. The company prospered (Bristol became known as "Bell City"), eventually opened a plant in Germany, and added ball bearings for bicycles and automobiles to its line, bearings becoming its principal revenue source. In 1907 Page engineered a transition from using outside agents to sell the company's products to having an in-house sales force. He became the division manager and showed exceptional creative energy as a salesman. His abilities resulted in further promotions, and when New Departure became affiliated with General Motors, Page became president of the company, as well as a director of General Motors (1923–40) and its vice president (1923–37).

Page married May Belle Rockwell in 1895, and the couple adopted a daughter, Nan. In 1933 the Pages donated Page Park to the city of Bristol and provided a $275,000 endowment for its upkeep. Page also enjoyed horse racing and through his Maemere Farm stables developed a reputation as a sportsman. His Mathis-Trumpy yacht appears to be the only vessel Page owned.

112 feet and built in 1929 for DeWitt Page. Designed and built by Mathis-Trumpy. Powered by a pair of 8-cylinder 8 x 10 Winton diesels.

TRAIL

93 feet and built in 1926 for William Wallace, Jr. Designed and built by Mathis-Trumpy. Powered by a pair of 150-hp Wintons.

Johan Trumpy didn't start producing graceful house-yachts right off. It took him two decades to achieve a certain fluidity of line that came to define Mathis-Trumpy, as shown here on *Trail*. This 93-foot 1926 design was one of the finest looking Mathis-Trumpys ever built.

In the image below, *Trail*'s plumb bow cuts an elegant wake; observe the distinctive scrollwork. Her sheer is perfection, a subtle sweep incorporating a detail peculiar to Mathis-Trumpy: the row of Pullman-type windows to brighten the staterooms. This row was vertical, as opposed to the gentle curve of the hull, and allowed two features: windows that could push open, and louvered wood screens, which disappeared into hidden side pockets.

This design feature incorporating the Pullman windows worked well visually on Mathis-Trumpy yachts because of myriad touches. Most important, note the double "sweeps" of the varnished mahogany toerail, which gracefully allowed the row of windows to break from the hull curve; no one did this better. The thin varnished strip atop the windows also pulled everything together, as did the larger scaled toerail above.

Other significant design considerations included the forward canvas awning, which highlighted *Trail*'s length, and, of course, the counterstern. Moreover, note the canvas under the stern handrail; its dark color didn't compete with the white hull. In the end, *Trail* was beautiful because of scale. Everything about her was just the right size and proportion.

An exciting close-up of a Mathis-Trumpy counterstern with bronze scrollwork intact (this vessel was launched as *Mariska*). However, note the white metal panel above the toerail, a feature that competes with the white hull and negatively alters the lines of any such Mathis-Trumpy.

Far left, a detail showing the hull curve contrasting with the vertical Pullman panel. In this contemporary image the mahogany toerail and "sweep" have been painted white, an unfortunate occurrence because it obscures their essential job: definition.

Near left, another contemporary image showing the sliding louvered screen covering the Pullman windows, a nice touch offering privacy and ventilation.

Neither of these images are of *Trail*.

Mathis-Trumpy house-yachts excelled in spacious interior accommodations, as shown here aboard *Trail*. This comfortable setting in the deckhouse offered a combined dining and living saloon, a typical feature. The furnishings reflect their late 1920s vintage and appear more the efforts of a land-based decorator than one familiar with yachts, although everything is inviting and plush.

I've yet to board a Mathis-Trumpy furnished like *Trail*, although such items can be readily obtained in secondhand stores and antique shops. And none of the items in this image would be terribly expensive today.

Opposite, *Trail*'s aft port bulkhead in the main saloon—an intimate corner for writing notes to one's yacht-less friends about what a wonderful and relaxing time one is having. Note the nicely done curtain, which was obviously purely decorative, as its brass rod was only as long as it was. The unusual patterned sheer fabric pulled tight against the glass was a thoughtful touch, offering privacy. The cut flowers were probably an addition for the photographers, but the peacock was perhaps a permanent resident. Note the carpet, its seam a telltale sign that in the days before wall-to-wall carpeting large rugs were sewn together in 27-inch-wide-strips.

Again, as the items in this image are readily available today, and inexpensive, why is no extant Mathis-Trumpy so furnished?

Right, *Trail*'s main deck pantry with a variety of shelves and hooks for cups and glasses (note the nicely detailed shelf edge in the upper right corner). Note also the drainboard on the Monel counter, the annunciator in the upper center, and the pull-up shelf on the lower right. And, because there was no kick-space (a standard galley/kitchen feature), the bottom of the white enameled cabinet was already badly scuffed on the almost new yacht.

Unfortunately, I've not seen one Mathis-Trumpy with an intact pantry or galley; they've all been altered.

These furnishings on *Trail,* while in themselves perfectly attractive (the pair of lamps are questionable),
offered no evidence that one was aboard something-
that-floated. And while the same type of furnishings

created an inviting atmosphere in the upper deck saloon, for some reason I dislike them in staterooms. Picture instead a built-in settee under the Pullman windows, bracketed by a pair of built-in cabinets. The

dressing table could have been easily built in, with a
mirror fitted into the recess of the paneling, all lighted
by a pair of bronze wall sconces. Better?

It's a rare yacht that survives decades of use without being "improved." Almost without exception, such changes are never for the better, as shown here on *Trail* in the 1980s. Most noticeably, she's missing her Pullman windows, which, if not carefully maintained, are prone to fresh water leakage—a yacht killer (fresh water eats wood as salt water preserves it). There are also more subtle changes, which, individually, may not seem of great significance but, when added up, collectively reduce the perfection that a yacht such as *Trail* once enjoyed. Such changes include the distinct thickening of both her rubrail (just below the ports) and her toerail, which is at least twice its original scale. Her bronze scrollwork on the counterstern is also gone, a profound loss. The davits are painted white and draw one's eye. Coast Guard regulations (the bane of classic yachts) are to blame for the increased height of the rail, which throws things off. Adding a further insult, another handrail had been added above. The stack is white with stripes, a far cry from the more subtle buff color sans strips. And the delicate canvas awning has been replaced with wood. *Trail* also appears hogged in this image. In short, a beautiful vessel, whose lines and details took decades to perfect, has been diminished.

CURMUDGEON COMMENTS:

I understand the importance of having classic yachts pay their way as much as possible, and, as such, understand that changes must be made to bring a sixty-year-old vessel into the modern age. What I don't understand is why such changes are almost without exception detrimental to a classic yacht. For example, hand-rails on a classic are much lower than the height now specified by the Coast Guard. The solution for many is to raise the rail, but this throws off the delicate balancing act of a classic yacht. An alternative might be to leave the rail as is, and add a thin, almost unnoticeable stainless steel cord at the required height, threaded through the stanchions. Most classic vessels have a hull with deckhouse above, and, possibly, a small pilothouse as level three. Yet many classics are pressed into having three full decks. This has been possible because the ubiquitous canvas awning stretching the length of many yachts has been, over time, invariably replaced by wood. It seems as if a lightbulb went off in someone's head who realized that—*gadzooks!*—the top of a wooden overhead could be pressed into more charter space. Great. Except there now will be a lot more happening on top where not much happening was the original intention (see 1980s *Trail*, above). People who charter classics will argue that this extra deck space is essential for guaranteeing the focus of our culture: more money. But, is this true? I wonder, with the proper marketing, if people couldn't be enticed to a classic vessel for all the reasons I am. Yet, I've not seen one yacht for charter that still looks like a classic in every respect. The furnishings are always an uneasy mix of period wannabe's and modern sofas. Even if there *is* wicker aft, it's never the same type that would have been there originally; more Pier One than Old World. And beamed overheads are covered with plastic laminate, curtains aren't linen but nylon, carpets aren't wool but more nylon, and lines aren't hemp but—you guessed it—nylon. Original berths have been discarded, replaced by large beds. Heads have been updated and in the process sturdy porcelain, Monel metal, varnished mahogany, and polished brass have been replaced by fiberglass, plastic laminate, and vinyl. As have galleys. More often than not, all this happens because people have no idea of what their yachts looked like decades before (part of the reason this book was written). Yet I strongly suspect that classic yachts for charter would do *better* if they took a lesson from the famed Orient Express. This train, in every respect, looks like it has time traveled. Yet people flock to it—at very high prices. And it doesn't have queen-size beds. I appreciate that the charter business is a competitive one; however, if someone wants acres of space, let them hire a big, modern, beamy fiberglass yacht. If someone wants something special, let them hire a classic yacht with plenty of varnished mahogany, canvas awnings, teak decks, and cabins outfitted with silk, wool, and cotton. Let them hire intimacy, graceful lines, and history.

TROUBADOUR

To show just how special the fluid lines of *Trail* were, this contrast is offered. Overall, much was the same, but note the area just aft of the Pullman windows: the sheer abruptly and awkwardly stopped short of the stern. On *Trail*, the toerail was a continuous and elegant sweep from port to starboard. Also note the aft portholes on *Trail*, which continued a theme from forward; on *Troubadour* a pair of peculiar horizontal windows introduced a discordant note. Otherwise, if you put your finger on the aft of *Troubadour* and then compare the image with *Trail*, there's hardly any difference, proof that God is in the details.

92 feet and built in 1925 for Webb Jay. Designed and built by Mathis-Trumpy. Powered by a pair of gas 6-cylinder Wintons.

MINOCO

While *Minoco* (later named *Idyl*) was similar to *Trail*, her stern was a modified counter. While still attractive, it hindered the toerail from gracefully sweeping around the stern.

108 feet and built in 1930 for Mills Novelty Company. Designed and built by Mathis-Trumpy. Powered by a pair of 8 x 10 Winton diesels.

115 feet and built in 1925 for Rodman Wanamaker. De-
signed and built by George Lawley & Son. Powered by
a pair of 8 x 11 Winton engines.

NIRVANA

To fully appreciate the excellence of Johan Trumpy in designing house-yachts, one need look at his competitors. This vessel (note the people on deck watching the photographer), designed by George Lawley & Son, had all the same features, but a crucial piece of talent was strangely absent during her design: a sense of scale. This was unusual, because Lawley produced beautiful yachts, yet everything about *Nirvana* was off just a bit. Her foredeck was too short. The forwardmost Pullman window was peculiar and attracted one's attention unnecessarily. The forward toerail "sweep" wasn't bright, and its reason for being—definition—was lost. The entire stern design lacked grace; the decks seemed too high, as did the stack; and the lack of canvas above the foredeck negatively differed from *Trail*. Even the masts were stubby.

Nirvana was commissioned by Lewis Rodman Wanamaker (1863–1928), son of the famed Philadelphia department store magnate, John Wanamaker. The younger Wanamaker, known as Rodman, had a variety of interests, including an involvement in the American Indian reform movement; he sponsored three photographic expeditions documenting Native Americans (1907, 1909, and 1913). Today, the Wanamaker Collection of over 8,000 of these images can be seen at the William Hammond Mathers Museum, in Bloomington, Indiana (see Sources). In 1916 Wana-

maker was the driving force behind the founding of the Professional Golfer's Association (better known as the PGA), and he donated $2,500 for the first PGA Championship and the trophy that bears his name. He also proved an able steward of the family business and assumed control of the Philadelphia, New York, and London department stores in 1920. Publishing was another interest; Wanamaker owned three Philadelphia newspapers. Upon his 1928 death, he was "the most insured person in the United States, with a policy valued at $6 million."

Wanamaker's first wife, the former Fernande Antonia Henry, died in 1908; the couple had three children. A second marriage took place in 1909 to Violet Cruger; the couple had no children and divorced in 1923.

Besides *Nirvana*, Wanamaker had previously owned *Lolomi*, a 112-foot Lawley gas engined yacht built in 1917; *Noma*, a 262-foot steam yacht (see page 125) built in 1902; and *Wakita*, a 37-foot Lawley gas engined yacht built in 1921. He was a member of the New York Yacht Club and the Corinthian Yacht Club, Philadelphia.

The massive organ—with 28,500 pipes—gracing the atrium of Wanamaker's Department Store in Philadelphia (now Lord & Taylor) has thrilled generations of people and is today undergoing an extensive restoration (see Sources).

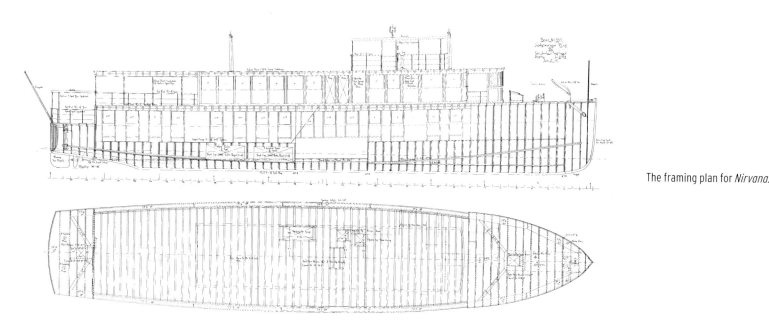

The framing plan for *Nirvana*.

IRWIN

To appreciate how important the pair of toerail "sweeps" on *Trail* are, note the lack thereof on *Irwin*; as a result, the Pullman windows seemed askew. And, like *Nirvana*, the details and scale of *Irwin* were off; even the counterstern wasn't proportioned attractively.

Note the owner's flag painted on the stack.

99 feet and built in 1925 for Julius Heilner. Designed and built by the Matthews Boat Company. Powered by a pair of gas 6-cylinder Wintons.

Scott J. Matthews founded the Matthews Boat Company (which designed and built *Irwin*) in 1890, building naptha launches in Bascom, Ohio; the company later moved to Port Clinton on Lake Erie's western shore. The Matthews Company built a variety of vessels, ranging from 12-foot rowboats to large luxury yachts such as *Irwin*, but their most popular model was a 38-foot single-cabin stock cruiser that sold for $8,500 in 1938. Earlier models, such as their 1927 28-foot cruiser, sold poorly, and the line was discontinued after three years. Scott Matthews died in 1959 and the company was sold. It continued operations until 1975.

ALPHA

100 feet and built in 1926 for George Marshall Allen, of New York. Designed by Henry J. Gielow. Built by Welin Boat & Davit. Powered by a pair of diesel 6-cylinder Bessemer-Atlas engines that drove her at 13.5 knots.

Again, the talent of Johan Trumpy is designing house-yachts is evident by this comparison image of *Alpha*. The sloping bulwark so far amidships was not attractive, and the large windows in the hull—serving the same purpose as the Pullmans aboard a Mathis-Trumpy in lighting the staterooms—seemed out of place and negatively contrasted with the portholes adjacent.

And her high, double-stacked deckhouses appeared top-heavy. An extraordinary feature of *Alpha* was that her upper deck housed an automobile, yet this unique addition wasn't mentioned in any contemporary literature. It's unknown why *Alpha*'s owner, George Marshall Allen (a member of the New York Yacht Club), installed this feature.

THE HUNT CONTINUES

The captain of *High Spirits* had enjoyed my wild, if misplaced, enthusiasm for impressively scaled Mathis-Trumpys and offered me tantalizing clues as to where others lay nearby. I bid adieu and set off to hunt for more. An hour later a target was spotted across the Intercoastal Waterway.

Unlike the shimmering *High Spirits*, the vessel before me seemed sad and tarnished. I came toward her but was stopped by a police officer, who regarded me with extreme suspicion. *What, I wondered, was going on?* The officer grilled me and my story only seemed to increase his suspicions.

"Come on, what do you know about the murder aboard this boat last night?" he asked, pointing to the forlorn Mathis-Trumpy adjacent to us.

The look on my face apparently conveyed more than any words could have, and the officer let me go.

An hour later I returned.

Walking along the dock, I saw, in black stick-on letters, the name *Sunset* rudely tacked onto the counterstern, which was missing its bronze scrollwork. I also observed two other important details: no one seemed to be around, and the cabin doors were wide open. I stepped aboard.

Sunset was a wreck. Cabin after cabin was full of clutter, a jumble of furniture, old, rusted gizmos and whatnots, and debris. I was fascinated that something once so beautiful could degenerate into such chaos. What had happened to this fine lady? When was she last owned by someone who lavished care and attention? What would happen to her?

As the sun crept toward the horizon, these questions would remain unanswered. I departed this sad vessel (launched as *Freedom*) without knowing that she'd remain an item of curiosity in my life for years to come.

FREEDOM

KNOWN AS SUNSET

Freedom was advertised as the first Mathis-Trumpy to have a "new-type full-deck" stern: a counterstern with fantail, bronze scrollwork, and triple portholes aft. Moreover, she sported the essential features that made *Trail* so attractive: the dark canvas above the toerail, double "sweeps" adjacent to the Pullman windows, a plumb bow, a canvas awning stretching almost her length, one buff-colored stack, and a raked mast.

Starting with *Freedom*, and continuing into the early 1930s, Trumpy-designed yachts reached a pinnacle of grace unmatched by competitors or even successors.

104 feet and built in 1926 for A. J. Fay. Designed and built by Mathis-Trumpy. Powered by a pair of gas 6-cylinder Wintons.

Unfortunately, by the time I caught up with her, *Freedom* was no longer her original self. Like *Trail,* she'd lost her Pullman windows, as well as the bronze scroll-work on her stern. The white painted deckhouse didn't help, nor did the white metal plates under the handrail, both of which conspired to make *Freedom* appear top-heavy. On the bright side, this picture was taken several years after I'd last seen her and she was in noticeably better shape.

Freedom was, in a way, a primer: a way to desensitize me for what lay ahead—the Haunted Yacht. Captain Eric had been mysterious about this vessel, which intrigued me all the more. Arriving in Miami, I drove up and down many potholed roads adjacent to small, obscure rivers looking for a particular marina. Once finding it, and after introducing myself, I asked to see this intriguing vessel, which I was careful not to call the Haunted Yacht but the name Captain Eric had given me: *Man-*atee. Like the day before, I was eyed with extreme suspicion.

Had another person been killed here? Did a serial killer exist who killed only aboard Mathis-Trumpys?

It developed that the marina was nervous because they couldn't guarantee my safety aboard *Manatee*—I couldn't wait to board!—and so I offered to sign a waiver. This accomplished, and my quest now having the allure of danger, I set out toward the vessel.

Walking into the huge metal shed that housed her, it was instantly apparent why *Manatee* was infamous. In the darkened light she did in fact appear a phantom. She was impressively huge and, as I later discovered, the second largest Mathis-Trumpy ever built at 121 feet. She floated with a sad list to port, was covered with dust—the first yacht I'd seen as such—her many stanchions were askew, and, ominously, a bilge pump was steadily discharging impressive amounts of putrid water. Moreover, the mahogany trim and deck cabin was 121 feet of peeling varnish.

To my surprise, she was in pretty good shape inside, apparently the result of a major facelift not long before. How, then, I wondered, had she fallen from grace so quickly? Walking through her main saloon, I marveled at its length and expansiveness. Passing by a fireplace on the forward bulkhead—*a fireplace!*—I entered a long starboard companionway lined with large ports (a space quite impressive). A galley that seemed too small for such a large yacht lay just forward of the main saloon. I returned to the long hall and opened a mahogany door into a cabin lined with large ports puncturing dark varnished woodwork. What had it originally been designed as? The smoking room? The space radiated intimacy, and I touched the bronze ports, delighting in their sizable scale. Nor did the relative darkness totally obscure the beauty of the woodwork and its fine condition. My soul was enveloped by this cabin of immense charm.

Forward of this was another impressive cabin, its diametric opposite. Where the "smoking room" was a dark and masculine environment, this half-circle cabin was filled with light from the wraparound windows. I walked back and forth between these two spaces and marveled at the contrast and brilliant juxtaposition. Stepping onto the deck, I climbed up to the pilothouse and its attached captain's cabin. Again, everything seemed in good shape. Peering out windows obscured with dust, I looked down to the majestic length of foredeck cluttered (appealingly) with impressively scaled hardware. Climbing down, I walked the length of the port deck and ran my fingers along the varnished deck cabin. Reentering the main saloon, I slowly descended the main stair while enjoying its fine detail. The hall before me was

dark and, as I soon discovered, dangerous; it was missing floor planks here and there. As my eyes adjusted to the light I started laughing nervously, excited by the proportions and length of the long, thin space. With careful steps, I entered cabin after cabin. These sad spaces were a contrast to the relative normalcy of the deck above and were covered with mildew, pulled apart here and there, and close to being disheartening.

I was enthralled. I've always been able to ignore superficial damage and dirt and appreciate the essence of any space. These many staterooms aboard *Manatee* were a delight, from the cozy charm of the aft cabin lined with those triple ports on each side, to the spacious main stateroom forward, behind the engine room. Moreover, *Manatee* was intact, original, and restorable.

After spending time in each cabin, I returned to the main saloon in the hope of discovering how to enter the forward part of the hull. Finding a stair that was almost a ladder, I went below and into—oh!—the *real* galley. It was huge; obviously, the space above was the pantry. Stepping aft and opening a heavy steel door, I was thunderstruck. Before me was a space seemingly copied from a 1930s Frankenstein movie, with a bewildering array of massively scaled mechanical devices. There was a pair of original Winton diesels, which, at 7 feet high and 13 feet long, dwarfed any I'd ever seen. A gigantic electrical panel attached to one bulkhead was studded with a plethora of definitely original knife-edge switches (and surely the same type used by Dr. Frankenstein to bring his monster alive). And, while the room was appalling—rusted, wet, and so filled with debris it appeared as if an explosion had occurred—it was also powerful and impressive.

My heart was pounding so hard I could feel it. Exiting this chamber, I continued my expedition. There was a crew's mess hall—the first I'd seen—and, forward, a row of cabins varying from semi-plush (for officers) to severely plain (for crew). What distinguished these spaces was the startling height of the overhead. In most yachts, the overhead will be just above one's head, but aboard *Manatee,* in this area, it reached twelve feet as the foredeck soared high above.

Wow.

TRUANT (II)

Truant—the second largest Mathis-Trumpy ever built—featured the overall details that made *Trail* so attractive, with the addition of thirty feet and a raised pilothouse. She was commissioned by Truman Handy Newberry (1864–1945), whose father was a lawyer and U.S. congressman (1879–81) and the founder of the Michigan Car Company. After graduating from college, the younger Newberry took a job with the Detroit, Bay City & Alpena Railroad and assumed a position managing his father's interests. In his twenty-third year Newberry succeeded his father as president of the Detroit Steel & Spring Company and took on numerous other directorships. He also became president of the Newberry Estate, Inc.

Newberry married Harriet Josephine Barnes in 1888, and the couple had three children, Carol, Barnes, and Phelps.

During the Spanish-American War, Newberry held the rank of lieutenant and was later made assistant secretary of the navy during the Theodore Roosevelt administration; his business acumen resulted in a promotion to secretary in 1908. During World War I he served as lieutenant commander in the U.S. naval fleet reserve.

In 1918 Newberry beat Henry Ford in Michigan's 1918 Senate race. Convicted of exceeding the campaign spending limit of $10,000 (an amount that seems laughable today), this conviction was overturned by the U.S. Supreme Court in 1921.

Truant II was the second Mathis-Trumpy owned by Newberry; a previous *Truant* was 105 feet and built in 1926.

During World War II Newberry made a gift of *Truant* to the U.S. Navy and the vessel was renamed *Idyl* (and later *Carnan*), serving as an executive recreation and entertainment facility until being sold in 1945 (Newberry died the same year), when she was renamed *Muriel B.* She was later purchased by Walter P. Chrysler, Jr. (the son of the automobile magnate who owned *Frolic*: see page 126), who renamed her *North Wales.* Chrysler sold the vessel in 1951 to Colonel and Mrs. Leon Mandel of Chicago, who cruised the East Coast extensively aboard the renamed *Carola* (Mrs. Mandel's name), spending much time in Palm Beach, Florida. After fifteen years of ownership—a record for *Truant*—the Mandels donated the yacht to the International Oceanographic Foundation, which had no use for it. For the next decade *Carola* (renamed *Manatee*) went through a variety of owners until being purchased by Boston Advertising executive Allen R. Hackel.

121 feet and built in 1930 for Truman H. Newberry, Detroit. Designed and built by Mathis-Trumpy. Powered by a pair of 8-cylinder Winton diesels.

This image, it is believed, is *Truant* under construction, a symphony of framing. The lattice of steel strapping helped the hull maintain its shape. Except the strapping doesn't continue to the stern, resulting in, over a period of time, the noticeable sagging of many Mathis-Trumpys in just this area.

The deckhouse (right top) aboard *Truant* showing the combined dining and living saloons typical of Mathis-Trumpy, although, because of *Truant*'s extreme length, a set of doors was added to divide the space (they were gone by the time I was aboard). Note the Moderne fabric on the curtains and pair of chairs (in the background). This offers a hint of a design revolution that would characterize the 1930s. Also, note the lack of seams in the carpet. Overall, this setting is less fussy than the one aboard *Trail* (page 180), built just three years before.

Forward of *Truant*'s combined living and dining saloon was a pantry, forward of that was an extraordinary womb-like cabin encased in dark woodwork and pierced by large bronze ports, perhaps unique for a Trumpy yacht. Finally, at the very forward end of the teak deckhouse was this sun-filled saloon (right bottom), a space occupied on most Trumpys by the pilot station. *Truant*'s extreme length afforded the option of a third deck for a pilot station with captain's quarters.

Left, the expansive aft deck, too large to offer much intimacy.

Above, the owner's stateroom, with the type of free-standing furnishings not my preference. It's possible that Mathis-Trumpy, because they designed house-yachts, delivered vessels with houselike interiors.

Right, the unidentified captain, officers, and crew aboard *Truant.*

This image (below), taken during the 1980s, shows the effect of fifty years on *Truant.* Observe how, as on *Trail,* all the Pullman windows, except two, have been replaced by large portholes, and the pair of toerail "sweeps" have been painted over. Otherwise, *Truant* is remarkably intact. Her deckhouses are still finished bright, the owner's private signal still graces a white stack topped by a colored strip, and the fore and aft awnings are still in place.

Truant as I found her in the late 1980s under a shed at Jones Boat Yard. *Truant* looks quite forlorn (note the askew and missing stanchions), but such problems are largely superficial. However, it's exactly this type of deferred maintenance that leads to the most tragic fate that can befall a yacht: a reputation. "You know, she's in really bad shape," is the phrase that starts getting around, and once it does, a yacht's days are numbered, regardless of the actual structural condition of the vessel.

Top right, a close-up of *Truant*'s bow in the late 1980s. While she looks grim, my poking couldn't penetrate the planking. And note also that the planks are tight to one another, another good sign. Obviously, though, the iron fastenings would have to come out.

A SLEEPING BEAUTY

Before New York's master builder Robert Moses* ruined Long Island with highways (setting a global precedent), those fortunate few New Yorkers with enough cash discovered that the most comfortable way of getting around was by owning your own private yacht. If this vessel was to be used primarily in speeding you to and from work—like a water taxi—and/or if it offered little in the way of interior accommodations, then it would be called a commuter. It could be on the small side, like the 68-foot *Saga*, or *really* large, like the 343-foot *Corsair*, where accommodations were, obviously, plush to the extreme.

In 1901, well before the term "commuter" came into vogue, Thomas Fleming Day called such vessels "general purpose steam yachts." Merchants and brokers, he wrote in *Rudder*, "reach their places of business in the early morning and return to their homes in the evening, to the great benefit of their health, temper, and spirits, if only by steering clear of the horrors of the crowded elevated railroads, the smoke-choked tunnels and the dusty abominations of railway travel during the hot months."

Yet, as C. Philip Moore comments in *Yachts in a Hurry*, "commuters were an extravagance in every way. Most of them were built and finished to the highest yacht standards. They were big speedboats engineered and powered with torpedo-boat sophistication. They burned extraordinary amounts of fuel and cost shocking amounts to maintain. They were tended by crews whose only business was to run them at wild speeds for a few hours each day and spend the time in between cleaning, polishing, oiling, and tuning these wonderful conveyances devoted to the whims and working routines of the titans of finance and industry."

Shortly before the morning sun rises, you walk in your silk robe, sleep still in your eyes, across the long expanse of carefully manicured lawn, through the lush gardens—delicately sprinkled with morning dew—and onto the long dock. Captain Smith offers a cheerful "Good morning, Sir," while helping you aboard. Almost immediately, the engines roar to life with impressive timbre. As you hold on to a bronze stanchion, the vessel pulls away from the dock and toward open water.

In your private cabin, you shower, shave, and dress, before moving forward to the dining saloon, where the first glint of sunlight ripples across the mahogany joinerwork varnished to a mirror-like finish. Sitting down in a rattan chair, you squint as the steward silently puts the neatly folded morning paper on the starched damask-covered table.

While breakfast is being served on custom-made china emblazoned with the vessel's name in elegant script, the chief engineer hovers over the twin 450-hp gas Wintons; the engine compartment is as clean as any hospital operating room. The captain, in the raised pilothouse, carefully scans the waves for obstructions. In the galley, the cook expertly goes about his work while the vessel slams against wave after wave.

By the time breakfast is over and cleared, the Manhattan skyline comes into view, its tall towers a dramatic vertical contrast from the horizontal sheet of choppy water—a view you never get tired of.

"Have a good day, Sir," says Captain Smith as you step onto the dock and toward your Pierce-Arrow. After the chauffeur closes the door, you settle into the luxurious mohair cocoon for the short ride to Wall Street, where, on the forty-fifth floor overlooking New York's harbor, you will continue to earn enough money to help maintain such expensive, but decidedly comfortable, modes of travel.

Commuters (a largely American phenomenon, as Europeans had a greater sense of leisure) became such a way of life that a person building a new estate concurrently ordered one. It would not be long before they littered the East River during working hours, as shown in this image of the New York Yacht Club landing at East Twenty-sixth Street.

While this image is often replicated, the yachts on moorings have not, to my knowledge, ever been identified. There is only one vessel I am sure of, and that is Harold S. Vanderbilt's *Vara* (in her original appearance), two vessels to starboard of the large, black-hulled yacht. This latter vessel was, I initially assumed, one of the Morgan *Corsair*s, but it actually appears to be *Vagabonia*, originally owned by W. L. Mellon. Starboard of *Vara* is, I believe, George K. Morrow's Mathis-Trumpy *Mono*, while astern of *Vara* is, possibly, *Shadow K*, originally owned by Carl G. Fisher, the prolific entrepreneur who created the Purdy Boat company (see page 95). On the far right is, perhaps, *Seaborn*, built for Richard F. Howe.

The fourteen yachts docked and rafted together remain unidentified.

CURMUDGEON COMMENTS:

*Robert "The Master Builder" Moses was responsible for more public works projects than any other. Indeed, Moses had a virtual lock on New York's public works from the late 1920s through the 1960s and was responsible for transforming the state through his beaches, highways, urban renewal schemes, dams, parks, and even the siting of the United Nations. Moses excelled at developing meticulous plans and cost estimates and at sniffing out funding sources; these combined talents afforded him a vast arsenal of public funds with which to reshape the world around him. Yet it's arguable that not only New York would have been better off had Moses never been born, but the world. He was virulently against public transit and designed his highways so that overpasses were too low to permit larger types of transportation, such as subway trains and buses. This "car supreme" attitude has been copied the world over, as has Moses's "Mega-Project" attitude. Moses leveled thriving neighborhoods to make way for what time has proven to be a fatal idea: urban renewal. It's ironic that most of what Moses built was paid for with public funds, yet Moses was extremely condescending toward this same public. He personified the old saying, "Power corrupts, absolute power corrupts absolutely." Robert Caro wrote a Pulitzer Prize–winning biography that makes for compelling reading, *The Power Broker: Robert Moses and the Fall of New York*.

CIGARETTE

Once upon a time there was a beauty known far and wide. She had many admirers. Yet, under mysterious circumstances, a spell was cast upon her, causing her to fall into a long decline.

The marina reminded me of a 1930s movie where gangsters dumped bodies, where boats, like elephants, went to die, where the docks were a threat to life.

I thought it grand. There were plenty of boats, albeit decrepit, half-sunk, and otherwise unloved.

Contained within this yacht graveyard was a vessel I'd heard rumors of, a once famous commuter owned by a dashing millionaire that had the lines and general appearance I'd been looking for. As it developed, she proved a sleeping beauty.

The vessel was, I would learn, the once formidable *Cigarette*, a commuter that sped between Port Washington and Wall Street. She'd been commissioned by Louis Gordon Hammersley, a man who had the good fortune to unexpectedly inherit seven million dollars while still in college. This windfall was used, in part, to finance Hammersley's passion for speed. He owned a series of vessels named *Cigarette* and won the Presidents Cup Race on the Potomac in 1926 (the cup was presented by President Calvin Coolidge).

75 feet and built in 1928 for Louis Gordon Hammersley. Designed by John H. Wells. Built by Nevins. Powered by a pair of 450-hp gas Winton engines.

Firmly held by her husband, Mrs. Hammersley breaks a bottle of Champagne across the bow of the newly launched *Cigarette* (opposite). Mr. Hammersley died in 1942, at forty-nine, and Mrs. Hammersley remarried. She reportedly maintained the Cigarette Trophy Room through at least the late 1980s.

Right top and bottom, *Cigarette* as I found her in the late 1980s. Beyond the obvious dereliction, one can see that the pilot station has been enclosed and the aft cockpit raised, thus raising its overhead.

Cigarette's pilothouse in pristine original condition (1). Note the raised teak deck and custom rubber mat.

Fast-forward six decades and you find this sad sight (2). About the only recognizable item is the knob (center), which once held the wheel.

Cigarette's dining saloon in 1928 (3). The wicker chairs were a nice tactile contrast to the otherwise polished setting.

The dining saloon in the late 1980s (4). The wicker chairs are long gone, as are the leaded glass windows on the attractive sideboard, and the lighting fixtures. However, contrary to appearances, everything is in good shape. The wood is sound and original, and even the mother-of-pearl call button (lower left) is still in place.

After accessing archival images of *Cigarette*, I was further pained by the contrast between what the photographs presented and what lay gently bobbing in murky waters. My concern for her led me to make an offer, even though she didn't possess the interior space I required (or thought I did). A survey was commissioned, and its conclusions scared me; my offer was withdrawn. It would take several more years, years during which *Cigarette* peacefully awaited an end to her plight, before I reboarded. By this time, I knew a little about boats. I crawled over, into, and under her every inch, looking for rot; to my amazement, I discovered almost none. Her double-planked hull was impressively impervious to my ice pick, and her exterior planks, under the peeling paint, showed tight and true. Even her deck cabins were startlingly intact. Sticking my hand deep into unspeakable mud, I found her keelson and frames were as hard as steel.

COMMUTERS

ARROW

130 feet and built in 1902 for Charles R. Flint. Designed by Charles D. Mosher. Built by S. Ayers. Powered by a pair of 3,500-hp steam engines.

Cigarette represented a late stage in commuter design. *Arrow*, an early commuter, achieved the then astonishing speed of 45.6 miles per hour, or 39 knots, in 1902. It would be another nine years before this record was eclipsed; her speed was compared to locomotives and something new, the automobile. This feat was achieved at considerable expense—$160,000—and because of her unusual construction. *Arrow*'s frames were steel below the waterline and aluminum above; all this was covered by a thin veneer of double-planked mahogany. She weighed only 67 tons, quite an accomplishment, considering her 130-foot length.

Arrow came about in a circuitous manner. Charles Ranlett Flint (1850–1934), a well-known entrepreneur of the era, had ordered a pair of 3,500-horsepower engines for a torpedo boat he hoped to sell to the U.S. Navy. After the Spanish-American War ended, and before Flint completed his engines, the navy decided that it required vessels in excess of 7,000 horsepower. Flint commissioned *Arrow* to house his orphaned engines. *Arrow*'s speed garnered enormous publicity, and Flint, ever the entrepreneur, harnessed this attention by selling Russia torpedo boats, munitions, and submarines.

Arrow was dropped from *Lloyd's* in 1921.

CIGARETTE

123 feet and built in 1905 for William H. Ames. Designed by Swasey, Raymond, and Page. Built by George Lawley. Powered by a pair of steam engines that drove her at 22 knots.

Another early commuter, also named *Cigarette* (and probably the first of that name), served her Boston owner, William H. Ames, for twelve years before being sold to the U.S. Navy in World War I. After the war, she was owned by, among others, Barron Collier,* until being dropped from *Lloyd's* in 1931. The plans below offer a wealth of detail on early commuter design. Again, note the extraordinary contrast between the 14.5-foot beam and 123-foot length. In 1911 *Cigarette* had 3 feet added to her length, her funnels were altered, and other changes were made, transforming her severe appearance into one more yachtlike.

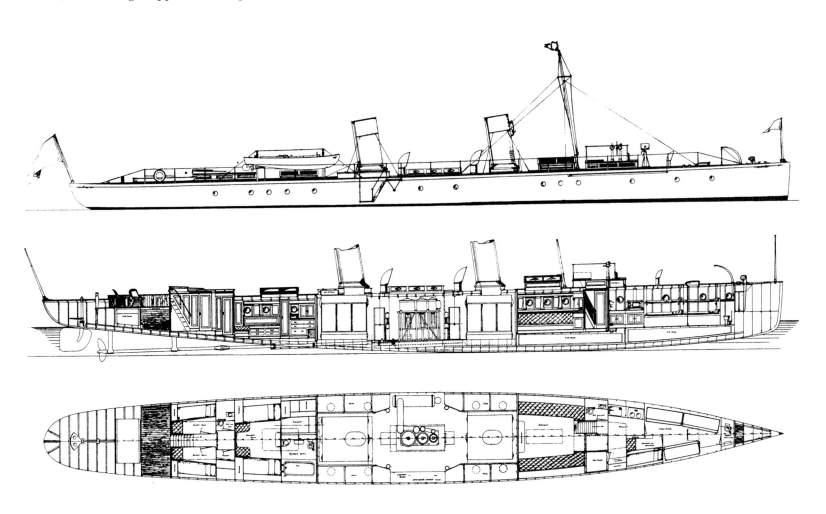

*Barron Collier, who owned *Cigarette* from 1921 to 1930, was a highly successful advertising executive, specializing in advertising placards on trolley cars. With this steady funding stream, Collier turned his attention to Florida real estate, purchasing Useppa Island off the Gulf Coast of Fort Myers and developing the luxurious Useppa Inn.

This venture was a spectacular success, and Collier later amassed 1.3 million acres of Florida property during 1921 and 1923 (now known as Collier County), becoming the largest landowner in the state. In the 1923 *Lloyd's Register of American Yachts* Collier is listed as owning six vessels; in the 1932 *Lloyd's*, Collier has, with one exception, six different yachts. While Collier experienced difficulties during the Depression, he managed to retain his empire, and upon his death in 1939 owned a hotel chain, newspapers, a telephone company, bus lines, numerous banks, and a steamship line. Today, descendants of Barron Collier control a fortune estimated at $2.5 billion.

WINCHESTER (I)

KNOWN AS ADROIT

147 feet and built in 1907 for P. W. Rouss. Designed by Henry J. Gielow. Built by Robert Jacob. Powered by a pair of steam engines that drove her at 21 knots.

There were four successive commuters named *Winchester* during the first two decades of the twentieth century, all commissioned by the same man, all black hulled, all fast, and all famous.

Peter Winchester Rouss, the heir to the Winchester arms fortune, liked to make high-speed dashes through Long Island Sound and down the East River that, according to Ralph Linwood Snow in *Bath Iron Works*, set a precedent. "Outraged shipowners and towboat operators prevailed upon the Coast Guard to impose a speed limit after *Winchester*'s wash caused damage to vessels tied up to some of the many piers lining both shores of the river."

The first *Winchester*, shown here passing under New York City's Brooklyn Bridge (below), sported the features that distinguished all her offspring: black hull, twin stacks, a single mast, and cruiser stern.

Barron Collier, who owned *Cigarette* (see page 213), also owned *Winchester (I)* from 1929 to 1937, and again from 1939 to 1941, at which point the thirty-four-year-old yacht was dropped from *Lloyd's*.

Note the canvas deck of *Winchester (I)*, as well as the imposing cowl vents, and open skylight over the engine room. The narrow beam (15 feet) was typical for the era, but *Winchester*'s extreme length (147 feet) accentuated this feature.

Looking aft aboard *Winchester (I)* (1).

What appears to be a luxurious private compartment aboard a train is the main saloon of *Winchester (I)* (2). While this type of arrangement—perhaps unique among yachts—offered little in the way of spaciousness, it nonetheless excelled in cozy comfort.

Winchester's dining saloon (3)—a setting of immense charm—in her forward deckhouse was deliciously narrow, but still could seat six in comfort. The drapes added an appealing tactile contrast to the highly varnished joinerwork.

The pilothouse (opposite) of *Winchester (I)* featured gleaming brass telegraphs and an equally polished wheel. Note the rolled charts tucked neatly in the overhead. This breathtaking image was taken after 1909; the formerly open pilot station had been partially enclosed.

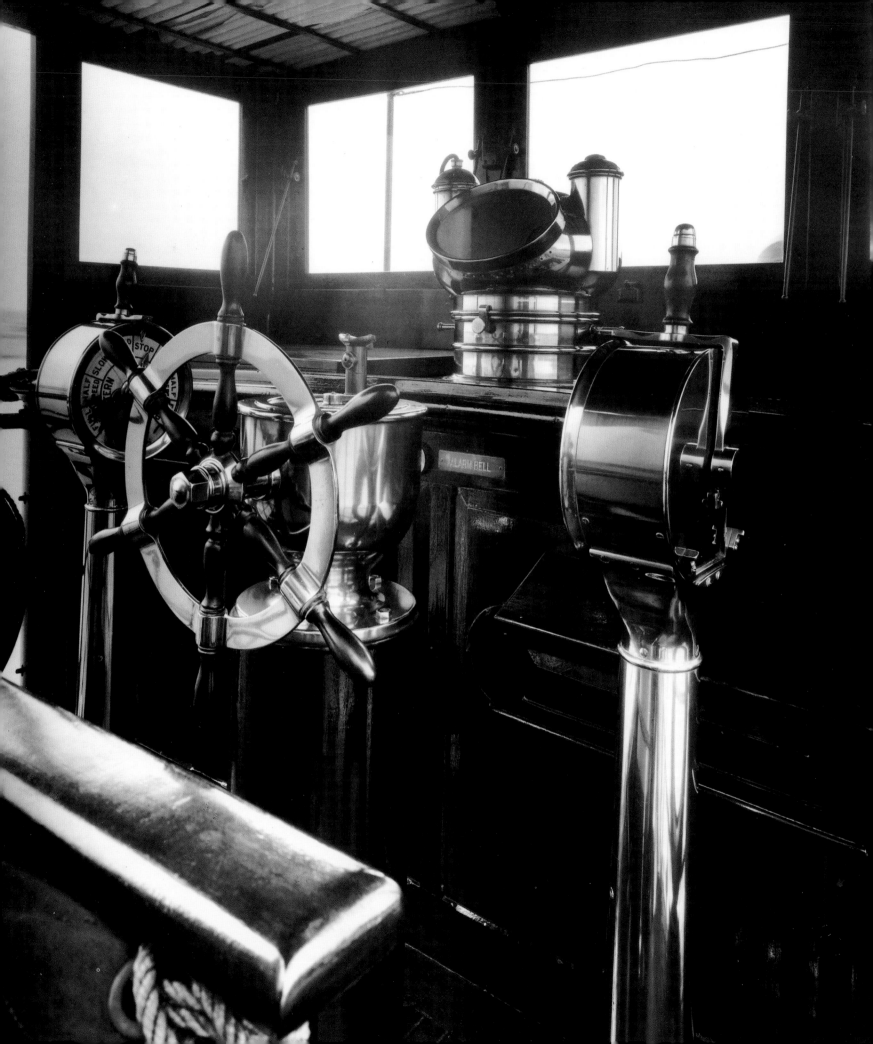

WINCHESTER (II)

KNOWN AS FLYING FOX

Peter Rouss enjoyed the Gielow-designed *Winchester (I)* for just two years before he took possession of a new commuter from designers Cox & Stevens; the result looked more destroyer-like than her predecessor, and much more formidable.

The image here shows *Winchester (II)* as *Flying Fox*, a name she was known by from 1913 through the 1930s, with her hull repainted gray.

165 feet and built in 1909 for P. W. Rouss. Designed by Cox & Stevens. Built by Yarrow. Powered by three Parson turbines, which drove her at 25 knots.

WINCHESTER (III)

KNOWN AS TRILLORA

Three years later Yarrow launched yet another Cox & Stevens *Winchester* (see also page 141) for Rouss; except for being faster and longer, she looks much like her predecessors.

In this impressive image *Winchester* (her hull repainted gray and another pole mast added) speeds past Manhattan's once-evocative lower skyline, now decimated by modern architecture.

Rouss owned *Winchester* for just three years before selling her to S. R. Guggenheim. Renamed *Trillora*, she remained in the Guggenheim family for sixteen years, from 1922 to 1938.

205 feet and built in 1912 for P. W. Rouss. Designed by Cox & Stevens. Built by Yarrow. Powered by two Yarrow turbines, which drove her at 32 knots.

The tradeoff of comfort for speed is best expressed by the plans of *Winchester (III)*. Even though she was 205 feet long, almost three-quarters of her hull was occupied by engines, coal bins, and attendant machinery, which could drive her at the then astonishing speed of 32 knots. As a result, her accommodations were comparable to a yacht of half the length and speed. Compare these plans with that of *Avalanche (IV)* on page 88.

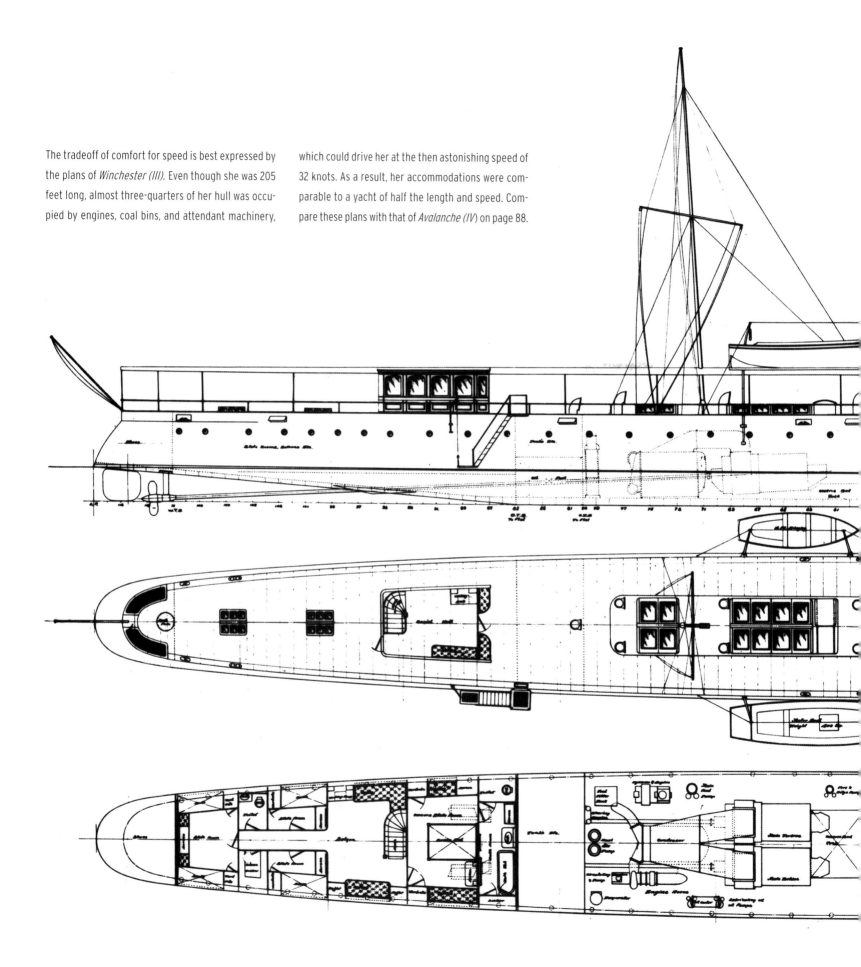

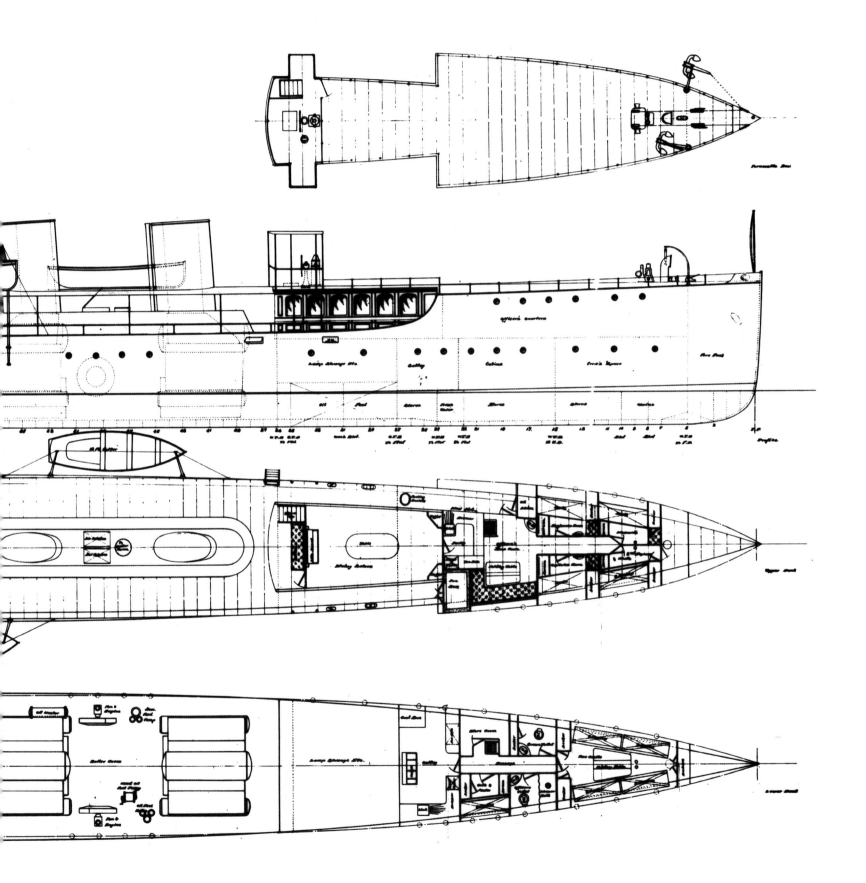

WINCHESTER (IV)

225 feet and built in 1915 for P. W. Rouss. Designed by Cox & Stevens. Built by Bath Iron Works. Powered by a pair of 7,500-hp steam turbine engines that drove her at 31 knots.

Originally, *Winchester (IV)* was black-hulled, which added to her fearsome appearance, a feature later subdued when her hull was repainted a kinder, gentler gray (see also front endpaper).

Rouss owned this *Winchester* the longest: a total of twelve years (excepting a stint in World War I). Her other owners included Vincent Astor, Cornelius Vanderbilt (a grandson of "Commodore" Vanderbilt), and the Canadian Navy in World War II. *Winchester (IV)* was last reported in service in Canada during the 1950s.

A nice close-up of the twin stacks and launches of *Winchester (IV)* (below).

Launching day for *Winchester (IV)* at Bath Iron Works (right top). Note the dashing cruiser stern and polished screws.

Right bottom, yet another of my favorite images, highlights the impressive length of *Winchester (IV),* an expansive awning, and, most significantly, imposing twin stacks surmounting a raised engine room casing.

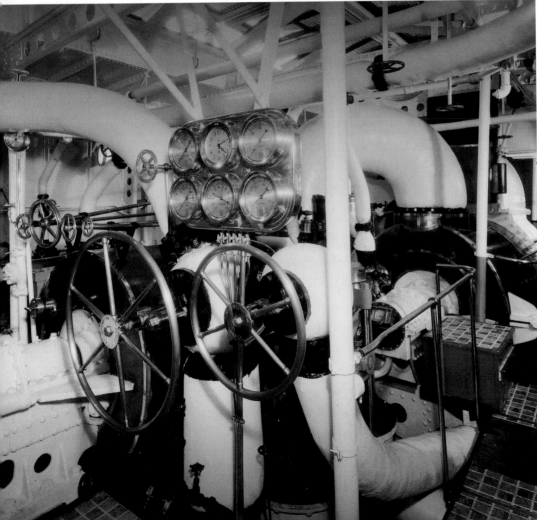

Winchester (IV)'s gleaming engine room (left top). The direct-drive Parsons turbines employed a reversing turbine that could bring the yacht to a quick halt when under full power.

Winchester's polished engine controls and gauges (left bottom).

Winchester (IV)'s galley (opposite) featured a contrasting dynamic I much favor: exposed steel shell plating studded with rivets played against simple, but elegant, cabinetwork; there's no denying this is a yacht. And, the galley seemed well equipped with every convenience, including a pencil sharpener (on the left).

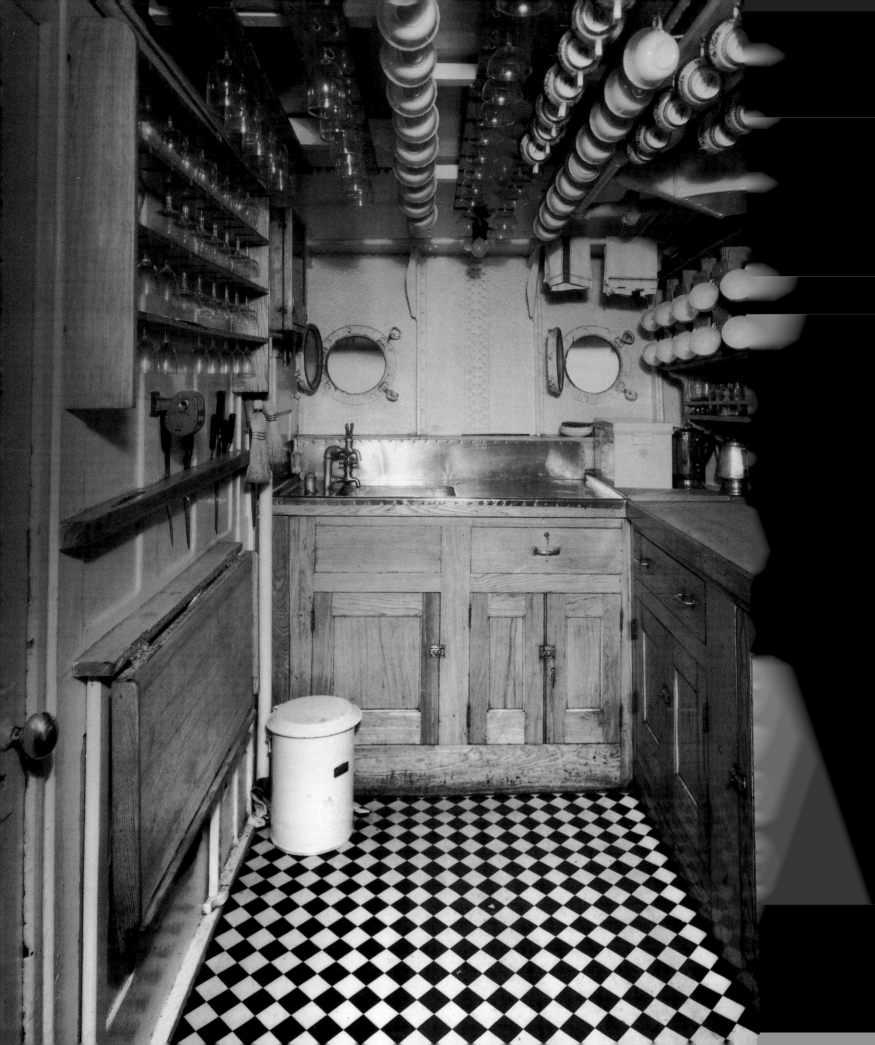

The 29-foot-by-15-foot main saloon (left top) was located in the aft deckhouse, a "comfortable living room in every sense of the word," paneled in Italian walnut.

Adjacent to the aft end of *Winchester (IV)*'s raised forecastle deck was a 20-foot-by-15-foot dining saloon (left bottom) paneled in Java teak finished natural with a "pleasing" neutral brown tint. The pantry (forward) had a dumbwaiter connected to the galley below.

The aft deck (right top) was graced by a canvas overhead and was not so large as to be overwhelming, a design feat impressive for the 225-foot *Winchester (IV)*.

The owner's stateroom (right bottom) featured two private heads and was further blessed with built-in furnishings. The open door offers us a peek into the companionway heading aft.

LITTLE SOVEREIGN (II)

Cotton magnate Matthew Chaloner Durfee Borden used *Little Sovereign (II)* to commute between his New Jersey home, New York, and his cotton mills in Fall River, Massachusetts. One fine day on Long Island Sound Borden reportedly was aboard the 24-knot *Little Sovereign (II)* when, much to his annoyance, he was passed by the mighty 25-knot *Winchester (II)*. Well, what's a millionaire to do, thus challenged?

Borden was said to have steeled himself and calmly ordered the captain to change course. Instead of docking at the New York Yacht Club launch on the East River, they continued to Morris Heights on the Harlem River, where Borden promptly ordered a 39-knot commuter from designer Charles L. Seabury (see page 88).

The rich *are* different.

A decade earlier Borden had commissioned a 250-foot steam yacht also named *Sovereign*, which he kept for just two years before she was taken over by the U.S. Navy, where she remained until being decommissioned in 1928, then scrapped in 1929.

137 feet and built in 1909 for Matthew C. D. Borden. Designed by Charles L. Seabury. Built by Gas Engine and Power Company and Charles L. Seabury Company, Consolidated. Powered by a pair of steam engines that drove her at 24 knots.

FROLIC III

By the 1920s the stark, almost naval, appearance of commuters was modified. A more elegant, yachtlike look, such as seen here, began to predominate. *Frolic III* was similar to *Cigarette*; both were designed by John H. Wells.

Walter Chrysler, who commissioned *Frolic III*, had a previous vessel of the same name (see page 126).

75 feet and built in 1927 for Walter P. Chrysler. Designed by John Wells. Built by Mathis. Powered by a pair of 8-cylinder Winton gas engines that drove her at 30 mph.

WOODLOVE

Finally, after many trips up and down the eastern seaboard, hundreds of calls, and dozens of letters, a tangible response to ephemeral longings was discovered. A yacht. And even though her topsides were streaked with stains from rusted fastenings, teak decks buckled with age, and mahogany cabins in immediate danger of collapse, she was purchased. When major areas of rot were discovered in her hull, decks, and cabins, my feelings did not waver. I would make her whole.

One of my reasons for this purchase was that she reminded me of a miniature *Titanic*. Over the years I had learned that the *Titanic* was built in 1912, was 882 feet, sported four imposing stacks, and had a steel hull and a vertical bow. Being a reasonable man, this was the baseline for comparison during my two-year search for a yacht. *High Spirits,* the 112-foot Mathis-Trumpy I'd found (see page 176), had come close with her plumb bow, counterstern, and stack. Yet her size, as was made clear to me by her captain, would have overwhelmed me financially. I was quite pleased that my new yacht met the *Titanic* criteria. Sorta. She *did* have a vertical bow, but . . . I worked hard overlooking her every other characteristic, none of which remotely matched the great liner. She was built in 1927 (still a good year), was only 68 feet (she *seemed* huge), had just one smokestack (stubby at that), and a wood hull (but long-leaf yellow pine!). Unfortunately, the similarity I insisted on seeing was soon stretched further when I had the stack removed—it wasn't original. Nonetheless, I was thrilled. While many collectors can find joy with books, posters, or artifacts, I could actually cruise the high seas aboard my *Titanic* facsimile.

Researching my new yacht, I realized that she had a history all her own, and my desire for a *Titanic* miniature slowly faded. The idea of naming her *Tinytanic* evaporated, and her lovely original name was restored. *Alondra.*

I purchased *Alondra* in New Jersey. After several weeks of preparation, she was set to begin her maiden voyage from Jersey, up the East River, through Hell's Gate, and to her new home in Port Washington, Long Island. With a hired captain, we awoke on board one early, chilly morning, cast the lines ashore, and set forth into the open water.

Watching the Manhattan skyline slowly glide by gave me a powerful sense of being on the other side of a mirror; as the majestic bow of *Alondra* cut through the choppy green waters, I was cruising past the city and, I sensed, away from a life there. Standing proud on the bow, I felt conflicting feelings of sadness, gratitude, and anticipation.

In a few short hours, and with a gentleness that seemed impossible for something 68 feet and buffeted by wind and currents, *Alondra* gracefully and precisely came into dock, a compliment to her captain and design. With lines secured, her "crew" cheered. Then, like the Robert Redford character in *The Candidate,* I asked, "What next?"

For the next eight weeks every opportunity was seized to visit with *Alondra,* sometimes with a few friends in tow. My life in Manhattan was draining me; arriving at the marina, I'd experience a mounting sense of excitement, a sensation of youthful exuberance and longing. Walking down the long dock, I'd puff up with pride and admiration. *Alondra*'s bulk, lines, and age dominated. While the dozens of small fiberglass boats around bobbed gently up and down on the never-ending wake, *Alondra,* regal and solid, hardly moved. Waves of such inconsequence wouldn't affect *her.*

I'd reach out to the varnished mahogany handrail and open a small section hinged on polished bronze fittings. Grabbing a cleat, I'd haul myself, friends, and supplies on board. There was the immediate but subtle sensation of no longer being on quite so firm ground. The sudden weight on the delightfully narrow teak deck would shift *Alondra*'s sense of balance, and she'd tilt gently to port. I'd steady myself by reaching out to a bronze stanchion and, walking forward as a gentle salt-tinged wind fluttered past, then open the mahogany-paneled door to the main saloon. As I stepped inside, the delicate proportions would envelop me with comfort and warmth.

The main saloon, like a sentinel, protruded above the main deck and was lined with windows. There were operable windows on her port and starboard sides, complemented by a gentle sweep of curved glass forward. Two bronze portholes punctured the aft mahogany bulkhead. Overhead was the rhythmic precision of arched mahogany beams supporting glossy white tongue and groove. I'd toss supplies onto a velvet built-in settee, walk across the yellow pine sole (floor), and collapse on the not original sofa between built-in mahogany cabinets.

And then it happened, as always. I'd smile. A great, big, full-face smile energized by a deep, gut-level happiness. *Ahhhhh. My beloved Alondra.*

Later, stepping down the deliciously narrow stair and around the mahogany newel post, I'd enter the dining saloon. Surely such an enveloping space had never before been created? Overhead lay more mahogany beams—delicate in scale—bisected by a glass and bronze skylight. Three bronze portholes lined each of the ceilings (walls) and a built-in L-shaped banquette filled a corner, its tufted cushions wrapping around a mahogany table with dropleaves. A pair of tall cabinets occupied the forward bulkhead, with felt-lined drawers below and glass-fronted sections held aloft by turned mahogany columns in front of beveled mirrors.

Often, with dozens of candles lit, I'd sit by myself in the dining saloon as *Moonlight Serenade* by Glenn Miller played on the cassette player, a glass of wine in hand, while the sound of seagulls joined in as additional musical accompaniment.

Retiring for the evening, I'd put guests in the forward stateroom (once the crew quarters but long converted). This compartment was a wonder of skewed angles and planes. The ceilings (walls), punctured by four portholes, angled both vertically and horizontally, following the sharp curve of the hull as it progressed to the grand finale of the bow and the keel below. The overhead arched and was further enlivened by a hatch. One had to jump up into the berth—36 inches wide at one end and 15 inches at the other—before snuggling in to read, helped by a small brass wall-mounted light overhead.

I'd return to the dining saloon and blow out the candles, turn off the music, and walk aft and down two steps into the galley, where I'd put the empty wineglasses. The galley was engineered to obtain maximum efficiency in a womblike space. It was fully outfitted with an array of cabinets, and, while well laid out and workable, it was the only cabin aboard *Alondra* I didn't like, principally because of the lack of light. Originally she had no ports in the galley, but a previous owner, slighted by this grievous insult, had brutally inserted four small, oval-shaped ports. The results helped, but not much.

After washing the wineglasses, I'd step down into the engine

Yachts, particularly from the 1920s and before, have a diminutive scale about their every feature, no matter their length. While land-based doors are invariably 32 inches wide or more and 6 feet, 8 inches high, on a classic yacht doors are 24 inches wide or less and usually not taller than a person, often less. The ceiling in your home is probably eight feet or more, but on *Alondra* the overheads tickled the hair of anyone over six feet. The same goes for cabinets, sinks, bunks, and seating. Like a child's playhouse, everything is slightly . . . askew. Aboard yachts, floors are called soles, ceilings are called overheads, and bathrooms are called heads.

room. Such cabins on yachts under, say, eighty feet are invariably cramped, inconveniently accessible, and with low overheads that force one to crouch. Aboard *Alondra* the twin engines sat regal among vast square footage and height—this was the largest cabin aboard. It was further blessed with four operable windows, one hatch with ladder access, and a full-height overhead reaching ten feet in one section. While I knew nothing about engines, mechanics, electrical systems, and plumbing, I looked forward to learning in such an oil-scented cathedral of yacht space.

Moving further aft and up one step, I'd enter stateroom number two. Originally two staterooms with single berths, at some point the dividing bulkhead had been removed, the berths cast overboard, and a queen-size bed inexplicably inserted. The scale of the bed would not earn the slightest notice in any home, but aboard *Alondra* it looked like a tufted beached whale.

Opening a small mahogany door, I'd enter the aft passageway and turn right into the main head. While the bathroom in a house is usually not less than five by seven feet, the head aboard *Alondra* was easily half that while still offering the same features. The porcelain sink was tiny but actually more convenient than mine at home (as it was closer to the mirror), while the head itself was just inches away. Alongside the aft bulkhead—painted a brilliant shiny white like the rest of the cabin—rested the tub. While not the scale to offer hours of deep lounging, it was large enough for a proper ablution. The three operable windows were the same height as my face—and just inches from it—and offered total privacy without curtains, as one's body was fully concealed. There was a pleasurable sense of freedom being in this space, naked, while boats passed by, a breeze tingling my skin, while the sun simultaneously provided warmth.

Aft of the head was the main stateroom, a pristine reminder of a bygone graciousness. The twin single berths were parallel to the hull, and between them was a built-in mahogany dressing table, surmounted by a three-panel hinged, beveled mirror. The joinerwork shown brilliant with its many coats of varnish, and the brilliant white lacquered overhead reflected the light from the six operable windows. And, two closets. And, another head. This former half-bath had been converted to a shower by the previous owner and lacked its original features, a conversion I anticipated undoing.

Before retiring, I'd climb up the steep stair opposite the main head, walk down the starboard deck to the aft deck, graced with several wicker chairs, and switch on the series of small lights attached to the wooden overhead covering almost three-fourths of *Alondra's* length (it had once been canvas). Unseen from my vantage point was the crowning feature of *Alondra*, the raised pilothouse. This feature, to my knowledge, was unique aboard a yacht of 70 feet, only appearing on larger yachts. The small cabin—windowed on four sides—contained the mahogany wheel, an array of navigational equipment, and even a single berth. And, like a treehouse, the cabin was only accessible by a steep bronze ladder and offered a narrow pair of teak decks on each side. I'd experience a special thrill while at her wheel looking at her length below me, high above the water and invariably above most other vessels. Surely the captain of the *Titanic* felt the same?

And so, with the evening breeze as company, a cocktail in hand, the gentle lapping of waves against hull as a reassuring presence, I'd marvel at this concoction of yellow pine, mahogany, copper fastenings, teak, varnish, mysterious mechanical systems, leather, beveled glass, and canvas. *Alondra* was a work of art, lovingly crafted, beautifully and sensibly detailed, and a pleasure to admire, touch, and even smell.

With stars flickering in the inky black sky and varnished deckhouses aglow from moonlight, I'd retire for another night. After snuggling into a berth, my thoughts would wander back in time to the Great Gray Shed, and one thought would surface: I'd brought a childhood fantasy to life.

ALONDRA

68 feet and first owned by George C. Smith, of New York, in 1927. Designed and built by the J. M. Densmore Company. Powered by a pair of 6-cylinder gas Sterling engines.

Alondra was built by the J. M. Densmore Company, of Quincy, Massachusetts. Densmore, like many such yacht builders during the booming twenties, lasted a very short time and is forgotten today, unlike others, whose names continue to resonate: Lawley, Consolidated, Trumpy, a.c.f., Elco, Chris-Craft. Densmore built five sister ships on speculation and gave each the working name of *Maya*. *Alondra*, pictured here, was *Maya III* until being renamed by her first owner, George C. Smith.

The original owner of *Alondra*, George C. Smith, was a member of both the New York Yacht Club and the Seawanhaka Corinthian Yacht Club, and he purchased the yacht for $60,000. In 1932, John H. Clowes became the new owner of the five-year-old vessel, and he and his family cruised Long Island Sound extensively before losing *Alondra* to the Fyfe Shipyard in 1940 (due to an unpaid $850 bill). The yard, in turn, sold the fifteen-year-old vessel in 1942 to Mr. and Mrs. Clarence S. Bruce, who renamed her *Sallie B*. The Bruces, members of the Corinthian Yacht Club in Washington, D.C., cruised *Sallie B*. extensively, shuttling back and forth between the Potomac river and their winter home in Fort Meyers, Florida. When Mr. Bruce died in 1962, his widow sold *Sallie B*. after twenty years of care and ownership.

During the ensuing quarter century, *Sallie B*., renamed *Mahogany Lady*, changed hands repeatedly, all the while declining, her forty-year-old hull in urgent need of repairs. Among her owners were Herbert P. Field, brothers Lee and Ray Bass, Captain Doug Kenny, Earl McMillen and his business partner, Arnold Guest, and Frank Rash, who donated the yacht to a church in Florida that lacked the resources to care for the vessel. Mr. and Mrs. W. Edward Guy rescued *Mahogany Lady*, refitted the yacht, and enjoyed her until 1986, selling her to Arthur and Ingrid Burch, of Morristown, New Jersey. The Burches renamed the sixty-year-old vessel *Somewhere in Time* and embarked on an extensive rehabilitation until Mr. Burch's poor health forced the family to sell the yacht after just one season of use.

After buying *Somewhere in Time* from the Burches (and restoring her original name after forty years), I wanted to see her place of birth. Traveling to the small town of Quincy, I was thrilled to discover a Densmore Street on the map, and headed there. Turning onto the short, narrow lane, I soon came upon a small tract of land fronting the Neponset River. Was this barren stretch where my *Alondra* had been crafted, where her long-leaf yellow-pine hull first touched the cold water, where her twin gas Sterling engines roared to life?

Walking along the pebble-strewn lot, something caught my eye. Coming closer, I kicked some dirt and small rocks out of the way, and to my astonishment a rail appeared—leading right into the water. A few feet away I uncovered another long-buried track. I knew that I'd discovered the launching ways to an old boatyard. But was it Densmore? To find the experts blessed with answers to these questions, I went to the one place they'd be—the local diner.

It *was* the Densmore yard.

Alondra's predecessor, built the year previous, was *Maya II* and named *Percianna* upon her purchase by Percy L. Hance. All the images that follow are of *Percianna*, an almost exact sister ship to *Alondra* except that she was two feet shorter, with a little less beam.

In the image opposite her foredeck is covered in canvas, which offered a nice tactile touch and a contrast to the bright mahogany adjacent. Canvas decks were common on smaller yachts, unlike the teak seen on larger and more expensive vessels. The skylight aboard *Alondra* lighted the dining saloon below, although *Alondra* didn't have cowl vents on her foredeck. The foredeck ends at the right angle of the main saloon, which featured a forward bulkhead of both curved mahogany and plate glass.

The main saloon looking aft. Aboard *Alondra* this aft bulkhead was mahogany and pierced originally (as far as I could tell) with two large ports at the edges. During the 1930s a picture of Long Island Sound hung between these ports, a picture given to me by Jack Clowes, the son of the then owner. The type of tufted settee shown here—nice—was long gone by the time I owned *Alondra*, having been replaced by a modern sofa in brown velvet.

This image is rich in details pertaining specifically to the decor of yachts from the 1920s. Note the radio (which doesn't quite fit the built-in table it rests on). A radio from the thirties would have been sleeker, more tall than horizontal, a cloth-covered speaker its central design feature instead of the dials shown here. The simple wicker chairs were typical for the decade. The dark gate-legged table, while a type dating back centuries, would not appear on a 1930s yacht (a more Moderne version would). Curtains from the Victorian era of yachting would have been much more elaborate, fringed, and not as sheer as the curtains shown here (probably cotton or linen), which were typical for yachts under 100 feet; aboard a larger vessel they would have been more detailed, and probably silk. (Modern synthetic materials wholly lack the ability to properly mimic the subtle characteristics of linen, cotton, and silk and should not be used aboard a classic yacht if one is hoping for an authentic restoration.) Note also the tufting on the settee, a detail surprisingly hard to manifest (an upholsterer's art). Modern versions are invariably too "tight" and look as though a penny would bounce off them—something quite unlikely to happen on this settee, where a tossed penny would just snuggle in for an afternoon nap. Even the doily, while a Victorian holdover, will vanish by the 1930s.

In short, 1920s yachts aren't as elaborate as their predecessors or as subdued as their descendants. They fit comfortably between an age of wonderful excess and Moderne simplicity.

The cozy aft deck and distinctive wicker chairs (matching the pair in the saloon). The style of this rattan and wicker set would still be a yacht feature during the 1930s, but not before the 1920s. Note also the glass ball (with built-in strike) holding matches. Can you imagine a more restful place to spend a warm afternoon, enjoying conversation with friends, the occasional shriek of gulls adding their song while you are gently rocked, like a baby in a mother's arms, by the steady waves?

This image of *Percianna* (the photographer is standing on the aft deck looking forward) offers more than just the pleasure of canvas awnings, detailing numerous delightful features prevalent on classic yachts: the pair of dinghies, finished bright, hanging on hemp—not nylon—lines; the nicely rumpled leather cushions seducing one into an afternoon snooze, the narrow beam not found on modern yachts, and as such, offering a coziness that "bigger" can't replicate; and, the final touch, the call button (bottom, center) connected to the galley annuciator and precisely placed just inches from the unseen wicker chairs so as to be convenient for calling the uniformed steward to fetch another after-dinner cocktail. Ahhhh.

The main stateroom aboard *Percianna* was identical to *Alondra*'s, except a little narrower. The two side mirrors (beveled) were hinged. I also like the cut-glass vase for flowers—remarkably, one was still aboard *Alondra*.

In the tiny space pictured above, there is all one needs to offer a comfortable and exceedingly intimate sleeping chamber. Of course, newlyweds may find twin beds a logistical challenge, but older married couples may find them a blessing. Why, then, are land-based bedrooms (as well as staterooms aboard modern yachts) vastly larger in size? Why aren't houses built like this? They'd certainly be cheaper to heat, to say nothing of taxing the global environment less. Yet the scale of bedrooms is increasing, and the charming lessons that this cabin aboard *Percianna* offers are overlooked. Architects, are you paying attention?

A ROTTING MENAGERIE

During my two-year search for *Alondra* I'd happened upon a number of other enticing yachts, and even though I was now, quite sensibly, preoccupied with a 68-foot hull, deck, and cabins in need of full-time focus, I couldn't stop two thoughts from swimming laps in my brain.

First, I missed the thrill of discovery. Of tracing subtle leads, finally pinpointing a location, heading out on the hunt, poking through stagnant backwaters, and then—the moment—discovering the object of desire: a forsaken yacht.

Second, once such a discovery is made, how to help? Like people who devote energy and resources to feeding children in faraway countries, like people who help animals or save rainforests/whales/bald eagles/ecosystems, I felt inexorably drawn to Saving Rotting Hulls.

My addiction became evident shortly after I bought *Alondra*. I'd happened upon a sad-looking vessel nearby. She was tied up, badly, to the end of a T-dock, and each wave rubbed her unprotected hull against the hard, unyielding wood, resulting in deep gouges that cried out for sympathy. Even before boarding,* I was a goner.

The sad vessel was, I'd later learn, built by American Car & Foundry (known as a.c.f.). Unlike the J. M. Densmore Company, which built my *Alondra*, a.c.f. was a well-known builder of yachts, a name still recognized today. They built production vessels, fully equipped and ready for an afternoon cruise (they also built the occasional custom craft).

Most of the yachts pictured in this book were unique, having been designed for a specific client. Others, like *Acania* (see page 258), were successful and encouraged their designers to develop near sister ships. The duplicates offered subtle differences here and there, and only a few would ever be launched. Production yacht builders (Chris-Craft being the most famous) built hundreds of identical craft. This method offered the advantage of honing a design, over and over, until it achieved an extremely graceful appearance. In my experience such yachts have a palpable sense of rightness about them and are blessed with a wealth of well-considered details.

It's bad form to board a yacht without permission. That stated, I break this rule of etiquette if the vessel is in danger (of, say, snapping her lines) or if she's owned by what appears to be an indifferent, unloving, or unintelligent person (three qualities that tend to go hand in hand). In such a case, I'll board and proceed with a preliminary structural analysis and ascertain how original the vessel is, using this information to try to find a more caring owner. However, I believe that it's a cardinal sin to break in (the vessel must be unlocked) or to remove any fittings—even if she's clearly abandoned. A derelict stands a chance of being restored if she retains much of her original hardware. I've known several yachts that were bulldozed because people said, "Well, if she'd just had all her hardware, I'd have taken her on."

To sell their production vessels, a.c.f. participated in a sales tool still very much in evidence today: the boat show, a type of event quite different than it is today, reflecting a manifestly changed era and sensibility. In the image opposite we have "The Boatman's Fairyland" (or so said the 1925 *Rudder*), held at the long-demolished Grand Central Palace in New York City, a setting more Imperial Rome than the basic industrial box one visits today. This image offers the delightful and surreal juxtaposition of Corinthian columns and things-that-float.

Besides boat shows, a.c.f. used its salon on New York's West Fifty-seventh Street as a marketing base (above left). Advertisements such as the one above right also promoted a.c.f., the galley shown here being from their 47-foot model. Note the blissfully innocent sexism: "give the Little Lady a galley."

American Car & Foundry (a.c.f.) was founded by Charles Land Freer (1854–1919), the son of a farmer, innkeeper, and horseman. With little schooling, Freer began working at the age of fourteen in a cement factory. From this inauspicious beginning he rose to amass a fortune, develop a discerning art collection, and found a museum. The underpinning of his fortune was a company he cofounded that produced rolling stock for rail cars. Freer later merged the company, the Peninsular Car Works, with twelve other car-building concerns to create a.c.f., which today is remembered for its rail cars as opposed to its yachts. After the merger, Freer retired (he was forty-five) and began a second career as an art connoisseur—one of the most knowledgeable of the period. His taste and intellect even

gained the notice of the hard-to-impress Harry and Louisine Havemeyer, the preeminent American collectors of Impressionist paintings. Freer became the chief patron to James McNeill Whistler and assembled 1,200 examples of the artist's work, including the famous Peacock Room designed by Whistler. Other holdings included ancient glazed pottery, Korean porcelain, Indian paintings, and a collection of Asian art that, in size and quality, was unmatched by any other private American collection. Freer, who never married, had an elegant home in Detroit (extant), and donated his collection, along with the funds to construct a museum, to the Smithsonian Museum. Today, the Freer Gallery, in Washington, D.C., houses more than nine thousand works of American and Asian art.

LORNA DOONE

The a.c.f. that I found near *Alondra* was built as *Panzola*. The images that follow are of *Lorna Doone*, an exact sister ship to *Panzola* and dozens of other 54-foot a.c.f.s and taken, probably, during the 1927 boat show at the Grand Central Palace in New York (excepting the image below).

The 54-foot a.c.f., being a production vessel, had evolved attractively, with every inch maximized for comfort, and it offered spacious accommodations for its length.

The downside of mass production, as least regarding the a.c.f.s that I saw during the 1980s were concerned, was under-building, which explained their deplorable structural condition.

When I first stepped aboard *Panzola* that fall after-noon, the forlorn vessel quickly listed to starboard, perhaps too much so. *Alondra* heeled upon being boarded, but nothing like this. Grabbing a stanchion, I walked the extremely narrow deck and opened the cabin door, which was ajar. (In this image, note how canvas has been draped over the windows to obscure the fact that *Lorna Doone* is sitting in a huge con-vention hall.)

I entered the pilothouse, encrusted with six decades of dirt, the once gleaming brightwork yellow and peel-ing, the sole layered with rubbish, and everything dank and wet from broken windows.

After recovering from my initial shock, I worked to look past the debris and erosion to what lay beneath. I moved broken furniture and mysterious, rusted me-chanical devices. This confirmed my suspicions: under all the junk was an original beauty. Every piece of hard-ware seemed intact. My excitement mounting, I de-scended a stair to starboard.

I stood in the main saloon (left), a cabin barely eight feet long. Sitting on the worn settee, I looked at the finely detailed arched ribs above (the varnish now mostly a fine powder), at the built-in desk and adjacent cabinets (some of the doors drooping from screws that had long ago lost their holding power), and toward the triple leaded-glass panels to my left, which seemed pristine, not a broken panel evident. Unable to resist, I opened one panel and was surprised to find myself looking into another cabin, the cabinet having no back.

Curious as to what other treasures lay behind the cabinet, I approached the tiny mahogany door to starboard, grasped the miniature bronze knob (a typical yacht feature), and stepped into a time portal: a 1920s galley (right). Never before had I seen a galley so original, so fantastically intact. My hands caressed the propane stove, gently brushing the dirt and dust away and revealing bright white enamel. Surrounding the stove was a well of Monel. Above this once shiny well, now oxidized to a dull green, were open doors, the other side of the leaded glass cabinet I'd seen in the saloon. Obviously, I now realized, dishes were stored in such a compartment after washing, leaving them instantly accessible when a meal was ready in the saloon. As a designer, I appreciated this thoughtful touch. After closing the doors, I turned to the ice chest, also intact. And the starboard sink and countertop—both Monel—were pristine under the muck, not having been replaced by inferior materials.

Before plastic laminate, before stainless steel, there was Monel metal, a nickel-copper alloy with a high nickel content. This durable surface was used in almost all yachts before the 1930s and required polishing, unlike today's stainless steel. However, it also had a warmth that its modern counterpart lacks.

1

3

2

Moving forward, I entered the crew's quarters (1), layered with filth and rubbish. But, like everywhere, under this grimy overcoat lay the most intact crew quarters I'd ever seen, a tiny, almost coffin-like symphony of odd angles and no-nonsense detail.

I retraced my steps to the pilothouse (2), its aft bulkhead graced by a full-width settee. Noting that the middle cushion was askew, I tried to right it, the tattered leather crumbling in my hand. In trying to reposition the seat cushion, I realized that a hatch was under. The wood was surprisingly strong. Lifting it up, I peered into the compartment below (3).

Looking back at me were a pair of formidable engines that seemed original, the dim light reflecting off embossed letters that spelled Hall-Scott. The shaft of light coming through the open hatch also revealed a sole so littered with debris, old batteries, and wires that I decided not to fully enter this cramped space with only enough headroom to crouch.

After putting everything in the pilothouse back in place, I stepped onto the starboard deck and headed toward the aft companionway. What, I wondered, was next?

A pair of hatch doors were flapping mildly in the

stiff wind. After securing them and pushing the hatch cover to port, I went below. Barely. The tiny passageway at the foot of the short flight of stairs was filled one-third high with debris. I spent ten minutes carefully making a path.

My efforts were rewarded. I first gained access to the head (4), graced with what seemed to be entirely original features. And what features they were. Most astonishing was the cast porcelain step tub to my right, a small, square, shallow basin one "stepped" into to take a shower. It was surrounded by a curtain (now in shreds) on a circular rod. I'd never seen such a feature on a yacht (or in a home, for that matter).

The adjacent head, a marvel of engineering art, came with an intricate mechanism of tarnished brass and still shiny porcelain. The lovely oval sink on the aft bulkhead had a pump faucet and brass soap dish cradling a porcelain dish. Attached to the bulkhead was a glass shelf. Even the wall "tiles," of pressed composite, remained. I moved some garbage on the sole aside, and the old checkerboard linoleum tiles peeked out.

Tearing myself away from this miniature marvel of a head, I turned to an open door directly aft and peered into a stateroom (above) filled with debris. Stepping over and around this affront, I realized that the cabin was intact, down to the pair of acanthus-leaf brass sconces. The furnishings were all built-in, and the cabin emanated that delicious intimacy so prevalent on yachts before the 1930s.

Forward of the head, I tried to open another door. After getting it half-open, it refused further effort. I peered into what was obviously a stateroom, although filled halfway high with junk, and realized that it was a near duplicate of the cabin I'd just seen.

Returning to the deck, I went aft with extreme caution—the decks were giving way. It was obvious that a canvas overhead had once graced *Panzola*, but only a fretwork of stanchions and pipes remained to offer a tantalizing hint of what had been. Using the toerail as a path, I inched toward the aft deck.

As I stood, careful that my weight wouldn't force a collapse into the lazarette, I felt the breeze against my cheeks while looking up the length of *Panzola* and knew one thing. I had to save this derelict, crumbling, rotting vessel.

The image at right reveals the truth: *Lorna Doone* high and dry at the boat show.

NOWANDA

This delightful image captured a moment during the launch of a 68-foot a.c.f., built in 1927. *Nowanda* cost $60,000, and while this amount might seem a trifle compared to the $1,455,190 cost of *Corsair (IV)* (see page 150), it was still a significant sum for the era, and many times the annual wage of the men who built her. Even the 54-foot a.c.f., at $32,500, was beyond the means of the average wage earner. While the design of motor yachts has changed considerably in the ensuing eight decades, one factor has remained constant: yachts are expensive.

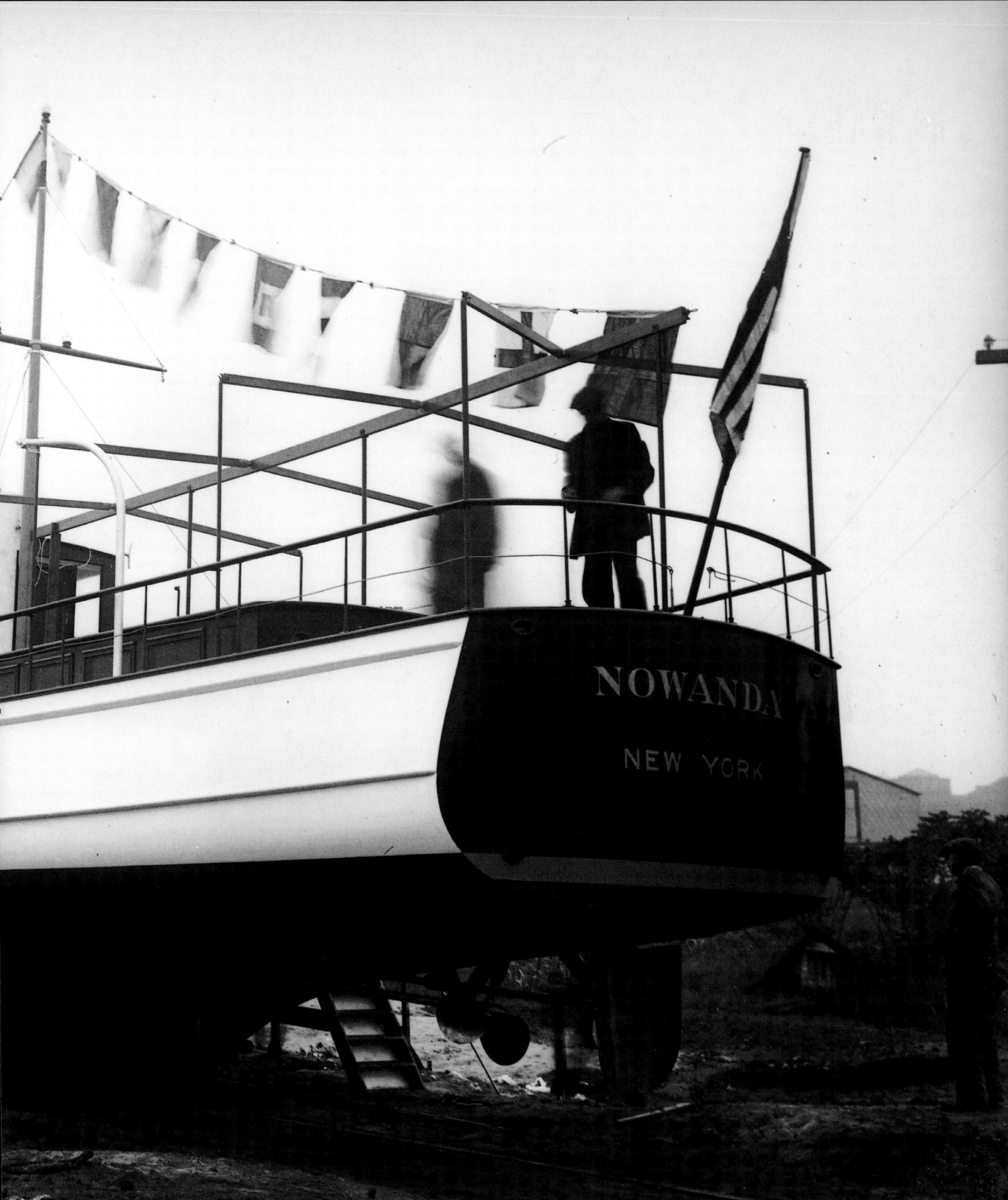
NOWANDA
NEW YORK

JAVEE

Not all a.c.f.s had the grace of *Panzola*. *Javee*, pictured below, suŷered from too much being stuŷed into a 47-foot hull; her foredeck seemed atrophied. Still, it's a nice image, capturing people on the aft deck having, I'm sure, a grand time.

POWSER

The image adjacent is that of *Half Moon*, which could be *Powser*, or an identical sister ship. *Powser* first appears in the 1953 *Lloyd's* (owned by J. Irving McDowell), and I've been unable to trace her previous name. It was rumored that she'd been owned by General George Patton and Cruising Club of America Commodore Alexander Moffat, but I can find no such evidence in any *Lloyd's*. What was her original name? A mystery!

I spent a great deal of time tracking down *Panzola*'s owner and making an offer. During these months, I also fell for another troubled craft, this one, luckily, just a hundred feet from *Alondra*. Her name was *Powser*, and the charm of her name contrasted with her deplorable condition. She'd come to my attention previously when she was scheduled to be sold at a yacht auction in Newport, and before I purchased *Alondra*. I'd planned to attend the auction, having been quite taken by *Powser*'s picture in the catalogue, but my schedule forced me to cancel. In retrospect, I wonder how different things might have turned out; if I'd gone, *Powser* might have become the yacht of my dreams instead of *Alondra*.

But God has a great sense of humor. After bringing *Alondra* to Newport for essential repairs, I was startled to discover two things. *Powser* was at the same yard, out of the water and looking sadder than ever. She was also a 1931, 40-foot a.c.f.

I was in trouble.

I found *Powser* under a torn, shredded, and wet canvas cover, sitting on blocks in the very back of the yard, a place boats go to die. Finding a broken ladder, I carefully positioned it and climbed into the aft cockpit. A full-beam settee butted up against her stern and after moving some debris and placing damp cushions back in place, I sat.

It was a tiny space, big enough for a small table and a pair of chairs, but that would have crowded things. As a gentle breeze carried over from the harbor, I marveled at how good I felt in this snug little cockpit and experienced a distinct sense of enclosure, of feeling nestled and safe.

Looking up, I could see that the overhead had once been canvas. Its tubing was intact (rare), the wooden cover simply attached to it. Ahead of me was a nicely detailed mahogany bulkhead with a door, ajar, enticing me. I ducked and went inside.

It was a stateroom with adjacent head. The one berth could have fit two in a tight, romantic squeeze; a fine built-in desk graced the forward bulkhead, and several wall sconces remained attached to the green painted paneling, each an unusual Art Deco design and worth a tidy sum. The head was quite small, but its fittings were entirely original.

Moving forward, I opened a pair of short doors and pushed back the hatch, stepping up into another cockpit. I later learned that this was intended as not only the pilothouse but the dining saloon; a fine mahogany table was once attached to the sole. The overhead arch of the beams was complemented by the delightful S-curve of the toerail, a surprisingly nice detail up close. And, the pilot controls seemed original—plenty of glass-covered dials and bronze switches and throttles.

Moving forward still, I opened another pair of short doors with hatch and stepped down into the main saloon. Before me was a setting eerily intact from six decades previous, including ice tongs in the ice chest; Monel counters and sinks; a tiny propane stove and adjacent tank; and, forward, a pair of built-in settees facing each other. Above was another pair of those wonderful Art Deco sconces, while light streamed in through eight ports and an overhead skylight. I opened a door and discovered another head, also intact.

FONTINALIS

LAUNCHED AS CAROLBAR

I'd been trying to track down any of *Alondra*'s sister ships, the five other *Maya*s that Densmore had built (*Alondra* was *Maya III*). Had any survived? While researching this, I was alerted to another Densmore vessel in Maine (although not a sister ship). Was I interested?

I entered the suburban driveway, turned a sharp left, and there she was, high on blocks and the only other Densmore yacht I'd been able to trace besides *Alondra*. She was for sale.

Her cabins, decks, and topsides were in excellent condition. Her bottom, however, was entirely missing, not just rotted, but not there. And her interior was an open shell, having been completely dismantled and placed in a nearby barn.

I wanted her. I wanted to put her back together. I wanted her to meet *Alondra* once again.

44 feet and launched in 1930. Designed and built by J. M. Densmore.

I went to work to secure *Powser*, and move *Fontinalis* and *Pan-zola* next to *Alondra*. Then, a fifth vessel caught my eye. She was in the same marina where *Powser* and *Alondra* were, appeared to have been built in the early 1960s, and was small, at least compared to *Alondra*. She was also, like *Powser* and *Alon-dra*, high up on blocks and, like *Powser*, seemed unloved by any-one. But her 1960s vintage didn't arouse my passion.

Still, I had to pass her every time I left the marina, and over the next few months she teased me with subtle flirtations. And then one day I realized that her curves, while not my preference, were attrac-tive, even stylish. The months passed, and eventually I made a vow: while I could acknowledge her appeal, I would not board.

I broke the vow.

Stepping into the moldering cockpit, I had to grab a cleat so as not to fall into the engine compartment below. Any wooden boat out of the water and left uncovered can rot in short order; *Rita* was no exception. I carefully maneuvered toward the pair of doors leading to the cabin and stepped down into the saloon— or jumped, as the ladder was missing. All around me was the dereliction typical of abandoned yachts: full of debris, cushions thrown about, papers, odd gizmos, and pulled-apart fittings.

I moved some things out of the way, pushed a cushion back in place, and then sat at the built-in dinette. Completely surround-ing me was a ribbon of windows, quite unlike the yachts I was used to and flooding the cabin with light—a floating greenhouse.

This one cabin aboard *Rita* housed all essential functions: a small head with shower (a pan folded down from the bulkhead); a tiny but well laid out galley; a dinette that converted to a double berth; a built-in settee, which also converted to a pair of single berths (one above, one below); and a V-berth for two. It was impressive that six people could be comfortably accommodated in such a small cabin.

When *Rita* was launched in 1962 she epitomized the very lat-est in design and equipment. Standing in the forlorn cabin, I remembered such vessels from my youth; they were gleaming, daring, and stylish. *Rita* was now three decades old, and her once-modern qualities were now overtaken by a distinct period charm. Her counters weren't Monel as in yachts from the 1930s and before but gold-flecked plastic laminate. The overhead lights weren't bronze or brass and based on classical examples but Atomic Age cones of brushed aluminum. And berths and settees weren't velvet or leather of dark green or burgundy but tight-fitting vinyl of orange and gray. These features now had a certain appeal, and *Rita* emanated a distinct "fun" quality quite different from the dignified grace of *Alondra*, *Powser*, or *Panzola*.

I was pursuing derelict yachts because *Alondra* was on hiatus. My grand dreams had been pushed aside by a unsettling reality: she had gotten worse under my care, the fault of my ignorance and a restoration team that talked better than they performed.

Work was halted and the restoration team let go.

While this development overwhelmed me, it was only, as I'd later discover, Debacle #1.

The troubles had begun after I'd been given an estimate and a six-month schedule to complete a certain number of repairs. After two months we had gone through, and surpassed, said esti-mate with 5 percent of the repairs completed. Moreover, *Alondra* was now a grim sight. I walked her decks (now pulled apart here and there), through her main saloon (its overhead partly removed), and sat forlorn in the pilothouse (now missing its aft bulkhead), an unaccustomed breeze blowing past the wheel sit-ting askew on the sole. Her decks, cabins, and bilges were filled with sawdust, piles of rotted original joinerwork that had been pulled out, and scraps of new wood. And even though impres-sively long, thick planks of new mahogany laid atop her trunk cabin, it was wood, as I'd later learn, that could not be used; it wasn't straight-grained, like *Alondra*'s original joinerwork, but random-grained. The former type of cut (quartersawn), once highly varnished, offers an elegant, even pattern, while the latter cut (pattern-grade) would have a busy, almost psychedelic pattern wholly out of keeping with a stately 1920s yacht.

Alondra was a mess. Sitting among the debris, I wondered how I could have allowed such a mistake to happen. Through my work as an architectural designer I regularly oversaw intricate multimillion-dollar renovations with confidence, although my work was constricted by the glass and stone exterior walls of New York's high-rise towers. Yet I felt intimidated by *Alondra*. (Some-one once told me that owning a classic yacht was like owning a beautiful wood armoire left out in the rain for years on end.)

The elaborate joinerwork that I regularly designed for apart-ments wasn't subject to the high levels of humidity standard on yachts, nor the stress (hulls move and twist, apartments don't). The electrical and plumbing systems of yachts are different from their land-based counterparts.

During my short ownership, *Alondra* had been transformed from a fully functioning yacht to a scrap heap candidate. I made a decision. At the very least, *Alondra* deserved her dignity back. I began by simply cleaning. Like a contortionist, I crawled into the 70-foot bilge with tools and the long hose of a wet/dry vac, scrap-ing and sucking away sixty years of slime. The congealed sameness of the bilge revealed disparate parts. Frames of unsuspected oak with copper fastenings appeared; long-leaf yellow-pine hull planks suddenly shone brilliant, seemingly just installed; while the tiny limber holes drilled between the frames to allow the passage of water were each reopened and cleaned by hand, allowing the passage of fresh salt water through the length of the hull and dispelling the stagnant pools. Pulling up the sole of the galley, I was shocked when the frames—the ones remaining—came apart easily in my hand, and a screwdriver effortlessly went through areas of the 2½-inch hull planking (quickly plugged). The cause of this catastrophic damage was traced to leaking freshwater tanks. I pulled out the not-original cabinets to access the tanks behind them. Once this task was completed, I discovered another cause for the damage: poor ventilation. Wooden hulls require that all internal/inaccessible compartments be ventilated and are usually designed as such. After dismantling *Alondra's* galley I found that these compartments, with tight-fitting bulkheads fore and aft, were like closed coffins. Her original designers, realizing this, had installed a pair of 6-inch copper pipes extending from the aft bulkhead to cowl vents perched on the trunk cabin. Yet at some point this crucial feature had been partially dismantled and the cowl vents removed. This, combined with the steady drip-drip of fresh water, guaranteed rot.

As I cleaned, an uncomfortable awareness dawned: vast sums had been spent on a wide variety of nonessential items, while the overriding problem—a virtual hull—had not even been checked. Surprisingly, the damage was not as severe as it might have been. In the engine room the frames and plank were like new, petrified by decades of oil and grease. The frames below the dining saloon were, surprisingly, less then a decade old, as were the frames below the forward and middle stateroom. In the main stateroom it was disconcerting to discover original framing moldering away, but the planking was resolutely impervious to my poking. In the huge lazarette the framing was again relatively new, as was her transom. In poking around at her overheads I discovered more rot but, more often, solid wood, although the mahogany pilothouse and main saloon needed almost total replacement.

I was in shock, exhausted, and my whole body hurt. . . . I also had had *the* time of my life. The great mysteries of *Alondra* were revealed; she no longer intimidated. I'd touched every inch of her skin, found her soft spots, her secret places, and knew how to restore her youth and glamour. And, while she still needed healing, she *looked* loved. People commented that they'd never seen a cleaner bilge—I took to showing it off—and her windows and ports gleamed in the sun, decks were kept washed and ropes coiled.

Dignity was restored.

Restoring structural integrity was another matter.

After a search lasting several months I had *Alondra* towed to Aquidneck Island, Rhode Island, a place known for its many yachting devotees, Newport Harbor, and, I hoped, qualified wooden boat restorers.

Alondra was hauled out of the water, thus ending my worry over *the* essential yacht function: flotation.

It was now apparent to me that a restoration would take years, perhaps even a decade (not the six months the initial restoration team had promised). It seemed sensible to construct a building that would keep *Alondra* dry, the workers comfortable, and materials safe. I hired another team to proceed with erecting a 100-foot greenhouse-type structure of pipes over *Alondra* that would then be covered with a vast space-age plastic sheet. A substantial check—in full—was issued.

The first plastic sheet lasted a few days until a strong wind blew it to shreds. The company that made it offered a replacement. It happened again, two weeks later.

The company that made the shed and the people erecting it were baffled. John Dalessio, my partner in *Alondra*, and an engineer, suggested that the problem was due to the fact that the pipe structure wasn't cross-braced and, so, moved too much in the wind, tearing the plastic sheeting.

At this point I had the wherewithal to ask how much had been spent on the now infamous shed (crowds had gathered to watch its brazen death-dances). I assumed a 10 to 20 percent increase and was willing to absorb this. Compounding my problems—as I was belatedly informed—was the fact that the restoration team had already spent 300 percent above our contract price to build the shed and expected that the figure would double before the shed was complete. This dark comedy was, of course, Debacle #2: another significant amount of money spent with no benefit to *Alondra*. Adding to the sideshow, within two weeks of bringing *Alondra* to Newport, her two-year-old $10,000 Onan generator was stolen. Later, her pair of engines vanished without a trace. All had been earlier removed by the restoration team. For safekeeping. Debacle #3.

I let go of the second restoration team. John and I erected a cover for *Alondra* attached to the hull itself, much smaller than the ill-fated dream shed, which towered high above, its lattice of cold gray pipes a stark and looming testament to my failures.

I then enrolled in a wooden boat restoration class.

A YACHT'S LIFE

ACANIA

126 feet and built in 1929 for Arthur E. Wheeler of New York. Designed by John H. Wells. Built by Pusey & Jones. Powered by a pair of 6-cylinder Winton diesels.

This John H. Wells design was built in 1929 at the Pusey and Jones Shipyard, and while there is nothing remarkable about her, the fact that she's so well documented makes for a compelling case study: the life of a yacht.

Acania was like many yachts launched at the end of the 1920s, possessing qualities both ancient and modern. While a few yachts built during this period sported more Moderne features, *Acania* represented nothing revolutionary. Her counterstern, of course, was a time-proven feature, but her plumb bow was of more recent vintage. Tall twin masts, which would have dominated just a decade before, have been reduced to an almost insignificant single pole. Still, her sheer was graceful, and the overall composition was subdued and elegant.

126 Ft. Diesel Yacht.
CONT. 1038
PROGRESS VIEW – Nov. 10. 1928
PHOTO 35-72

CONT. 1038
DEC. 18. 1928
PHOTO 3579

Arthur E. Wheeler, who commissioned *Acania*, had owned numerous previous vessels, such as *Sequoia*, a 1923, 45-foot auxiliary yawl designed by Tams & King. A few years later he purchased *Gannet*, a 1925, 100-foot diesel yacht, also designed by Tams & King, which he renamed *Bienestar*. Concurrent with his ownership of *Bienestar*, Wheeler owned *Skai*, a 1924, 34-foot single gas engine yacht.

Wheeler, a member of the New York Yacht Club, owned the 126-foot *Acania* for just a year before commissioning another vessel of the same name and from the same designer, John H. Wells. The second *Acania* (extant) was quite similar, and just ten feet longer, while her interior was almost an exact match with the first *Acania*, even down to identical furnishings. It's unknown why Wheeler commissioned this near replica.

In these images, *Acania* takes form at Pusey & Jones.

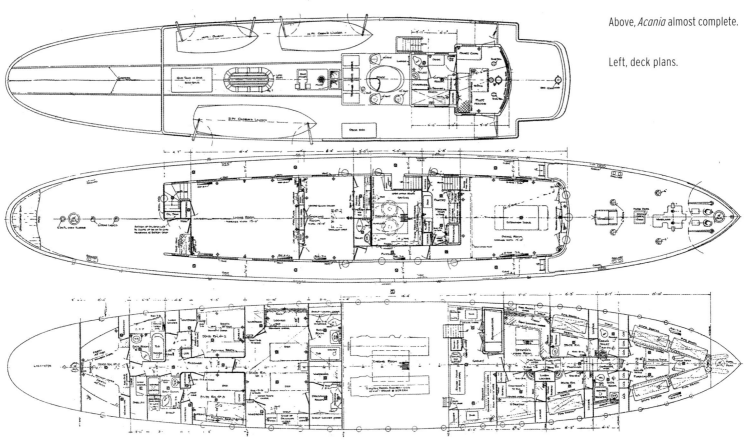

Above, *Acania* almost complete.

Left, deck plans.

Any yacht six decades old invariably acquires, like barnacles, stories that purport to be true. For example, *Acania* was reportedly purchased by a French film director in the 1930s and then given as a gift to the film star Constance Bennett, who used the yacht to entertain lavishly. Yet a search through *Lloyd's* indicates no such chain of ownership. A year after her launching, *Acania* was sold to Donald Woodward, who renamed the vessel *Murdona*. Two years later, in 1932, Frank H. Woods purchased the yacht and renamed her *Nellwood II*.

When G. W. Skinner purchased the yacht in 1941, he retained the name. During World War II the U.S. government acquired *Nellwood II* and continued ownership for an extraordinary forty years. Returning to private hands in the 1980s, the aged vessel was refurbished, but she'd long ago lost her yachtlike appearance. The images above show the effects of sixty years.

For all that she's been through, *Acania*'s exterior remains relatively unaltered. The most obvious change has been the painting white of her varnished deck

cabin and a forward extension to the upper pilothouse. More subtle alterations include the removal of the aft and forward canvas overheads, the pole mast, and many of the portholes. It wouldn't take much effort to return these elements to their original condition.

The beautiful counterstern was punctured for sampling nets—a sad sight, which could be remedied.

Shown above is a close-up of *Acania*'s pilothouse, in surprisingly original condition (although the raised portion in the upper left is an addition).

1

2

Acania's main saloon (1) and quite typical for the period, detailed simply with a few elegant touches (such as the pair of arched cabinets) and a nice mix of overstuffed chairs and sofa that invite rather than intimidate. And, in an age before air conditioning, observe the all-important fan attached to the forward bulkhead.

Forty years of government ownership obliterated much of the beauty that *Acania*'s interior once possessed (2). The main saloon was a dry lab and its walnut paneling was gouged, punctured, and vandalized by the time the nonprofit Intersea Foundation (which conducts whale research expeditions in Southeast Alaska) formed a for-profit offshoot and purchased *Acania* from the U.S. Navy in 1987. Cynthia D'Vincent, the founder and director of Intersea, had hoped to restore the main saloon but realized that the damage was too extensive. Its interior was gutted (except for the pair of arched cabinets), white oak installed, and a soapstone fireplace on quartzite was installed in place of the long-missing original.

Another image of the main saloon in its original incarnation (3).

The same view sixty years later (4). Changes—done with sensitivity—include extending the bulkhead aft (losing the shelter deck), opening up the stairwell.

The dining saloon, 1929 (1). This image is of the nearly identical sister ship commissioned by Arthur E. Wheeler in 1930.

The dining saloon today (2 and 3).

The smoking room (4). Note the "masculine" leather in this male domain, which contrasted with the "feminine" fabric in the main saloon. The linoleum floor was a typical touch.

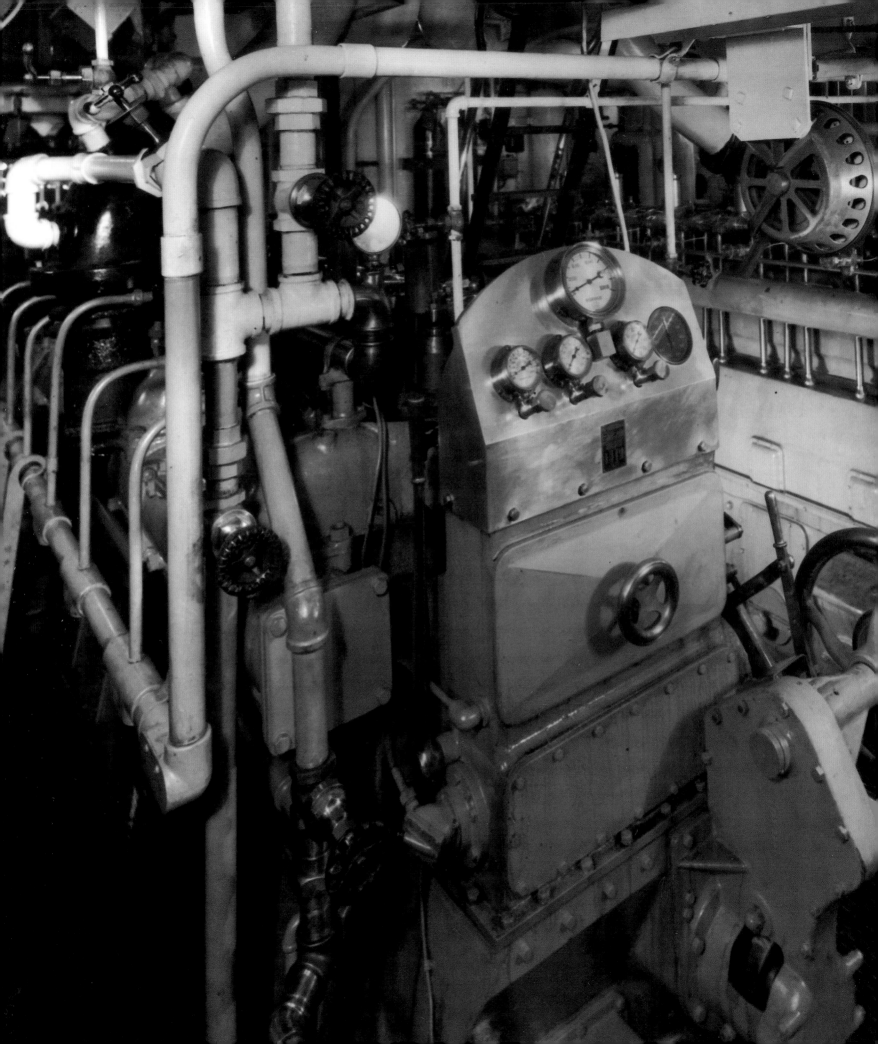

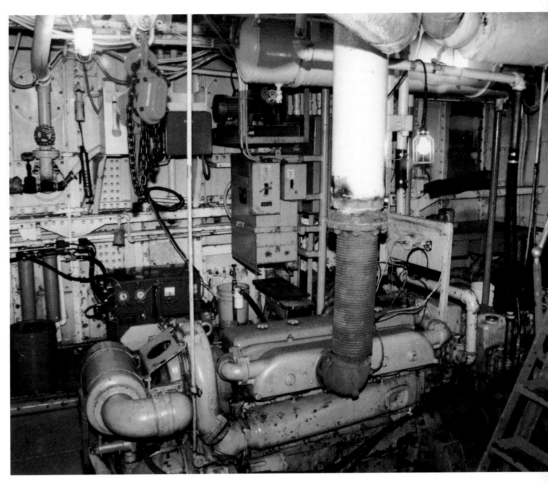

Left, the engine room with its pair of enormous Winton diesels, a veritable symphony of machines, pipes, dials, and gears.

Above, today, the engine room lacks the huge, powerful Winton engines, their replacement a pair of distinctly smaller GM diesels. The polished nature of the room in 1930 has been modified over sixty years of extensive use.

The owner's stateroom in 1929 (1). The built-in settee is a nice, nautical touch, but the freestanding beds aren't as much to my liking. And, again, note the fan, a now extinct yacht feature once omnipresent. This pleasant cabin, as well as all the staterooms aboard *Acania*, was gutted during her government ownership to provide for more berths.

The dressing room adjacent to the owner's cabin (2). Note the seam in the "wall-to-wall" carpeting, and the camera reflected in the mirror. This type of dressing table, while not my taste (I'd prefer a built-in cabinet), is attractive and typical for the era, yet no such item is ever seen aboard a classic yacht today. This is surprising, as such an item would be less than $800 in most antique shops.

The owner's head (3), with imitation marble, a rare ceramic tile floor (linoleum was more common), and a set of white-handled tub fittings that would be quite valuable today. But, what's the electric cord adjacent to the medicine cabinet for?

My favorite kind of stateroom (4), obviously nautical and blessed with fittings fully built in. Yet there are two features I dislike. First, the unfortunate windows obscuring the ports, and, second, an overhead that covers the supporting beams (compare this image with that of *Radiant*, page 134). It's sad to think that everything in this image has been destroyed.

A single cabin (5), again, no longer extant in this form. I like the water pitcher and two glasses resting on their own shelf, a detail that typifies the period.

The aft stateroom (6), a wonder of skewed angles. This cabin is so charming that's it's hard to imagine its destruction.

The same cabin today (7).

It's impressive that *Acania* has managed to reach such an old age. Her transformation from a privileged and elegant yacht to the no-nonsense working vessel she's become has enabled her continued existence. Intersea sold *Acania* in 1994 but continued to operate the vessel for new owners until 1997. Since then, *Acania* has been out of service and her future is in question. This grand yacht, photographically documented to a degree that few vessels are, is an excellent candidate for restoration. (Fraser Yachts, Seattle, may have a current listing for *Acania*. Call (206) 382-9494 or E-mail: frasersea@frasersea.com.)

HATCHING A PLAN

My addiction to Saving Rotting Hulls grew steadily worse in the early 1990s, a period coinciding with a dramatic slump in my income, two dynamics that fight against each other.

I didn't work on *Alondra* for several years. She was secure under her plastic cover held aloft by an elaborate custom frame, allowing full headroom on her decks. During heavy rainstorms I'd drop everything, race out to her, climb the tall ladder to her deck, unlock the plywood door, and step aboard. Under the plastic sheeting all noise was muffled, light diffused, and the steady raindrops created a pleasing song. I'd carefully walk the length of *Alondra* and look closely at her cover, checking for even minute leaks; finding such an offense, I'd duct-tape it into submission while the raindrops continued their plit-plat, plit-plat against this forcefield.

After a business deal gone spectacularly bad in 1992 (and an overall economic slump), an unsettling thought occurred to me: What if I could no longer afford my addiction? What, then, to do with the three boats I now owned (I'd taken over *Powser* and *Rita*) and the others I wanted to save?

The Classic Boat Collection (CBC) seemed the answer. I woke one morning with the idea formed in my head, waiting to be typed up and presented. It entailed having dozens of restored vintage craft available in one place as a floating B&B—Berth & Breakfast. The numbers on this idea indicated the potential for profit and at the same time (my real goal) saving large wooden boats from destruction.

Dick and Jane arrive at the Classic Boat Collection dock and are checked in aboard Truant, *an elegant 1930 121-foot Mathis-Trumpy houseboat. A steward in a starched white jacket emblazoned with the CBC logo appears as if by magic and attends to their bags. After having refreshments aboard the aft deck, they're shown to their own yacht for the weekend. Stepping aboard* Powser, *a crisp 1927 cruiser, they find an aft cabin and double bunk layered with linens, down pillows and comforter; adjacent is a head. Aft of the cabin they discover a cozy cockpit with a pair of wicker chairs designed for comfort while sipping evening brandies. In the main saloon forward, they find arched mahogany beams bisected by a skylight, while a deeply tufted settee in green corduroy offers comfort.*

Dick and Jane are delighted with the music offered for the evening: waves lapping against the hull, the droning of the harbor foghorn, seagulls talking, and footsteps along the dock. While

Powser gently rocks at her mooring, the couple are lulled to sleep; shafts of moonlight coming through the bronze portholes watch over them.

I envisioned that the CBC Marina would be located adjacent to a former Air Force Base.* Inside an old airplane hanger would be vessels awaiting restoration, while others, too far gone, would simply be preserved as is, the whole open as a museum with raised "docks" surrounding the vessels to allow for better viewing (yachts not structurally sound enough to withstand cutting through waves might be perfectly fine sitting up on blocks under cover).

I thought it all a grand idea: a classic boat museum and floating Orient Express. It also seemed likely that a dozen large classic motor yachts moored together—unique, to my knowledge—would attract international publicity and had the potential for a considerable return on investment.

But … not one person agreed with me. "Wooden boats *can't* make money," was something I heard over and over again for the next few years. People ignored the theory that while *one* yacht couldn't make a profit, dozens *together* might. My argument went unheeded. Any hopes for my rotting menagerie faded.

*It's possible to acquire former military bases, sometimes quite inexpensively. The late Donald Judd, a sculptor, did just that in the small town of Marfa, Texas. The massive artillery sheds and gymnasium were transformed into housing and spacious—to the extreme—art galleries (see Sources).

What follows is an update on some of the yachts listed in these pages.

LADY MARY

Page 179. This 93-foot 1927 Mathis-Trumpy (built as *Mariska*, I believe) was, by the 1980s, one of the few Trumpys remaining, perhaps the only, with her distinctive stern bronze scrollwork intact. She was reported burned and sunk in North Carolina's Intercoastal Waterway in the 1990s.

MAEMERE

Page 176. This 1929 Mathis-Trumpy (known as *High Spirits*) was purchased by Hornblower Dining Yachts and traveled to San Diego, California, where, after extensive renovations, she is available for day and evening dinner cruises (see Sources).

TRAIL

Page 178. This 1927 Mathis-Trumpy (known as *Southern Trail*), one of the finest ever designed, was burned and sunk at Windsor, Canada. She was reportedly raised and is undergoing restoration, although I haven't been able to confirm this.

FREEDOM

Page 192. This 1926 Mathis-Trumpy remains in Florida (known as *Sunset*). While far from her original elegance, she is maintained decently by her long-term owner.

CIGARETTE

Page 207. After I reboarded her and recognized that she was in better shape than appearances indicated, Earl McMillan also recognized this. A few years later, and after enormous effort (a great sales pitch and some cash), he was able to release *Cigarette* from her murky prison (assisted by Elizabeth Myer and Bob Tiedeman) and have her towed to Newport, Rhode Island, and hauled out of the water at the International Yacht Restoration School (see Sources). This dashing commuter was covered, her hull repainted, and scrollwork regilded; she sits, safe, but awaiting an enlightened soul who can fund her resurrection.

TRUANT

Page 196. I tried for several years to re-spark the owner's enthusiasm for restoring the Haunted Yacht, yet this extraordinary vessel was cut up, bits and pieces of her being salvaged by Nautical Furnishings, in Fort Lauderdale, Florida. Her pilothouse, completely restored and in one piece, is available (see Sources)—a sad end to a great yacht.

PANZOLA

Page 242. After trying to buy *Panzola* from the marina where she was abandoned, I was dismayed to discover that she'd been bulldozed to bits.

FONTINALIS

Page 254. I was unable to secure this Densmore vessel, and she was destroyed in the late 1990s.

ALONDRA

Page 233. After shutting down my architectural design business in 1991, I moved to Newport, in part to be closer to *Alondra* and closely oversee her restoration. My mistake, in retrospect, was buying a three-story 250-year-old house that needed a complete restoration. For the next few years I poured money and time into this house while my *Alondra* sat high and dry, patiently awaiting the return of my senses.

They never surfaced.

As the years went by I replaced *Alondra*'s cover annually, including one smashed by a hurricane. (*Alondra* was unscathed except for one broken window.) I also took an original Rosenfeld image of her, placed it in a waterproof frame, and attached it to her hull. The idea was that people drawn to this huge, mysterious, beached, wooden creature would see the picture, read the accompanying text, and know that *Alondra* was loved. It seemed to work; she was never vandalized or damaged by curiosity seekers.

Finally, in 1995, three years after a business deal gone sour, my finances were so bad that when *Alondra*'s cover needed replacing, I had no funds to accomplish this vital task. She was foreclosed on by the marina (an unpaid storage bill) and auctioned. There were no buyers.

My original instinct had been to berth *Alondra* in Hoboken (across the Hudson River from Manhattan), give up my expensive duplex apartment, move aboard, and work for a decade to slowly restore her. If I had done so, I believe that she'd be completed by now.

In an ironic twist, my original desire to have a *Titanic* clone ended with one extraordinary similarity to the doomed ocean liner: I enjoyed one voyage aboard *Alondra*.

However, I'm immensely pleased to report that *Alondra* lives on. She was purchased by Earl McMillen, who helped save *Cigarette* and has restored several vessels. Earl's father had owned *Alondra* during the 1970s, when Earl was a teenager, and he was delighted to regain this vessel from his formative years. Her long-delayed restoration is under way on Aquidneck Island, Rhode Island (see Sources). There remain only two Densmore-built vessels, *Alondra* and *Trilby* (built as *Maya I*).

POWSER

Page 253. Well before my finances collapsed, I'd taken over this charming, 44-foot a.c.f., had her moved next to *Alondra* (the "mother ship"), and spent weeks meticulously cleaning her every inch, scraping her bilge clean of debris and encrusted sludge, putting all her fittings back in order, and covering her with a vented cover over a custom wooden frame. As with *Alondra*, I attached a picture of *Powser* to her hull detailing her history.

Structurally, *Powser*, like all a.c.f.s I knew, was in very poor condition. I envisioned three possibilities. First, that she could be preserved as is in the CBC Museum. Second, that if another such a.c.f. was discovered, somehow, in better condition, but missing most of its fittings and hardware, then *Powser* could be "parted out" to restore what was lost. And third, my preference, that *Powser* could be restored.

After I lost *Alondra*, *Powser* was cruelly bulldozed by the marina.

RITA

Page 256. I'd also taken over *Rita*, cleaned her every inch, and was pleased to discover that she was in very good shape, structurally. Her mahogany hull was sound, all her hardware and fittings were intact, and, while she had a few deck leaks, these could have been easily remedied. She remained a few hundred feet from *Alondra* and *Powser*, was protected by a vented cover over a custom wooden frame, an identifying picture attached.

Rita was also cruelly bulldozed by the marina after I lost *Alondra*.

EPILOGUE

CAN THESE YACHTS BE SAVED?

I believe classic yachts are works of art. They represent an era and level of craftsmanship that have much to teach us in today's hectic, plastic, cheaper-is-better world. To me, bulldozing a *Powser* is like doing the same to a Matisse painting—unthinkable. Yet every year classic yachts are smashed to bits, sunk, set ablaze, or otherwise allowed to drift into oblivion. Often, such a downfall can happen swiftly. One season a yacht is nicely maintained, a season later it's caught in an argument between the owner and yard hired to do some repairs, and, as so often occurs, the frustrated owner becomes paralyzed, years pass, and the yard, needing the railway, cuts the yacht into bits. Or a new owner enthusiastically pulls apart his or her classic yacht to begin a restoration and, never having attempted such a project before, becomes overwhelmed. Years pass, and the once intact and reasonably sound vessel begins to deteriorate. The owner, his or her enthusiasm long turned to frustration and embarrassment, has the yacht cut into bits.

One of these fates almost befell *Alondra* in the 1930s when her owner couldn't pay an $850 bill. The yard seized her and resold her a few years later for $6,000, a rare happy ending under such circumstances (it helped that *Alondra* was then only fifteen years old). When I lost *Alondra* in the 1990s, she would have been destroyed except for the fact that Earl McMillen wanted her and had the wherewithal to negotiate a deal with the yard. Otherwise, she'd be dust today.

I suspect that many yachts that are destroyed are structurally sound. *Rita* was one example. It's not a coincidence that every vessel I've been aboard that was later bulldozed also *looked* like hell: trash everywhere, furniture strewn about, moldy clothing stacked in closets, backed-up heads, rusted fastenings staining topsides, and bilges filled with decades of unspeakable muck. Even a yacht in perfect structural condition filled with such rubbish will seem like a sure candidate for the scrap pile.

When people toured *Alondra* shortly after I purchased her they always said, "Oh, I see that her bottom and frames will need replacing." After I laboriously cleaned her, the comments—without exception—shifted to "I can't believe *Alondra's* in such good shape after all these years." Even seasoned restoration experts reacted this way.

An early 1980s survey on *Truant* (see page 196) commented more on her disorderly appearance than on her structural condition:

"I was hindered by the tremendous amount of trash.... There are literally tons of old engine parts, boards, cans, and other trash.... The framing is almost entirely obscured by the junk and debris.... A tremendous quantity of old rusted engine parts prohibits the possibility of inspecting the frames.... The large quantities of engine parts and lumber [limit] visibility.... The bilge is completely filled with ... old batteries, radiators, solidified bags of concrete, and general rubble."

The survey concluded that *Truant* had "deteriorated to the point where she is not worth investing substantial sums of money to restore her." Yet the survey also repeatedly indicated that the majority of the hull couldn't be inspected because of all the debris.

I later met a man who'd been aboard *Truant* a year after me. He, like me, sees the essence of an old yacht through the debris and muck. He concluded that *Truant* was a very worthy candidate for restoration, that her immense size would make her the premier Mathis-Trumpy on the charter circuit, and that the ominous gallons of water being pumped out of her on a steady basis was the result not of a decayed hull (as everybody had told me) but of stuffing boxes that needed reconditioning.

Once a yacht is declared "not worthy," word gets around quickly, and her death sentence is sealed, even if such a declaration isn't true. "Everyone *knows* she's a wreck!"

Today, in rural Kansas, I have noticed the same phenomenon with old houses. When I started working on an early Federal-style gem, people asked, "Why don't you just burn it down?" After I meticulously cleaned the interior, carted away all the junk, washed the floors, cleaned the windows, mowed the lawn, cut away the overgrowth, and even hung curtains, the comments changed: "My. It'll be a mighty pretty house once you're finished."

CONCLUSION

Since the 1930s, naval architects have transformed the way yachts are designed. Today, sleek and aerodynamic dominate. As such, the elegant majesty of the yachts contained within these pages seems particularly relevant—photographically frozen in time—with the ability to teach us anew about the beauty, grace, and visual allure of a clipper bow, a seductive counterstern, and brilliant varnished deckhouses. After all, who decreed that all modern power yachts have to be ruled by identical aesthetic guidelines?

I once lunched with a noted interior designer who'd been retained to develop a $25 million, 215-foot motor yacht. The designer and his client wanted a vessel like the fabled *Corsair*: black hull, clipper bow, and counterstern. When they conveyed these ideas to the respected naval architect hired, he was aghast. In the end, another white-hulled, sleek, beamy behemoth was launched, its interior a stark Edwardian contrast.

How many times has this dynamic taken place in the last few decades?

Since the late 1970s, similar "rules" have been smashed in the architectural profession. No longer are classic lines, proportions, and materials taboo, and cities are once again graced with works the likes of which haven't been seen since the 1930s. And in the last decade a number of beautiful sailing yachts have been launched that could be mistaken for vessels from seventy years previous. Yet the people who commission and design grand motor yachts seem locked in an aesthetic that prevents anything other than one type of creative expression.

My aim in writing this book, and the volumes that follow, is threefold.

First, I want to illustrate the seductive beauty of yachts before 1930 with the hope of shattering a mandate: All modern motor yachts must look like Nike sneakers.

Second, I hope to generate interest in classic motor yachts and prevent them from being abandoned or destroyed.

Third, I wish to offer historic guidelines for people who own a classic yacht and desire an accurate restoration. As this volume will, I hope, show, subtle details—and scale—make a world of difference.

To help save classic yachts from destruction, a Web site has been developed detailing endangered vessels. This site acts solely as an information exchange and is not a brokerage company. If you are interested in restoring a classic or know of one in danger, please contact us.

Moreover, if you have any information regarding the vessels depicted in these pages, know of a yacht that you'd like to see in future volumes, or have old family photographs of a motor yacht pre-1930, contact me at: www.thegoldencentury.com.

TIMELINES

The *Lloyd's Register* was my principal resource for tracing the history of yachts included in these pages. During World War II, *Lloyd's* suspended publication (from 1942 to 1947). Many yachts do not reappear in post war editions. While a number of vessels were lost in war service, such as *Alva*, or not worth the cost of a refit, other yachts simply vanished from the printed record for unexplained reasons. *Arcadia* was last listed in 1940, although she was reported extant until 1969. (Being converted to a commercial vessel would offer an explanation, as happened with *Acania*.) *Alondra* disappears from *Lloyd's* in the late 1960s, but she is extant. Even well known yachts, such as *Haida*, are not listed in *Lloyd's* for long periods of time, forcing the author to rely on unconfirmed records in tracing owners. The disappearance of other vessels leaves a historian with a lingering, annoying curiosity. *Zapala*, one of the most beautiful motor yachts of the 1920s, is last listed in the early 1970s. Could she be extant?

Lloyd's suspended publication after its 1977 edition, forcing a historian out of elegant libraries and into the arms of a small cadre of classic motor yacht enthusiasts. "Hey, what ever happened to . . . ?"

(Yachts can be traced after 1977 through the Coast Guard; due to time constraints, this resource was unexplored.)

ACANIA

	extant
1929–1930	Arthur E. Wheeler
1930–1932	Frank H. Woods *(Murdona)*
1932–1941	Donald Woodward
1941	G. W. Skinner *(Nellwood II)*
1942–1987	U.S. Government
1987–1994	Intersea Foundation *(Acania)*
1994–	Norman Volotin

AEGUSA

1896–1897	I. Florio
1898–1914	Sir Thomas Lipton *(Erin)*
1915	British Navy *(Aegusa)*
	Torpedoed in 1915.

AGAWA

1907–1916	C. W. Harkness
1916	U.S. Navy World War I
1917–1941	W. A. Harkness *(Cythera)*
1942	U.S. Navy World War II
	Lost at sea during World War II service.

ALOHA

1910–1938	Arthur Curtis James
	U.S. Navy World War I

ALONDRA

	extant
1927–1932	George C. Smith, New York
1932	Charles E. Proctor
1932- 1940	John H. Clowes, New York
1940–1942	Fyfe Shipyard, Long Island, New York
1942–1962	Clarence S. Bruce, Washington, D. C. *(Sallie B)*
1962–1966	Herbert P. Field *(Mahogany Lady)*
1966–1970	Edwin S. Mooers, Lee Bass, Ray C. Bass (respective owners)
1971–1986	Captain Doug Kenny, Earl McMillen, Arnold Guest, Frank W. Rash, W. Edward Guy (respective owners).
1986–1988	Arthur Burch *(Somewhere in Time)*
1988–1996	Ross MacTaggart, John Dalessio *(Alondra)*
1997–	McMillen Yachts, Inc. (see Sources: Classic Yachts Under Restoration)

ALPHA

1926	George Marshall Allen, New York
1927	not listed
1928	LeGrand S. DeGraff
1929–1930	James W. Perry, Pebble Beach, California
1931	Robert H. Morse *(Rosinco)*
1932–1933	W. R. Swissler, Chicago, Illinois
1934	Wilbert Melville, New York
1935–1936	George L. Batchelder, Boston, Massachusetts; Miami, Florida *(Pia)*

ALVA

1930–1943	William K. Vanderbilt II
	U.S. Navy World War II (USS *Plymouth*)
	Torpedoed in 1943.

APHRODITE

1928–1936	John Hay Whitney
1937	Charles H. Oshei, Detroit, Michigan *(Avalanche)*
1938–1942	Charles H. Oshei, Detroit, Michigan *(Selarch)*

1947–1949   Anthony DeLorenzo, Daytona, Miami, Florida

1950–1960   F. Nelson Blount, Warren, Rhode Island *(Aphrodite)*

A R A S

              extant
1930–1941   Hugh J. Chisholm, Greenwich, Connecticut
1941   U.S. Navy (USS *Williamsburg*)
1945–1953   presidential yacht *(Williamsburg)*
1953–1962   decommissioned and laid up
1962–1966   National Science Foundation *(Anton Bruun)*
1966–1972   Marlboro Machine Company, Salem, New Jersey
1972–1982   Goldstein Brothers, Philadelphia, Pennsylvania
1982–1985   USS Williamsburg Company, Inc., Alexandria, Virginia
1985–1988   Clyde's Restaurant Group, Washington, D.C.
1988–1993   Presidential Yacht Trust, Washington, D.C.
1993–1996   USS Williamsburg Corporation
1996–1999   Italian Bankruptcy Court
1999–   Navalmare SRL, LaRicci, Italy (see Sources: Classic Yachts in Need of Restoration)

A R C A D I A

1926   Galen L Stone
1927–1939   Mrs. Huntington Reed Hardwick, Brookline, Massachusetts
1940   Stuart B. Playfair, Toronto Reported scrapped in 1969.

A R R O W

1902–1906   Charles R. Flint
1907–1914   E. F. Whitney
1915   J. Stuart Blackton
1916–1917   Theodore Krumm
1918–1920   V. S. Briggs

A T A L A N T A

1883–1892   Jay Gould
1893–1901   George Gould
1902–1950   Venezuelan Navy *(Restaurador, General Salmon)*

A T H E R O   I I

1926–1927   Jesse L. Livermore, New York
1928–1931   Eldridge R. Johnson. Essington, Pennsylvania *(Caroline)*
1932–1936   Joseph A. MacDonald, New York
1937   Joseph M. Schenck, New York
1939–1940   Dr. Jno. R. Brinkly, Galveston, Texas *(Dr. Brinkley)*

A V A L A N C H E   I I I

1926–1929   Anson W. Hard
1930–1931   Alexander Dallas Thayer, New York *(Lone Eagle)*
1932–1942   Frederick H. Bedford, Jr. *(Kikai)*

A V A L A N C H E   I V

1929–1935   Anson W. Hard.
1936–1940   Arthur V. Davis, New York *(Elda)*
1941–1947   not listed
1948–1949   Marcross Corporation

A V A L O N

1930–1939   Ogden L. Mills, New York
1940   Delta Transportation Company, Gulfport, Mississippi

C A L U M E T

1903–1915   Charles G. Emery
1916–1927   James A. Farrell, New York
1928   A. Atwater Kent
1929   Alecio Serentino
1930   DeNeal H. Samuels, Boston, Massachusetts

C A N G A R D A

              extant
1901–1903   Charles J. Canfield, Manistee, Michigan
1903–1941   George and Mary Fulford, Brockville, Ontario *(Magedoma)*
1948–1954   J. Gordon Edington, Toronto, Ontario; London, England
1955   S. Burtis Smith, Toronto, Ontario
1956–1974   Frederick B. Smith. Rochester, New York *(Cangarda)*
1983–1999   Richard Reedy
1999–   J-Class Events, Newport, Rhode Island (see Sources: Classic Yachts in Need of Restoration)

C A R O L B A R

1930–1939   not listed
1940   Matthew P. Whittall, Marion, Massachusetts *(Fontinalis)*
1948–1950   Mrs. Ralph Haller, Duxbury, Massachusetts
1951–1952   Stuyvesant Fish, New York
1953–1974   Thomas H. MacWhinney, Essex. Connecticut
1975–1976   John E. Swanstrom, Portsmouth, New Hampshire *(Raven)* Later renamed *Fontinalis*. Destroyed late 1990s.

C I G A R E T T E

1905–1917   William H. Ames
1918–1920   U.S. Navy
1921–1930   Barron Collier *(Pocantino)*

C I G A R E T T E

              extant
1928–1931   Louis Gordon Hammersley, New York
1932–1941   William Deering Howe, New York *(Nepenthe* after 1933)
1942   not listed

1947–1969	Henry R. Stadler, Fairhaven, New Jersey (*Philijean*)
1970–1972	William Hampson, City Island, New York
	Now at the International Yacht Restoration School, Newport, Rhode Island (see Sources: Classic Yachts in Need of Restoration)

C L E R M O N T

1892–1901	Alfred Van Santvoord
1902–1903	Alfred Van Santvoord (estate)
1904–1910	Charles G. Gates
1911–1921	(estimated) Commercial interests. Scrapped in the early 1920s.

C O R S A I R   (I I I)

1899–1913	J. Pierpont Morgan, Sr.
1913–1917	J. Pierpont Morgan, Jr.
1917–1919	U.S. Navy
1919–1930	J. Pierpont Morgan, Jr.
1930–1942	U. S. Coast & Geodetic Survey (*Oceanographer*)
	Scrapped in 1944.

C O R S A I R   (I V)

1930–1940	J. Pierpont Morgan, Jr.
1940–1946	British Navy
1946–1949	Commercial interests
	Wrecked in 1949, later scrapped.

D E L P H I N E

extant

1921	Horace E. Dodge
1921–1968	Mrs. Anna Dodge Dillman
	U.S. Navy World War II (USS *Dauntless*)
1968–1986	Seafarer's Harry Lundeberg School of Seamanship, Piney Point, Maryland (*Dauntless*)
1986–1989	Travel Dynamics, New York
1989–1993	Sea Sun Cruises, Singapore
1993–1997	Groupe Georges Michel
1997–	Marine Cruising, Jacques Bruynooghe (*Delphine*)
	(see Sources: Related Books)

D R E A M E R

1899–1903	Thomas W. Lawson
1904–1905	L. C. Ledyard (*Rambler*)
1906–1912	Pliney Fisk, New York
1913–1915	Charles T. Thorne, Chicago, Illinois
1916–1917	Kenneth B. Van Roper, New York
1918	no owner listed
1919	U.S. Navy

E D A M E N A   I V

1926–1933	Earle P. Charlton
1934–1936	Bernard W. Doyle, Marblehead, Massachusetts (*Margelou*)
1937–1940	Harry E. Noyes, Marblehead, Massachusetts (*Seyon*)
1941–1942	Cymro, Inc., Washington, D. C. (*Sayon*)
1947–1948	Patricia Rowe Richter, Washington, D.C.
1949–1955	Sal C. Mirenda, W. M. Priest, Miami, Florida

F R E E D O M

extant

1926–1932	Aubert J. Fay, Boston, Massachusetts
1933-1939	Mrs. J. P. Donahue, New York
1940–1941	S. A. Lynch (*Sunset*)
1947–1950	Herbert M. Plimton

1950	Hollis W. Plimton, Miami, Florida
1951–1968	Yachts, Inc., Wilmington, Delaware
	Currently owned by Ashley E. Howes.

F R O L I C   I I

1925–1928	Walter P. Chrysler
1929–1947	F. T. Bedford, Great Neck, New York (*Phantom*)

F R O L I C   I I I

1927–1940	Walter P. Chrysler
1941–1942	Walter P. Chrysler estate

G E M

1913–1922	William Ziegler, Jr.
	US Navy World War I
1922–1926	Jesse Livermore (*Athero*)
1926	Russell A. Alger (*Gypsy Jo*)
1926–1935	A. E. Mathews (*Condor*)
1935	J. E. Smith (*Carolus*)
1936–1941	H. P. van Knauf (*Condor*)

G L A D Y S

1884–1885	Neil Mathieson, Port Glasgow
1886–1888	Mrs. R. E. Stewart, Southampton
1889–1892	Edmund B. Liebert, Southampton
1893–1895	Charles Barton, Southampton
1896–1908	Sir John Mowlem Burt, Southampton
1909–1915	H. H. Barlett, Southampton
1919–1920	James McKelvie, Southampton
1921–1922	William Gislow, Stockholm
1923–1926	William Griffiths, Cowes
1927–1936	Capt. Alwyn Foster, Cowes
1937–1939	Robert Kemp, Cowes
1947	Acquired by his Majesty's government, Cowes
1948	D. E. White, Cowes
1949–1951	Robert Kemp

HAIDA

extant

1929–1939	Max Fleischmann
1940–1946	U.S. Navy (USS *Argus*)
1947–1952	Eastlane Shipping Company, Panama (*Sarina*)
1953	dropped from *Lloyd's*
1969–1978	Loel Guinness
1978–1981	Robert Stigwood
1981–1988	owner unknown (*Rosenkavalier*)
1988–1992	Isaka Family, Yokohama, Japan
1992–1999	Andres Dion Liveras
	Sold in 2000 and renamed *Haida*. (see Sources: Classic Yachts for Charter. Please note that this listing may no longer be current.)

HAPPY DAYS

1927–1942	Ira C. Copley, New York

HOHENZOLLERN

1893–1918	German Admiralty, Imperial Royal Yacht Fate unknown

HUSSAR

extant

1930–1935	Edward and Marjorie Hutton
1935–1955	Joseph E. Davies, Marjorie Post Hutton Davies (*Sea Cloud*)
1955–1961	Rafael Leonidas Truillo Molina (*Angelita*)
1961–1963	Dominican Government (*Patria*)
1963–1978	Operation Sea Cruises (*Antarna*)
1978–	Sea Cloud Cruises, Inc. (*Sea Cloud*) (see Sources: Classic yachts for Charter)

IOLANDA

1909–1911	Morton F. Plant
1912–1919	Mme. E. Terestchenko British Navy World War I
1920–1927	Camper & Nicholson
1920–1939	Mr. and Mrs. Moses Taylor British Navy World War II
1947	Commercial interests

IRWIN

1925–1934	Julius Heilner, New York
1935	Jerome A. Thirsk, New York
1936–1937	Katherine Young, Fisher Island, New York
1938–1941	Glenfield S. Young, Fisher Island, New York
1942–1947	R. C. Huffman Construction Company, Buffalo, New York (*Allo*)
1948	Franc B. Jackson, Buffalo, New York
1949–1950	Frank Davis, Inc. (*Frank Davis III*)
1951–1955	Laurence D. Ely, New York (*Ballerina*)
1956	Post Publishing Company, Marblehead, Massachusetts
1957	Sidney Svirsky, Marblehead, Massachusetts
1958	New England Marine Finance Company, Marblehead, Massachusetts
1959–1965	Ballerina, Inc. (Leon F. Shelby), Marblehead, Massachusetts

KANAWHA

1899–1901	John P. Duncan
1901–1910	Henry H. Rogers
1911–1914	Abram Baudouine, New York
1915	Morton F. Plant
1916–1917	John Borden
1918	U.S. Navy (USS *Piqua*)
1919	John Borden
1920	James A Briggs

LITTLE SOVEREIGN (II)

1909–1911	Matthew C. D. Borden
1911–1917	Charles L. Seabury
1917–1922	F. W. White
1923	owner not listed (*Sovereign*)
1924	John Hart (*Vereign*)

LORNA DOONE

1928–1929	H. C. Dechant, Marblehead, Massachusetts
1930–1934	O. C. Doering, Boca Grande; Miami, Florida (*Lucy*)
1935–1961	Mort Kallis, Chicago, Illinois (*Laejack*)

LYSISTRATA

1900–1914	James Gordon Bennett
1914	Russian Navy (*Yaroslavna, Vorovsky*) Listed in *Jane's* until 1966.

MAEMERE

extant

1929 1939	DeWitt Page
1940–1941	Mrs. Dewitt Page
1947–1956	Edward S. Moore (*Big Pebble*)
1956–1962	Mrs. Edward S. Moore
1962–1967	Oscar F. Holcombe (*Sea Panther*)
1967–1971	John J. Atwater, Jr.
1971–1973	Richard Wallace
1973–1975	Arnold & Sons (*High Spirits*)
1975–1985	Charles Cauthen, Hilton Head, South Carolina Now owned by Hornblower Dining Yachts, San Diego, California (see Sources: Classic Yachts for Charter)

MAID OF HONOR

1907–1912	William K. Millar, Southampton
1913–1921	Mrs. Marion G. Thorton, London
1922	M. Grahame-White, London
1923–1924	Lord Tredegar, London (Sylvana)
1925–1936	Miss K. A. Mackinnon, London
1937	J. Anderson Miller, Glasgow
1938–1939	Hubert Scott-Paine, Glasgow
1947	Acquired by his Majesty's government, Glasgow
1948–1952	Bury Court Shipping Company, Glasgow

MARGARET F III

1928–1938	Lawrence P. Fisher, Detroit, Michigan
1939–1952	The Glenn L. Martin Company, Baltimore, Maryland (Glenmar)
1953–1958	The F. C. Russell Company, Baltimore, Maryland (Rusco)
1959–1975	Creighton's Restaurant, Ft. Lauderdale, Florida (Sunrise)

MARISKA

1927	F. D. Owsley
1928	not listed
1929–1931	Anton E. Walbridge, New York (Heigh-Ho)
1932–1938	Fred W. Weller (Truelove)
1939	Howard Bonbright (Dolphin)
1940–1942	Allen P. Green (Josephine)
1947	Nelson M. Davis (Windswept)
1948–1949	Lee Johns, Ruby Johns, Miami, Florida
1950–1974	Bruce Dodson, Kansas City, Missouri; Miami, Florida (Helma)
1975–1976	Edward S. Dobson, Kansas City, Missouri; Boca Raton, Florida (Lady Mary)
	Reported sunk in the 1990s.

MEDEA

	extant
1904–1911	William Macallister Hall, Carradale, Argyll
1911–1913	Frederick G. Todd, Troon, Ayrshire
1914–1917	John Stephen, Govan, Glasgow
1917–1919	War service French Navy (Corneille)
1919–1920	M. Graham-White, Warsash, Hants (Medea)
1921	H. Dudley-Ward, London
1922	F. E. Guest, Templeton, Roehampton
1923–1926	A. M. Symington, Almada, Lisbon
1927–1929	B. H. Piercy, London
1930–1933	Fred J. Stephen, Rhu, Dunbartonshire
1934	A. A. Paton, Liverpool
1935–1941	Job Longson Wild, London
1941–1942	War service with British Royal Navy
1942–1943	War service with Royal Norwegian Navy
1943–1945	War service with British Royal Navy
1945–1960	Job Longson Wild, Kenley, Surrey
1961	Estate of Job Longson Wild
1962–1964	C. E. Reffitt, London
1965–1969	Captain N. P. S. Millar, Padstow, Cornwall
1969–1971	Captain K. G. Holmberg, Jarnforsen, Sweden
1971–1973	Nelson Paul Whittier, British Columbia
1973–	The Maritime Museum Association of San Diego

METTAMAR

1930–1935	Ransom E. Olds
1936	W. L. Kellog
1937–1942	Miss Frances C. Griscom
1947–1963	E. Harold Greist, Bridgeport, Connecticut (Harolyn)
1964–1969	Robert D. Huffman, Washington, D.C. (Mettamar)

MINOCO

1930–1940	Mills Novelty Company
1941–1942	Walter P. Murphy (Idyl)

NAHLIN

	extant
1930–1938	Lady Yule
1939	H. M. King Carol II of Romania (Luceafarul)
	No owner listed in *Lloyd's* after 1940. Vessel not listed after 1950. Later became a school ship in Romania (Liberatatea). Restoration underway in England.

NIRVANA

1925–1937	Rodman Wanamaker
1938	F. Linden, New York
1939–1941	Sutton Line, Inc., New York
1942	M. H. Tallman, New York (Pirateer)

NOMA

1902–1908	William B. Leeds
1908–1910	William B. Leeds (estate)
1910–1912	John Jacob Astor
1912–1921	Vincent Astor
	US Navy World War I
1921–1926	Rodman Wanamaker
1927–1933	N. B. Worden
1934	Commercial interests (Salvator Drimo)

NOURMAHAL

1921–1927	Vincent Astor, New York
1928–1929	William Boyce Thompson, New York (Alder)
1930	Carle C. Conway, New York (Conseco)
1931–1939	John W. Hubbard, New York
1940	Philip S. Ross, Montreal

PANZOLA

1928–1929	not listed
1930–1934	Nicholas M. Schenck, New York
1935	Edward J. Churchill, Great Neck, New York
1936–1942	Clarence G. Crispin, New York *(Cris II)*
1943–1946	owners unknown, name changed to *Bitsy* and *Tarbet II*
1947–1960	Arthur A. Brown Greenwich, Connecticut; New York *(Stymie II)*
1960–1974	George K. Gould, New York *(Eltee)*
1974–1976	Adelphi University, New York
1984–1990s	Arthur M. Pecchioni, New York *(Zostera II)*
	Destroyed in the early 1990s.

POWSER

	launched in 1931, first listed in Lloyd's in 1953
1953–1976	J. Irving McDowell
	Destroyed in the mid-1990s.

RADIANT

1926–1928	Clifford R. Hendrix, Larchmont, New York
1929	John W. Hanes, New York *(Tar Heel)*
1930	*(Mommie)*
1931–1933	Herbert J. Adair
1934–1942	Alfred DeCozen, Newark, New Jersey *(Charlotte II)*

RAMNA

1926–1929	Walter P. Lasher
1930–1932	B. F. McGuckin, New York *(Alta Rocca)*
1933–1936	Sinclair G. Stanley, New York
1937–1938	Gordon C. Thorne, Miami, Florida and New York *(Marimont)*
1939	Anna Schaeffer and Lois May Jacobson, Chicago *(Annlo)*
1940–1942	Anna Schaeffer

ROAMER

1902–1911	N. G. Herreshoff
1912–1915	Lyman E. Warren, New York
1916–1919	not listed
1920–1922	Frank A Egan, New York
1923–1930	F. D. M. Strachan

SAGA

1927	Hugh C. Creswell
1928	Charles S. Payson
1930	Charles S. Payson *(Sinbad)*
1931–1933	James H. Ottley *(Varramista)*
1934–1935	Royal Yacht Chartering Company, New York
1936	Gerald A. Kelleher, New York *(Serene)*
1937	George F. Trommer, Manhasset, New York
1938	Harold S. Goldsmith, Manhasset, New York
1939	Serene Corporation, New York
1940	Gerald A. Kelleher, New York
1941–1942	F. W. Flood, New York
1947–1949	Benjamin E. Cole, Palm Beach and Miami, Florida.
1950	Herbert Wilson, Ft. Lauderdale and Miami, Florida
1951	Philip W. Parker, Elizabeth City, New Jersey
1952–1957	Janet Megrew Elcock, Miami, Florida

SCOUT

1900–1918	August Belmont

SIVAD

1926	D. P. Davis
1926–1927	Victor Emanuel *(Vidor)*
1928	Carll Tucker, New York
1929	Charles A. Bolot, New York *(Hi-Esmaro)*
1930–1933	Caddo Company, Houston, Texas *(Hilda)*
1934–1937	William Leeds, Oyster Bay, New York *(Moana)*
1938–1949	Leslie L. Irvin, New York *(Velda)*

TRAIL

	possibly extant
1926–1928	William Wallace, Jr.
1929	David A. Schulte, New York
1930–1934	DeVer H. Warner, Bridgeport, Connecticut
1935–1941	Henry Hemmerdinger
1942–1954	not listed
1955–1956	Mary Sue McCulloch Oakes
1957–	Southern Builders of Houston, Inc. *(Southern Trail)*
1958–1977	Castro Convertible Corporation
1991	Ken Kreisler
	Reported burned and sunk, raised and towed to Toronto.

TROUBADOUR

1925–1930	Webb Jay
1931–1933	I. C. Elston, Jr. Miami, Florida; Chicago, Illinois *(Ilderim)*
1934–1971	Sabine Towing & Transportation Company, Port Arthur, Texas; Baltimore, Maryland

TRUANT

1930–1945	Truman H. Newberry, Detroit, Michigan (renamed *Idyl* and *Carnan* during World War II service)
1948–1951	Walter P. Chrysler, Jr., Warrenton, Vermont; New York *(North Wales)*
1951–1966	Colonel and Mrs. Leon Mandel, Chicago, Illinois; Miami, Florida *(Carola)*
1966	International Oceanographic Foundation
	Not listed in *Lloyd's* after 1967. Later owned by Advertising Agency Associates, Inc. (Allen R. Hackel). Destroyed in the late 1980s.

UTOWANA

1883–1886	not listed
1887–1917	Elias Cornelius Benedict (*Oneida*; *Adelante* after 1914)
1918	Theodore Krumm, New York

VALDA

1900–1901	Frank B. McQuesten
1902–1905	Charles W. Henry (*Wissahickon*)
1906–1917	Mrs. Charles W. Henry
1918	no owner listed
1919	U.S. Navy
1920	Mrs. Charles W. Henry
1921–1922	Frank B. McQuesten (*Valda*)
1923–1930	James A. Ross, Boston, Massachusetts

VANADIS

	extant
1924–1925	C. K. G. Billings, New York
1926–1928	Harrison Williams, New York (*Warrior*)
1929	Sidney S. Whelen, New York
1930–1935	Harrison Williams, New York
1936	Sandoma Gasoline Company, Los Angles, California
1937–1938	Hekor Investment Holding Company, Montreal
1939	N. V. Maats. tot Exploitatie van Yachten, Antwerp
1947–1948	Acquired by his Majesty's government, Panama (*Troubadour*) Extant today as *Lady Hutton* (the Malardrottningen Hotel) in Stockholm, Sweden (see Sources: Classic Yachts Open to the Public)

VARA

1928–1940	Harold S. Vanderbilt
1941–1946	not listed
1947	Walling Hamilton, Florida (*Susie Mae*)

VIRGINIA

1930–1939	Sir Stephen Courtauld
1940–1946	not listed
1947	Acquired by His Majesty's Government
1948–1958	Viscount Camrose
1959–1968	Government of Liberia (*Liberian*)

WAKIVA

1907–1918	L. V. Harkness, H. S. Harkness U.S. Navy World War I. Lost at sea in 1918.

WAYFARER

1929–1940	Winthrop W. Aldrich
1941–1942	Charles B. Levey, Margaret B. Levey, Jamestown, Rhode Island (*Wild Duck*)
1947	J. O. Larsen, New York
1948	Larsen, Inc., New York
1949–1951	Charles B. Levey, Margaret B. Levey, Jamestown, Rhode Island
1952–1955	Barret Crockett, Miami, Florida (*Bahama Queen*)
1956–1959	Henning O. Nielsen, Boston, Massachusetts
1960	Bahama Queen Corporation

WINCHESTER (I)

1907–1909	Peter Winchester Rouss
1909–1914	Alfred G. Vanderbilt (*Adroit*)
1914–1916	Alfred G. Vanderbilt (estate)
1916–1928	I. E. Emerson
1929–1937	Barron Collier
1938	Melville Cannon
1939–1941	Barron Collier (*Aera*)

WINCHESTER (II)

1909–1912	Peter W. Rouss
1913–1915	Irving Cox, et al. (*Flying Fox*)
1916–1920	C. K. G. Billings
1920–1929	Dr. J. A. Harriss
1930–1937	William B. Leeds
1938–1955	Columbian Navy (*Mariscal Sucre*)

WINCHESTER (III)

1912–1915	Peter W. Rouss
1916–1921	Canadian Navy (HMCS *Grilse*)
1922–1938	S. R. Guggenheim (*Trillora*)
1939–1941	Merritt, Chapman & Scott

WINCHESTER (IV)

1915–1927	Peter W. Rouss U.S. Navy World War I
1928	Vincent Astor
1929	Russell A. Alger
1930–1939	Cornelius Vanderbilt
1940	B. P. McCurdy Canadian Navy World War II (HMCS *Renard*)
1951–1957	W. N. MacDonald (Margaree S. S. Company) (*Renard*)

ZAPALA

1928–1933	Howard E. Coffin
1934	Alfred W. Jones, Sea Island Beach, Georgia
1935–1941	Richard J. Reynolds
1947–1954	John J. O'Freddy, New York
1955–1968	S. H. Plaskon, Miami, Florida

SOURCES

PHOTOGRAPHS

Barge House Museum

Including a large collection of material from John H. Trumpy & Sons

133 Bay Shore Avenue

Annapolis, Maryland 21403 USA

(410) 295-0104

Bath Iron Works

700 Washington Street

Bath, Maine 04530 USA

(207) 442-5327

Web site: www.biw.com

Boston Public Library

Print Department, Photo Collection

P. O. Box 286

Boston, Massachusetts 02117 USA

(617) 536-5400 x280

E-mail: prints@bpl.org

Deutsches Museum

Bildstelle

80306 München, Germany

(089) 2179 220

Glasgow Museums

Photolibrary

The Burrell Collection

2060 Pollokshaws Road

Glasgow G43 1AT

Scotland, UK

(0141) 636 0086

The Hagley Museum and Library

Including the Pusey and Jones archives

P. O. Box 3630

Wilmington, Delaware 19807 USA

(302) 658-2400

Web site: www.hagley.lib.de.us

Historical Collections of the Great Lakes

Center for Archival Collections

Jerome Library, 5th Floor

Bowling Green State University

Bowling Green, Ohio 43403-0175 USA

(419) 372-9612

Web site:

www.bgsu.edu/colleges/library/hcgl/hcgl.html

Lyndhurst

A National Trust Historic Site

(The Gould Estate)

635 South Broadway

Tarrytown, New York 10591 USA

(914) 631-4481

Web site: www.lyndhusrt.org

Maine Maritime Museum

243 Washington Street

Bath, Maine 04530 USA

(207) 443-1316

Web site: www.bathmaine.com

The Mariners' Museum

Including the Edwin Levick Collection

100 Museum Drive

Newport News, Virginia 23606-3759 USA

(757) 591-7784

Web site: www.mariner.org

Maritime Museum Association of San Diego

Home of the restored steam yacht Medea

1306 North Harbor Drive

San Diego, California 92101 USA

(619) 234-9153

Web site: www.sdmaritime.com/index.html

Millicent Library

45 Center Street

P. O. Box 30

Fairhaven, Massachusetts 02719 USA

(508) 992-5342

E-mail: millie@ma.ultranet.com

The Pierpont Morgan Library

29 East Thirty-sixth Street

New York, New York 10016-3403 USA

(212) 685-0008

Web site: www.morganlibrary.org

Museum of the City of New York

1220 Fifth Avenue

New York, New York 10029 USA

(212) 534-1672

Web site: www.mcny.org

Mystic Seaport Museum

Including the Rosenfeld Collection

74 Greenmanville Avenue

P. O. Box 6000

Mystic, Connecticut 06355-0990 USA

(860) 572-0711

Web site: www.mysticseaport.org

National Maritime Museum

Greenwich, London SE10 9NF

England, UK

(020) 8858 4422

Web site: www.nmm.ac.uk

San Francisco Maritime National Historic Park

National Maritime Museum Library

Building E, 3rd Floor, Fort Mason Center

San Francisco, California 94123 USA

(415) 556-9874

Suffolk County Vanderbilt Museum

The former home of William K. Vanderbilt I, see page 83

180 Little Neck Road

P. O. Box 0605

Centerport, New York 11721-0605 USA

(631) 854-5555

Web site: www.vanderbiltmuseum.org/welcome.html

University Of Glasgow

Archives and Business Records Centre

13 Thurso Street

Glasgow G11 6PE

Scotland, UK

Web site: www.archives.gla.ac.uk

R E L A T E D   B O O K S

Encyclopedia of Yacht Designers

Edited by Lucia del Sol Knight and
Daniel B. MacNaughton.
Available from W. W. Norton (USA) in 2001.

(800) 223-2584

Trumpy

Author Robert Tolf and illustrator Robert Picardat
wrote an excellent book detailing the history of
Trumpy yachts; published by Tiller Publishing (USA).

(410) 745-3750

Web site: www.tillerbooks.com

Yachts in a Hurry

Another excellent and related book (on commuters)
is by C. Philip Moore; unfortunately, it is no longer in
print. However, copies may be obtained through used
books dealers or from—

Web site: www.abebooks.com

Web site: www.bibliofind.com

Chronicle of Dodge's Steam Yacht Delphine

Ineke Bruynooghe has extensively researched the
steam yacht Delphine (see page 105), which her
father owns. She has gathered this material into a
book, which should be available in 2001 from—

E-mail: i.bruynooghe@wanadoo.be

Web site: www.ssdelphine.com

The Steam Yacht Delphine and Other Stories

Another book on Delphine—and quite delightful and
informative—is available from author Jay Ottinger,
who once crewed aboard.

Jay Ottinger

The Sailor's Snug Harbor

P. O. Box 150

272 Highway 70 E

Sea Level, North Carolina 28577-015 USA

(252) 225-4411

R E L A T E D   I T E M S

The pilothouse from Truant (see page 196) has been
restored and is available, along with many other
yacht fittings, at Nautical Furnishings.

(954) 771-1100

E-mail: nautical@gate.net

C L A S S I C   Y A C H T S
F O R   C H A R T E R

Shamrock V

See page 42

J-Class Management

28 Church Street

Newport, Rhode Island 02840 USA

(401) 849-3060

Web site: www.jclass.com/shamrock/shammain.htm

Gleam

See page 77

Seascope Yacht Charters

Bob and Elizabeth Tiedemann

103 Ruggles Avenue

Newport, Rhode Island 02840 USA

E-mail: aboard@earthlink.net

High Spirits

ex-Maemere; see page 176

Hornblower Cruises and Events, San Diego

1 (800) On The Bay

Web site: www.hornblower.com

Medea

See page 69

Maritime Museum Association of San Diego

1306 North Harbor Drive

San Diego, California 92101 USA

(619) 234-9153

Web site: www.sdmaritime.com/index.html

Haida

See page 153

Thierry Voisin from Partnership, Quai Amiral Infernet

Port de Nice, 06300 Nice, France

33 4 92 00 42 40

Sea Cloud

ex-Hussar; see page 154

SEA CLOUD CRUISES GmbH

D-20095 Hamburg, Ballindamm 17

Germany

49 (0) 40 309592-0

E-mail: info@seacloud.com

SEA CLOUD CRUISES, Inc.

32-40 North Dean Street

Englewood, New Jersey 07631 USA

(201) 227-9404; toll free: (888) 732-2568

E-mail: seacloud@att.net

CLASSIC YACHTS OPEN TO THE PUBLIC

Malardrottningen Hotel And Restaurant

The former Vanadis; see page 119
Riddarholmen, 111 28 Stockholm
08-545 18 780
Web site: www.malardrottningen.se

USS Potomac

See page 142
FDR Pier, Jack London Square
Oakland, California USA
(510) 627-1215
Web site: www.usspotomac.org

Coronet

See page 77; undergoing restoration and available
for public viewing
International Yacht Restoration School
449 Thames Street
Newport, Rhode Island 02840 USA
(401) 848-5777
Web site: www.iyrs.com

CLASSIC YACHTS IN NEED OF RESTORATION

Aras

See page 142
Mr. Kim Nielsen
Director
U.S. Navy Museum
805 Kidder Breese Street
Washington, D.C. 20374
(202) 433-3973
Web site: www.history.navy.mil

Cangarda

See page 114
J-Class Events
28 Church Street
Newport, Rhode Island 02840 USA
(401) 849-3060

Cigarette

See page 207
International Yacht Restoration School
449 Thames Street
Newport, Rhode Island 02840 USA
(401) 848-5777
Web site: www.iyrs.com

CLASSIC YACHTS UNDER RESTORATION

Alondra

See page 233; McMillen Yachts is accepting
partners in their fractional ownership program
featuring a number of finely restored classic
yachts including Alondra
Earl McMillen
McMillen Yachts, Inc.
P. O. Box 1495
Newport, Rhode Island 02840 USA
(401) 846-5557
Web site: www.woodenyachts.com

MISCELLANEOUS

Henry H. Rogers owned the steam yacht Kanawha,
shown on page 48. Three of his descendants have the
following homes or collections open to the public—

Coe Hall

Mai Rogers, the daughter of Henry H. Rogers, married
William R. Coe, and the couple lived at Coe Hall. After
Mai Coe's death in 1924, William Coe remarried a third
time. He donated Coe Hall and its 406-acre estate to
New York State. It is today open to the public.
Planting Fields Arboretum State Historic Park
P. O. Box 58
Oyster Bay, New York 11771 USA
(631) 022-9206
The Planting Fields Foundation may be reached at—
E-mail: coehall@worldnet.att.net

The Henry H. Rogers Ship Models Collection

The son and namesake of Henry H. Rogers donated
an extensive collection of ship models to the U.S.
Naval Academy Museum
U.S. Naval Academy Museum
118 Maryland Avenue
Annapolis, MD 21402-5034 USA
(410) 293-2108
Web site: www.nadn.navy.mil/Museum/
     rogersshipcollection.html

Millicent Rogers Museum

Millicent Rogers was a granddaughter
of Henry H. Rogers
P. O. Box A
Taos, New Mexico 97571 USA
E-mail: mrm@millicentrogers.org

Auditorium Theater

The Auditorium Theater in Chicago (discussed on page 53) is one of the finest and most impressive late-nineteenth-century interiors extant, a must-see for any person living in or visiting the city. Tours are available.
50 East Congress Parkway
Chicago, Illinois 60605 USA
(312) 431-2354
Web site: www.auditoriumtheatre.org
(note the web site spelling "theatre")

Mills Mansion

The elegant McKim, Mead and White mansion designed for Ogden Mills (see page 82) is open to the public.
Old Post Road
Staatsburg, New York 12580 USA
(914) 889-8851
Web site: www.hvnet.com/houses/mills

Eltham Palace

Sir Stephen and Virginia Courtauld (see page 92) built Eltham Palace, a remarkable Art Deco house in England, before World War II. After a slavish restoration, the home is now open to the public.
Eltham, London SE9 UK
0181 294 2621
Web site: www.aboutbritain.com/ElthamPalace.html

Yale Center for British Arts

Many of the paintings (including Turners) collected by the Courtaulds may also now be seen by the public.
1080 Chapel Street
New Haven, Connecticut 06520-8280 USA
(203) 432-2800

Rodman Wanamaker (see page 189) left two enduring legacies: a 28,500-pipe organ and 8,000 images of Native Americans.

Wanamaker Organ

(Lord & Taylor, Philadelphia, Pennsylvania)
Friends of the Wanamaker Organ
224 Lee Circle
Bryn Mawr, Pennsylvania 19019-3726 USA

William Hammond Mathers Museum

416 North Indiana Avenue
Bloomington, Indiana USA
(812) 855-6873
E-mail: mathers@indiana.edu

The Chinati Foundation

The minimalist sculptor Donald Judd, who died in 1994, created a unique home and museum on a former army base, Fort D. A. Russell, near the small town of Marfa, Texas (see page 271). Now owned and operated by the Chinati Foundation, exhibits include works by Judd, light artist Dan Flavin, John Chamberlain, Claes Oldenburg, Ilya Kabakov; there are also poems by Carl Andre and drawings and paintings by Ingólfur Arnarsson.
P. O. Box 1135
Marfa, Texas 79843
(915) 729-4362
Web site: www.chinati.org

South Street Seaport

The library at the South Street Seaport has a large John H. Wells archive.
207 Front Street
New York, New York 10038
Norman Brouwer, Librarian
(212) 748-8648
E-mail: nbsailship@aol.com
Web site: www.southstseaport.org

Fisher Mansion

The Lawrence P. Fisher mansion (see page 166) is now the Bhaktivedanta Cultural Center and open to the public for tours. A vegetarian restaurant, Govinda's, is located in the main dining room.
383 Lenox
Detroit, Michigan 48215
(313) 331-6740

BIBLIOGRAPHY

Arnold, Craig. *Medea, The Classic Steam Yacht.* California: The Maritime Museum Association of San Diego, 1994.

Barnes, Eleanor, C. *Alfred Yarrow, His Life and Work.* New York and London: Longmans, Green & Company, 1923.

Blair, Clay. *Hitler's U-Boat War, The Hunters 1939–1942.* New York: Random House, 1996.

Bowbrow, Jill, and Dana Jinkins. *The World's Most Extraordinary Yachts.* Maine: Concepts Publishing, 1986.

Brannock, Earl. *Queen of the Chesapeake and Hudson.* USA: Frank Gumpert Printing, 1986.

Couling, David. *Steam Yachts.* Maryland: Naval Institute Press, 1980.

Crabtree, Reginald. *The Luxury Yacht from Steam to Diesel.* New York: Drake Publishers, 1974.

Crane, Clinton. *Clinton Crane's Yachting Memories.* New York and Toronto: D. Van Nostrand Company, 1952.

Dear, Ian. *The Great Days of Yachting.* London: B. T. Batsford, Limited, 1988.

Drummond, Maldwin. *Salt-Water Palaces.* New York: The Viking Press (in association with Debrett's Peerage Limited), 1979.

Eskew, Garnett Laidlaw. *Cradle of Ships.* New York: G. P. Putnam's Sons, 1958.

Feversham, Lord. *Great Yachts.* New York: G. P. Putnam's Son's. 1970.

Grobecker, Kurt, and Peter Neumann. *Sea Cloud, A Living Legend.* Great Britain: Collectors' Books Limited, 1991.

Herreshoff, L. Francis. *Capt. Nat Herreshoff, the Wizard of Bristol.* New York: Sheridan House, 1953.

Hofman, Erik. *The Steam Yachts, An Era of Elegance.* Lymington, Hampshire, England: Nautical Publishing Company, 1970.

Hoyt, Edwin P. *The Goulds: A Social History.* New York: Weybright and Talley, 1969.

Jaffee, Captain Walter W. *The Presidential Yacht Potomac.* California: Glencannon Press, 1998.

Klein, Maury. *The Life and Legend of Jay Gould.* Baltimore and London: The John Hopkins University Press, 1986

Lawton, Thomas, and Linda Merrill. *Freer: A Legacy of Art.* Washington: Freer Gallery of Art, Smithsonian Institution in association with Harry N. Abrams, Inc., New York, 1993.

Lipton, Sir Thomas. *Lipton's Autobiography.* New York: Duffield and Green, 1932.

Lloyd's Register of American Yachts. Lloyd's Register of Shipping, various years.

McCutchan, Philip. *Great Yachts.* New York: Crown Publishers, 1979.

Meisel, Tony. *Yachting, a Turn of the Century Treasury.* New Jersey: Castle, 1987.

Moore, Philip C. *Yachts in a Hurry.* New York: W. W. Norton & Company.

O'Conner, Richard. *The Scandalous Mr. Bennett.* New York: Doubleday & Company, 1962

Ottinger, Jay. *The Steam Yacht Delphine and Other Stories.* North Carolina: Jay Ottinger, 1994

Paine, Ralph D. *The Corsair in the War Zone.* Houghton Mifflin Company, 1920.

Phillips-Birt. *The History of Yachting.* New York: Stein and Day, 1974.

Robinson, Bill. *The Great American Yacht Designers.* New York: Alfred A. Knopf, 1974.

Robinson, Bill. *Legendary Yachts.* New York: The MacMillan Company, 1971.

Robinson, Bill. *The World of Yachting.* New York: Random House, 1966.

Rosenfeld, Stanley, and William H. Taylor. *The Story of American Yachting, Told in Pictures.* New York: Bramhall House, 1958.

Rousmaniere, John (and the editors of Time-Life Books). *The Luxury Yachts.* Alexandria, Virginia: Time-Life Books, 1981.

Rubin, Nancy. *American Empress: The Life and Times of Marjorie Merriweather Post.* New York: Villard Books, 1995.

Smitten, Richard, *The Amazing Life of Jesse Livermore.* South Carolina: Traders Press, Inc., 1999.

Snow, Ralph Linwood. *Bath Iron Works, The First Hundred Years.* Bath, Maine: Maine Maritime Museum, 1987.

Strouse, Jean. *Morgan, American Financier.* New York: Random House, 1999.

Tolf, Robert, and Robert Picardat. *Trumpy.* Maryland: Tiller Publishing, 1996.

Walker, Fred. *Song of the Clyd:, A History of Clyde Shipbuilding.* New York: W. W. Norton & Company, 1984.

Waugh, Alec. *The Lipton Story: A Centennial Biography of England's Great Merchant Sportsman.* New York: Doubleday & Company, 1950.

ILLUSTRATION CREDITS

Page 148: Archives of the Pierpont Morgan Library, NY

Page 150: © Mystic Seaport, Mystic, CT

Page 151: Courtesy of Maine Maritime Museum, Bath, Maine

Page 152: Courtesy of San Francisco Maritime NHP, ships, P82–019 2320PL

Page 155: Deutsches Museum, München

Pages 157, 158–59: The Edwin Levick Collection, The Mariners' Museum, Newport News, VA

Page 160: © Mystic Seaport, Rosenfeld Collection, Mystic, CT

Page 161: © Mystic Seaport, Ships' Plans Collection, Mystic, CT

Pages 162–65, 167–69: © Mystic Seaport, Rosenfeld Collection, Mystic, CT

Pages 170–71: *Trail*, © Mystic Seaport, Rosenfeld Collection, Mystic, CT

Page 177: Morris Rosenfeld image, The Barge House Museum, Annapolis, Maryland

Page 178: © Mystic Seaport, Rosenfeld Collection, Mystic, CT

Page 179: Jay Benford

Pages 180–84: © Mystic Seaport, Rosenfeld Collection, Mystic, CT

Page 185: Jay Benford

Page 186: © Mystic Seaport, Rosenfeld Collection, Mystic, CT

Page 187: © Mystic Seaport, Mystic, CT

Page 188: © Mystic Seaport, Rosenfeld Collection, Mystic, CT

Page 189: Hart Nautical/MIT Museum

Pages 190, 191: © Mystic Seaport, Rosenfeld Collection, Mystic, CT

Page 193: The Barge House Museum, Annapolis, Maryland

Page 194: Jay Benford

Page 197: © Mystic Seaport, Rosenfeld Collection, Mystic, CT

Page 198: The Barge House Museum, Annapolis, Maryland

Pages 199–201: © Mystic Seaport, Rosenfeld Collection, Mystic, CT

Page 202: top, © Mystic Seaport, Rosenfeld Collection, Mystic, CT; bottom, Author's collection

Page 203: Author's collection

Pages 205–8: © Mystic Seaport, Rosenfeld Collection, Mystic, CT

Page 209: James Mairs

Pages 210, 211: top, © Mystic Seaport, Rosenfeld Collection, Mystic, CT; bottom, James Mairs

Page 212: © Mystic Seaport, Rosenfeld Collection, Mystic, CT

Page 213: *Rudder* Magazine

Page 214: The Edwin Levick Collection, The Mariners' Museum, Newport News, VA

Pages 215–17: © Mystic Seaport, Rosenfeld Collection, Mystic, CT

Pages 218, 219: The Edwin Levick Collection, The Mariners' Museum, Newport News, VA

Pages 220–21: © Mystic Seaport, Ships' Plans Collection, Mystic, CT

Page 222: © Mystic Seaport, Rosenfeld Collection, Mystic, CT

Page 223: top, *Yachting* magazine; bottom, © Mystic Seaport, Rosenfeld Collection, Mystic, CT

Page 224: top, *Yachting* magazine; bottom, © Mystic Seaport, Rosenfeld Collection, Mystic, CT

Page 225: © Mystic Seaport, Rosenfeld Collection, Mystic, CT

Pages 226, 227: *Yachting* magazine

Page 228: © Mystic Seaport, Rosenfeld Collection, Mystic, CT

Page 229: The Edwin Levick Collection, The Mariners' Museum, Newport News, VA

Pages 233, 235–39: © Mystic Seaport, Rosenfeld Collection, Mystic, CT

Pages 240, 241: *Rudder* magazine

Pages 242–51: © Mystic Seaport, Rosenfeld Collection, Mystic, CT

Page 252: The Edwin Levick Collection, The Mariners' Museum, Newport News, VA

Page 253: © Mystic Seaport, Mystic, CT

Pages 254–55, 258: © Mystic Seaport, Rosenfeld Collection, Mystic, CT

Page 259: Courtesy of Hagley Museum and Library

Page 260: top, Courtesy of Hagley Museum and Library; bottom, *Rudder* magazine

Page 261: Courtesy of Cynthia D'Vincent

Pages 262–64: top, © Mystic Seaport, Rosenfeld Collection, Mystic, CT; bottom, Courtesy of Cynthia D'Vincent

Pages 265, 266: © Mystic Seaport, Rosenfeld Collection, Mystic, CT

Page 267: Courtesy of Cynthia D'Vincent

Page 268: © Mystic Seaport, Rosenfeld Collection, Mystic, CT

Page 269: 4, 5, 6, © Mystic Seaport, Rosenfeld Collection, Mystic, CT; 7, Courtesy of Cynthia D'Vincent

Pages 274–75, Epilogue: *Aras*, The Edwin Levick Collection, The Mariners' Museum, Newport News, VA

Back endpaper: *Arcadia*, The Edwin Levick Collection, The Mariners' Museum, Newport News, VA

INDEX

Page numbers in italics indicate illustrations.